RELIGIOUS EDUCATION AND DEMOCRACY

BY

BENJAMIN S. WINCHESTER

Chairman Commission on Christian Education of the Federal
Council of the Churches of Christ in America and Assistant
Professor of Religious Education in Yale School of Religion.

THE ABINGDON PRESS

NEW YORK   CINCINNATI

Copyright, 1917, by
BENJAMIN S. WINCHESTER

CONTENTS

276

4   CONTENTS

PART II

SUGGESTED PLANS AND PROGRAMS OF WEEKDAY
RELIGIOUS INSTRUCTION

PREFACE

THE present world situation compels a serious reexamination of the foundations of democracy. Especially does it necessitate a consideration of educational processes and materials. In the haste to achieve efficiency may it not be that some indispensable values have been sacrificed? The words of Jesus sound again with a new emphasis: "What shall it profit a man, if he shall gain the whole world, and lose his own soul?" The same applies to a nation as well as to the individual. "Has democracy failed?" men are asking to-day. Has Christianity failed? These have not failed, but, as one recent writer has said, they have been found difficult and have not yet been fairly tried.

Under the conviction that a fresh study of the relation of religious education to democracy would just now be especially timely, the present writer prepared for the Commission on Christian Education of the Federal Council of the Churches of Christ in America a Survey of Week-day Religious Instruction. In this task many valuable suggestions and criticisms were made by the members of the Commission. The writer would express his peculiar obligation to the chairman, Dean W. F. Tillett, D.D.; the secretary, the Rev. H. H. Meyer, D.D.; and to the chairman of the special subcommittee appointed for this purpose, Professor W. J. Thompson, D.D.

This Survey, which appeared as a part of the Quadrennial Report of the Commission, has been carefully revised and is now contained in Part I of the present volume.

For those who are contemplating a more adequate program of religious education there is provided in Part II a selection of documents drawn from a wide field of observation. Among these are typical curricula illustrative of systems of religious and moral education which are under state control, in Germany, France, and England; copies of legislative enactments from Australia and Canada; syllabi giving full requirements for voluntary instruction in the Bible for state credit, as in North Dakota and Colorado; supplementary programs, for situations such as exist at Gary, Indiana, and plans for vacation schools; suggested reconstruction of public school curricula to develop a sense of religious values; and plans of organization, denominational and interdenominational, community and national, to suit a variety of conditions, rural and urban.

It is hoped that the material thus assembled may be of some real service to those who in this critical moment of the world's history are striving to develop through educational methods a religion that shall be vital and genuine.

PART ONE

A SURVEY OF THE RELIGIOUS EDUCATION IN ITS RELATION TO DEMOCRACY

CHAPTER I

COMPULSORY EDUCATION AND RELIGIOUS FREEDOM

Two principles seem to be firmly established in the life of the American people: the principle of compulsory education and the principle of religious freedom. We may regard it as a settled conviction that the nation is responsible for providing educational facilities for all its children, and for compelling them, if need be, to avail themselves of these advantages. It is also a settled conviction that any form of religious instruction which may be given under public auspices must not interfere with the religious freedom which is the birthright of every American citizen. The problem is, how to reconcile these two principles in practice. If the state undertakes to include religious instruction as an integral part of the educational system, it lays itself open to possible criticism from those who stand as the guardians of religious freedom. If, on the other hand, it refrains from offering religious instruction, it must then be admitted that the state system of education is defective at a vital point, for all will agree that any system of education which is designed to prepare youth for the responsibilities of citizenship in a democracy, but which fails to include religion, is an imperfect and incomplete system. Thus far the people of the United States have found it more expedient to follow the second course than the first, relying upon private agencies to supply the religious element in education which the state itself has omitted from its public school system.

RELIGIOUS EDUCATION AND DEMOCRACY

Three great types of faith are represented in the United States: Judaism, Roman Catholicism, and Protestantism. Probably a majority[1] of the people in the United States would acknowledge at least a nominal connection with some religious body standing for one or the other of these faiths. Upon these adherents of religion rests the responsibility for providing religious instruction for the entire citizenship. None of these three faiths would repudiate this responsibility, at least in so far as its own constituency is concerned. All alike recognize the obligation to instruct the child in the essentials of religion. And while all these three types of faith have much in common, being based in part upon the same Scriptures, each has addressed itself to the problem of religious education in its own way, providing agencies and material and working out methods which are in harmony with its own peculiar point of view in religion and its conception of education.

In obedience to their ancient law,[2] the Jews, in home and in synagogue school, have been faithful in the discharge of their teaching responsibility, a fact which goes far to explain the remarkable persistence of the Jewish faith in its essential characteristics, in spite of long-continued opposition and oppression. In the United States, in many communities, the Jews require their children to attend week-day sessions of the religious schools. In New York city there is a Bureau of Education of the Jewish Community, which proposes to provide not less than five hours a week of religious instruction, in well-equipped buildings, under well-trained teachers who are paid salaries not less than those received by public school teachers. At the present time, there are over four hundred organized Jewish schools for week-day instruction, in

---

[1] The number of communicants for 1915 is reported by Dr. Carroll as 39,380,670. If children were also included the number might possibly reach a total of 47,000,000.
[2] Deut. 6. 4-9.

10

which more than three thousand paid teachers are employed, at a cost of approximately $2,000,000 annually
—a sum which is made possible only through great personal sacrifice. In addition to the week-day school, many
synagogues also maintain Sunday schools, but, in spite
of all effort, it is said that not more than one fourth of
the children of Jewish parentage in this country receive
regular religious instruction.[1]

The Roman Catholic Church has always emphasized
the importance of religious instruction, but has never
looked kindly upon the American public school system,
with its artificial distinction between secular and religious instruction. The Roman Church has refused to
recognize this distinction, insisting that all education
should be under the supervision of the church. It voices
its protest against the public school in the parochial
school, which it maintains wherever possible, submitting
to what it regards as double taxation for this purpose,
in order that Catholic youth may be taught in an atmosphere of religion and under the eye of the priest. But
the Roman Catholic Church does not, on this account,
neglect the public school; many of the priesthood are to
be found upon school boards, and many Roman Catholics
are teachers in the public schools; in one instance known
to the writer, practically the entire teaching force in a
school situated in the midst of a Roman Catholic section
in one of our large cities is drawn from the adherents of
this faith, and the school is, to all intents and purposes,
a parochial school, supported by public funds, but practically, though not officially, under the control of the
Roman Catholic Church. Effort has often been made in
the United States to secure a division of school funds, a
part being set aside as available for the parochial school,
but the suggestion has never yet met with favor. Such

_____
[1] Religious Education, XI, p. 227.

11

a plan is held by many Catholics themselves to be fundamentally opposed to the genius of the public school as a democratic institution. It is not known how large a proportion of the children of Roman Catholics remain untouched by the church's efforts to supply religious instruction. Although many Catholic children attend the public schools, it is probable that the great majority even of these are for a considerable period brought under the church's teaching influence.

Protestants, no less than Roman Catholics and Jews, acknowledge their responsibility for providing religious instruction. It is generally admitted, however, that the instruction thus far provided has been less effective than it should be, and far from adequate. There are several reasons why this is so. In the first place, the members of Protestant churches have devoted themselves to the cause of freedom in its larger aspects, and to this end have been instrumental in the extension and development of the public school system and in the establishment of colleges, universities, and other institutions of higher learning. Jealous of their freedom in religion, they have been content to see the growth of general education, trusting that religious instruction would be supplied in some way by private agencies. From this element in the population has come also, in large measure, the initiative in the social-settlement movement and other democratizing agencies. Thus, both leadership and financial support have been required which otherwise might naturally have been available for the development of religious education.

Again, among Protestant bodies there is often uncertainty as to where the responsibility for religious instruction properly lies. In the Roman Catholic Church there is no such uncertainty; the priest has his duty clearly marked out for him. The Jewish rabbi also perceives his duty with equal clearness. But Protestant pastors sometimes boast that "they do not meddle with the Sunday school," and many Protestant churches make no provision in their budget even for the cost of lesson material, leaving to devoted laymen and women the whole responsibility for the instruction of the church's children in religion.

Undoubtedly, the most serious obstacle to effective religious education has been the weakening of the Protestant forces through excessive division. This is a part of the price paid for religious liberty. The whole Protestant movement has been a movement toward freedom, and freedom in the church, as elsewhere, has too often been interpreted as being synonymous with individualism. The one hundred and fifty Protestant denominations in the United States to-day all testify to this spirit of independence in matters of religious faith and practice. But this very division of forces has so reduced the strength of any one denomination in most communities as to make it impossible to provide the essentials of effective religious instruction, such as proper lesson material, suitable classrooms and equipment, and trained teachers. On the other hand, such has been the divergence between denominations in their theory of education, some holding strongly to the principle of Christian nurture and emphasizing the catechism as a preparation for confirmation, others exalting conversion and looking with distrust and even disparagement upon all educational methods of developing the religious life, that it has been in many instances impossible to unite upon a practical program of cooperative religious instruction.

There are indications, however, that this overemphasis upon superficial and often accidental differences between the various branches of Protestantism is giving place to a keener appreciation of those great fundamentals which underlie all types of Christian faith, and to a spirit of cooperation in the great common tasks of the kingdom of

God. One evidence of this is seen in the association of the Sunday schools which are to be found in practically every Protestant church, binding them together for the achievement of a common task. Although the instruction in the individual school has been too brief and often desultory, its influence has been enhanced by the sense of mutual support which has come through association with other churches in the same community, and through such association the churches have been feeling their way toward closer cooperation along new lines, making for practical efficiency while preserving religious liberty. Organizations like the Federal Council, the Sunday School Council, the Missionary Education Movement, and other similar federated movements, are illustrations of the new spirit which is permeating the Protestant denominations, and through them the life of the nation.

Within the last few years great advance has been made in Protestant circles. With the perfecting of the means and methods of public school education, the disparity between this and Sunday school instruction became more apparent. The official societies and boards of the Protestant denominations began to concern themselves seriously with the production of graded lesson material, the improvement of equipment and the conditions of teaching, and with the preparation of teachers. All this has made only the more evident the impossibility of providing adequate instruction in religion within the space of thirty or forty minutes on one day a week, and that a rest day.

A comparison of the actual time devoted to instruction and training in the Christian faith with either the total school time or the recreation time of the average pupil, reveals an astonishing discrepancy and makes one wonder that so much is actually accomplished for religion in so brief a period. The same conclusion is reached upon comparison of the time devoted to the study of the Bible with the time required for the study of any common subject like mathematics, or even penmanship, in the public schools. Already there are many among the Protestant forces who are turning their eyes toward the other days of the week in the hope of discovering somewhere an opportunity for inserting at least a limited program of religious instruction among the many studies and activities planned for children and young people.

The Sunday School Council minutes for January, 1917, give 18,601,103 as the number now enrolled in the Sunday schools of the twenty-eight constituent Protestant denominations. This number includes a considerable number of adults. According to the census reports of 1915, there are 22,000,000 children enrolled in the public schools. This, of course, does not include all of the children of school age; allowance must be made for the pupils in attendance upon private schools and parochial schools. All things considered, it is a large task confronting the Protestant churches, first, to provide a religious instruction which shall reach all who are entitled to it; and, second, to provide an instruction which shall be adequate.

It is a significant fact that just at the time when the officials of the Protestant denominations are turning their attention with a new solicitude to the task of making religious instruction more adequate, a new interest in this same problem is manifest in another quarter. At its convention in 1903, the National Education Association took the following action with reference to religious instruction:

We must conclude, therefore, that the prerogative of religious instruction is in the church, and that it must remain in the church, and that in the nature of things it cannot be farmed out to the secular school without degenerating into a mere deism without a living Providence, or else changing the school into a parochial school and destroying the efficiency of secular instruction.

Since then, however, the impression has been gaining ground that something is wrong with the educational situation. However successful the public schools may be as disseminators of information, the realization is being forced upon us that knowledge does not insure morality, much less religion. Many close students of education have been growing increasingly solicitous over the fact that dishonesty, a spirit of lawlessness, lack of loyalty and true patriotism—not to mention more serious lapses into immorality—are to be found in schools which otherwise seem to have conformed to requirements. Moreover, the popular ignorance of the Bible has been widely deplored, no less by teachers of literature and history than by zealous representatives of the church. It was also observed that boys and girls attending the public schools were drawing the altogether logical but fatal inference that, inasmuch as attendance upon the public school is required, while attendance upon Sunday school is optional, therefore, "secular education" is important, but religious instruction is a matter of indifference.

Several interesting experiments have recently been made in the field of general education, such as the North Dakota plan for securing a better knowledge of the Bible, the Colorado plan for increasing the effectiveness of Bible teaching, and the Gary plan, which offers to leave unoccupied a portion of the pupil's week-day program on condition that this be filled with appropriate religious instruction by the church, at the option of the parent.

The members of the Protestant churches have approached the task of education in general from the point of view of civic necessity; religious instruction they have regarded too often as a matter of denominational concern.

16

EDUCATION AND RELIGION

The time is at hand when religious education also must be regarded in the light of its relation to democracy and civilization. The experiences of the Great War have brought home to the nation the realization of the fact that many questions long supposed to be settled are now to be reopened. The very principles fundamental to democracy must again be defined. The meaning of democracy, the meaning of religion, the meaning of education, and the relation of each of these to the other, must all be made clear. Before entering upon the task of reconstructing civilization out of the remnants and ruins which shall remain, it is expedient to inquire: What is democracy? What is the relation of the Protestant churches to democracy and to those new problems which democracy must face? What can these churches contribute to the solution of these problems of democracy through education? What agencies are available for their use? And what should be the educational program of the churches for meeting this crisis in democracy? As shedding light upon these problems, it will be well to consider the development of the ideal of democracy in the United States and the attitude of the great religious bodies respectively toward this ideal. It will then be in order briefly to review historically the relation of the church to education, the development of popular compulsory education as a function of the state, and the rise of typical state systems of education. Finally, we may consider the significance of recent educational experiments in the United States, whether from the side of church or state, looking toward a more generous provision for religious instruction. With these facts in mind, the churches will be in a position to address themselves constructively to the task of formulating a program.

CHAPTER II

THE ESSENTIALS OF DEMOCRACY

THE Pilgrim Fathers came to these shores in the quest of a country where every man might be free to worship God according to the dictates of his own conscience, and the same spirit found its political embodiment in the state which was later developed. The assertion in the Declaration that "all men are equal," though often misunderstood and frequently misapplied, has been fondly cherished, while the pronouncement that they are "endowed by their Creator with certain inalienable rights," among which are "life, liberty, and the pursuit of happiness," has served as a kind of irreducible minimum for democracy.

The Constitution of the United States combined, in a skillful and remarkable manner, provisions for the safeguarding of individual liberty with others designed to secure national strength. At the same time the adoption of the Constitution, which provided for a republican or representative form of government, was in itself a recognition of the limitations of pure democracy, or direct government by the people, as originally embodied in the town meeting.

As time went on, however, the very machinery of government which was originally devised with great care so as to conserve the rights of the individual, on the one hand, against the encroachment of tyranny, and, on the other hand, to maintain the authority of the state, has, in fact, so developed as to leave the individual often exposed to a tyranny, not of the state, but of other individuals who were shrewd, designing, and unscrupulous, while the state

18

has been itself an unintentional and unwilling party to the oppression, even protecting these offenders in their exploitation of the ignorant and weak.

So far as the political development is concerned, therefore, the tendency has been, at least until recent years, to emphasize the rights of the individual as the characteristic feature of democracy, and to think of the government as an instrument intended for the convenience of the individual. From an individualistic point of view, the line between rights and wants is a very hazy one, and under such a conception politics is likely to become a scramble between the stronger and the weaker for the attainment of their personal desires. Nothing could be more dramatic than the struggle as it has been actually carried forward in the United States, for the stakes have been large and the competition correspondingly keen.

Visitors from other countries who were accustomed to a monarchical form of government naturally found much to criticize in what they saw here. Democracy in America was said to be extravagant, inefficient, wasteful, and, although it claimed to secure to each individual his rights, there were few modern states where the individual submitted to so many kinds of personal inconvenience. Therefore, it was easy to pass the hasty judgment that democracy is a failure. But true lovers of democracy are not content to have it judged by its superficial appearance at a particular moment. It is argued that the function of democracy is not primarily to produce the best government, but to produce the best men. Moreover, democracy is itself in a state of evolution, and its results are best seen by comparing it with itself at intervals, rather than by comparing it with some long-established monarchy which may have succeeded in perfecting certain details of governmental procedure. It was hardly to be expected that a whole people should become at once proficient in all the intricate details which hitherto have been left largely to the attention of a comparatively small ruling class. And when one takes this long look at the history of democracy in the United States there is no doubt that it is developing men into better citizens. Notwithstanding the diluting of the earlier idealism by the influx of great masses of humanity, sometimes at the rate of a million a year, speaking different languages, bringing with them other traditions and customs, often so poor and so ignorant as to become a serious charge upon the body politic, democracy has thus far succeeded, in the main, in assimilating this vast company of new Americans to its own life, and has infused into them the "American spirit."

A few illustrations will suffice. In the first place, there has been a steady movement toward a more effective popular control of the machinery of government. The emphasis has been shifted from the thought of public office as a means of private advantage to the conception of office as a public trust and of the officer as a servant of the people. The temptation to corruption has been lessened by the adoption of the secret ballot, and attempt is being made still further to curtail the power of the boss through advocacy of the direct primary. Effort is being made to compel public officers to be more immediately responsible to the voters electing them, and thus to free democracy from the evils of special privilege and boss rule, and make it efficient in providing for the common good. Forces are at work, designed to reduce the extravagance of governmental expenditures. In order to bring home to the individual a keener appreciation of his personal share of the burden of government, and further to check the making of huge appropriations for purely private or sectional advantage, there has been a steady tendency to substitute direct for indirect methods of taxation. It is becoming the custom to appoint commissions, endowed with large discretionary powers, to deal directly with matters too intricate and pressing to await the slow action of law-making bodies. Perhaps the most conspicuous example of such service is that rendered by the Interstate Commerce Commission, as a result of which the railroads have been brought so completely under popular control as to seem now somewhat in danger of falling outside the field of profitable investment, and hence unable to command the capital necessary for their development and maintenance. Relief from the oppression of vast combinations of capital is urgently demanded, and the disturbance of the public convenience through the disputes of labor and capital is becoming increasingly subject to adverse public criticism which finds expression in boards of arbitration and restrictive legislation.

Back of all these is a far deeper concern for the life of the people, and a determination to safeguard those interests which are common to all. Take, for example, the matter of public health and public morals. Closely connected with such service is that of the public parks and playgrounds commissions, which have done so much in recent years to provide wholesome recreation for those in the community who need it most. Within a decade the movement for getting entirely rid of the saloon with all its vicious and corrupting appurtenances has proceeded so silently and swiftly that there is good reason to hope that a few years more may see it absolutely wiped out. The management of prisons is becoming more humane, and the establishment of juvenile courts, with their friendly probation officers, is another step toward the recognition of the duty which democracy still owes to those who are largely the victims of its own inadequacy. Of a similar nature has been the legislation abolishing child-labor, all of which is a part of the whole great movement for conservation of all natural resources. The day for the free exploitation of all natural resources is passing.

Thus it appears that, while the earlier stages in the development of democracy in the United States were characterized by an undue emphasis upon individual rights, and by a widespread tendency to exploitation, during recent years a great change has quietly been taking place in the spirit of the people, a change which looks in the direction of a corresponding emphasis in the future upon the duty of the individual as a citizen of the democracy, the duty of willing service and faithful cooperation for the welfare of all.

Real democracy must ever rest upon two great correlative principles, each of which is fully recognized and generally accepted: first, the right of every individual to life, liberty, and the pursuit of happiness, without encroachment thereupon by any other individual; and, second, the duty of the individual not only to respect this right of every other, but also to join with all others in the whole-hearted endeavor to secure for all those blessings which are the fruit of cooperative effort, and can be secured only by such effort. Overemphasis upon the first principle leads to individualism or the exploitation of society by one or a few of its members, while overemphasis upon the second principle leads to socialism, the logic of which tends toward the subordination of the individual to society as a whole, and the possible restriction of individual initiative. Somehow the balance between these two extremes of democracy must be maintained in the administration of the commonwealth.

The maintenance of this balance requires a high average of intelligence, and wide diffusion of knowledge in the citizenship of a democracy. The problems regarding which the individual is called upon to express himself are often highly complicated. And he should at least be able intelligently to aid in the selection of men who are especially qualified to deal with them, and to give to them loyal and effective support when once they have been chosen.

But more is demanded than mere intelligence. Some of the most intelligent have turned out to be the worst citizens. A true democracy involves the voluntary subordination of individual interests and desires to the requirements of social welfare. In a growing democracy this will be increasingly true, which means that more and more exacting standards of behavior must constantly be imposed upon the individual by society. A recent writer has said :[1] "Democracy has assumed an express responsibility for the achievement of the stupendous task of making this world a better place in which more human beings will lead better lives than they have hitherto had an opportunity of doing. It will never succeed in making better men and women, unless an unprecedentedly large number of citizens seek to be better men and women." This is something which cannot be brought about by legislation or the application of external force. Real democracy is the resultant of forces which are within the life of the individual, forces which are spiritual and religious in their nature.

At the heart of democracy there must be faith, the same kind of faith which is attributed to Abraham when he went forth, not knowing whither he went, but seeking a better country, that is, a heavenly; the same kind of faith which made the Protestant and the Pilgrim. It is the free spirit of the pioneer, rather than the plodding submission of the subject, that is characteristic of democracy. To quote again the words of the writer just referred to,[2] "A democracy becomes courageous, progressive, and ascendent, just in so far as it dares to have faith, and just in so far as it can be faithful without ceasing

---

[1] Herbert Croly, Progressive Democracy, p. 406.
[2] Progressive Democracy, p. 168.

to be inquisitive." And this faith must be a faith in the possibilities of human nature, in the development of individual and social values, rather than in the accomplishment of specific results. Such a faith "means the assumption of large risks, and the making of large sacrifices," risks and sacrifices which the new demands laid upon democracy by recent developments of world-wide significance will more than ever require of the Christian churches of America.

CHAPTER III

THE CHALLENGE OF DEMOCRACY TO THE PROTESTANT CHURCHES OF AMERICA

IT has not been easy for a composite people like those of the United States, whose sympathies are naturally divided, to analyze calmly the causes which led up to the war, to estimate justly the issues at stake, or to interpret correctly the trend of events. But whatever may have been the motives originally behind the war, it is certain that the nations who have done the fighting have undergone the severest kind of discipline, a discipline which cannot but result in a more intense feeling of nationality in each of these peoples, a clearer conception of the ideals for which nationality is the symbol, and a deeper loyalty to these ideals. There is bound to be a closer understanding between all classes of citizens as they share in the terrible democracy of the battlefield; a more intimate understanding also between those nations which have fought shoulder to shoulder as allies in a common cause, which ought to facilitate a larger degree of peaceful cooperation between them in the future. Even between those nations which have opposed each other, there is likely to be a feeling of increased respect, for, irrespective of results, the costs have been so stupendous that each side must recognize and admire the genius and valor of the other. Thus from the crucible of war there is likely to be gained a clearer conception of values or ideals, a more intense loyalty, a spirit of comradeship and cooperation, all of which are essential to the spread of real democracy. The main question now is whether, in the final analysis, these values shall be interpreted in terms of individual freedom, or in terms of governmental supremacy and of centralized force.

This war has tried the soul of America as well as the soul of Europe. Through all the terrible days, the United States was confronting a great moral problem—the problem involved in attempting to maintain its honor as a nation and remain true to its democratic ideal, while profiting by the world's misfortune. The question was, Will America declare herself with reference to her ideals? The call came, summoning the people to a new patriotism, bringing a challenge to American citizenship. Had America, then, something worth sacrificing for? Were there values here, ideals, which not only had cost precious life, but were worth such price again to maintain? The United States professed to be eager to render service, a world service. Was she ready for it? Was she fitted for the task? Surely not while those things which the world saw as most characteristic of America were her sordid commercialism, her boastful egotism, her selfish individualism. If she aspired to perform some really noble task, she must first of all be true to herself. Out of the raw and uncouth mass of American strivings must, somehow, be disclosed an ideal, beautiful, lofty, and worthy to command the devotion of the world's chastened spirit.

There was danger lest the summons of the new patriotism be interpreted too narrowly and degenerate into a mere tool of the demagogue. If the motive appealed to were self-interest, even though it were national self-interest, then we should have had merely a nationalized selfishness, the projection into the sphere of national life and relationships of the old spirit of individualism and self-seeking which had been too characteristic of American democracy. But as the time had come to reassert in the sphere of private life the obligation to work with equal diligence to secure the welfare of all, so now the United States as a nation had finally to take its place among the other members in the family of nations, not as an isolated unit to strive to secure from this association merely such benefits as it can appropriate for its own use, but as a vigorous and willing sharer in the world's burden, a participant in the struggle to secure for all humanity everywhere equal justice and opportunity.

As we have seen, if America is to justify herself as a democracy in the eyes of the world and of her own people, she must have faith, a faith that means "the assumption of large risks and the making of large sacrifices." Still more is this true if she is now to be a participant in the conduct of the world's affairs, a contributor toward the solution of the world's problems. Such a faith is something more than the glorification of a particular form of government, or devotion to a particular political program. It is the kind of faith which is loyal to an ideal, an ideal in which are comprehended all those things which to the free man are of most worth: justice, opportunity, unhampered initiative, and the joy of working together for the common good. It is a faith both reverent and humble, acknowledging its dependence upon God, looking to him for guidance and insisting upon the right of every man to immediate approach to God. But it is a faith which is saved from arrogance by the firm conviction of the essential unity of human nature, and by the belief that the highest and most enduring satisfactions are attained by anyone only when he is working with others that all may accomplish for all men the will and purpose of God. The real question for America, as for any democracy, will be this, Can she instill such faith in the hearts of her citizens?

Faith, in a democracy, is not propagated by governmental or any other kind of authority. Laws are not the cause of progress; they merely register the advance already made under the compulsion of faith. The agencies most directly concerned in the fostering of such faith are the churches. Through their teaching office the churches undertake to transmit to each new generation their heritage of faith, the story of the men of faith who have sought and found God and have tried to order their lives in harmony with his purposes, the writings and teachings of patriarchs, prophets, and wisemen, the principles and ideals which have won recognition as of divine origin; in short, the background of ideas and feelings which constitutes the faith of any particular church.

The most venerable of the faiths largely represented in the United States is, of course, the Jewish. A religion based upon an immediate and intimate relation to God, and with a strong emphasis in its teaching upon righteousness and justice, Judaism possesses many of the elements required to-day by the new patriotism: reverence, loyalty to the laws of God, a virile and persistent faith. Nevertheless, the influence of the Jewish church in America, as a church, is confined largely to the members of the Jewish community. Within these limits, its influence may be said to be helpful to the cause of democracy.

The autocratic system of the Roman Catholic Church is, on the other hand, the antithesis of democracy. As an institution, it not only does not teach democracy, it does not believe in democracy. It does not believe in the immediate approach of the individual to his God, but teaches that approach must be made through the person of a mediator, the priest. It does not believe that the individual can be trusted to assume directly for himself the responsibility of ascertaining what the will of God is, nor of formulating for himself a program of conduct. The church assumes that responsibility for him, and the individual must accept its teaching and conform to its program on pain of being denied the satisfactions which the church has to offer in its sacraments. According to its theory, man is not safe, society is not safe, except as it yields implicit and unquestioning obedience to authority, the authority of the church as expressed through the utterance of the supreme and infallible pontiff. It is evident that an institution which embodies such a conception of religion can hardly be in sympathy with the kind of individual freedom for which true democracy stands. America can hardly depend upon the Roman Catholic Church to supply the kind of teaching and influence which make for democracy.

The responsibility for this teaching task falls mainly, then, upon the Protestant churches of America. These churches, in their very variety of worship, creed, methods of work and organization, are an expression of the freedom which is characteristic of democracy. And while some lay greater stress upon the observance of the sacraments and the ritual of worship, and others lay stress upon the preaching function, in either case they are dependent upon the work of teaching, to raise up the church of the future. Still more necessary is it that this teaching function should be emphasized if the Protestant churches are to meet their full responsibility as represented in the demands of the new patriotism.

We have traced briefly the growth of democracy in the United States. We have noticed the tendency to over-emphasize individual rights in the interest of selfish advantage. We have seen democracy reasserting the duty of the individual to labor for the common welfare. For the securing of this welfare, for maintaining the balance between self-interest and the interests of the community; in short, for the successful working of democracy, we have pointed out the necessity for a high degree of intelligence in its citizenship. Hence, the American system of compulsory education.

But, on the other hand, we have noticed that democracy, in order to meet the strain to which it is subjected in practice, must be permeated with another quality: idealism, faith, religion; a faith not only in democracy, but a faith in God which is free to grow and to express and to propagate itself in democratic fashion. Such a faith cannot do for democracy what it should, if there is any suspicion, on the one hand, that it is hampered by considerations of expediency or subserviency because of any dependence upon the bounty of the state, nor, on the other hand, if there is suspicion that it assumes to employ the sanctions of religion in such wise as to control the policies of a free government. Hence the separation of church and state in America.

Again, we have seen why the country must largely depend upon the Protestant churches as possessing in preeminent degree those qualities necessary for building up the ideals of freedom, and for expressing and extending the freedom of the faith. This does not imply a disparagement of other churches; still less is it an indorsement of intolerance and sectarianism. The fact remains that the influence of the Jewish church is naturally limited to its own constituency, and that the genius of the Roman Catholic Church is autocratic, not democratic. The strength of the Protestant churches lies in their freedom to discover, to appropriate, and to disseminate truth, while their apparent weakness lies in their divisions, these likewise an expression of their freedom. The question is, in view of the present critical situation in American democracy and in world relationships, can these churches find such a basis of common, cooperative effort as shall enable them effectively to teach the faith which is both Christian and democratic, and thus to discharge to the full their responsibility? Any plan of cooperative teaching effort must have due regard for the prerogative of the state in its work of education, for the churches themselves as interpreters of the truth, and for the actual moral and religious needs of children and youth in the conditions in which they find themselves to-day. At this point it will be instructive to consider what has been, historically, the relation of the church to education.

CHAPTER IV

THE TEACHING INHERITANCE OF THE PROTES-TANT CHURCHES

Jesus was the embodiment of the ideals of democracy. He thought of God as a kind and loving Father, and of all men as his children. As a child of God, every person, however exalted or humble, was alike the object of God's care and solicitude. True life, as he thought of it, involved two things: an intelligent sharing of the life and work of God, and a sharing by men with each other of the good things which are God-given. To do this one must know God, and every individual must be free to come to God, to inquire of him, to commune with him, directly and immediately. And for the rest, God would hold each one responsible for his own life and for the use made of opportunity.

Jesus was preeminently a teacher. He had the spirit of the true teacher, the desire to expand, to *educate* the life of every person, to free it of its limitations and constraints. He taught with a peculiar power and authority, because he embodied in his own personality the things he undertook to teach. Indeed, we may say that Jesus anticipated very nearly all that has since been advocated in educational method and illustrated it in his own teaching; the importance of personality, the grading of pupils, the appeal to interest, the use of the story, the stimulation of observation by the laboratory method, the study and interpretation of facts, the use of questions, the organization of ideas, the development of the power of discrimination toward differing values the enlistment of self-

32

activity, the encouragement of initiative, and the providing of opportunity for motor expression—all these may be found, together with an earnest admonition not to neglect the child, in the teaching of Jesus.

The primitive Christian community was a democracy in miniature. Its members had caught the Master's spirit sufficiently to make them concerned for those outside and desirous that as many as possible should identify themselves with the Kingdom before the King should return to replace the existing social and political order with the benign rule of the Messianic age. At the same time the missionary propaganda of the primitive church was thoroughgoing; those who were to be reckoned as members of the Kingdom must be able to qualify as citizens; they must be acquainted with its ideals, accept its responsibilities, and order their lives according to its requirements. It was therefore imperative that these Christian communities should also become teaching centers, partly to maintain their own integrity and purity, and partly to accomplish the larger task of winning men for citizenship in the Kingdom.

The members of the Christian communities needed themselves to be taught, first, to discriminate between Christian ideals and Jewish ideals; between the broad, democratic spirit of Jesus and the narrow, intolerant spirit of the Pharisee; they needed to *see Jesus,* through the eyes of a Jew, but appreciatively, sympathetically. In the second place, the Christian communities needed to be taught to discriminate between the Christian life and the common life about them. Again, there was need of instructing the church to discriminate between Christian thought and other popular types of thought. Religion, on its intellectual side, was in danger of becoming a composite of Oriental beliefs—Persian, Indian, Egyptian, Babylonian—"a mythological and fantastic dress for the doctrines of Greek philosophy." The very controversies, therefore, to which the primitive Christian communities were exposed—controversies with Jewish ecclesiastics, with their pagan neighbors and fellow citizens, and with the leaders of contemporary thought—threw them back upon the original story of Jesus and of the beginnings of the church, and compelled them to give to it a permanent form, which could be appealed to as authentic and authoritative, and could be utilized as the basis upon which to prepare the material to be used in teaching. Thus were developed the New Testament canon, the standards of thought which soon took shape in the form of creeds, and the standardized forms of government and worship.

But the church had a wider teaching mission than simply to instruct its own adult membership, necessary and important as that was. There was a duty also which it owed to childhood and youth. Not only must the church insure the perpetuation of its own life through the teaching of the young, but here, in fact, lay its most fruitful field for the enlargement of that life. The church came to this teaching work with perfect naturalness, for it found a model close at hand in the schools connected with the synagogue. Provision was therefore made in every local church for instruction.

The foremost minds of the age gave themselves to this work of catechizing, and children of heathen parents as well as the children of the Christians were freely admitted to instruction. Among others were such names as Clement, himself a great teacher and trainer of teachers, and Origen, renowned as preacher, commentator, dogmatist, and especially as teacher. These men gave themselves to the careful study of the teaching work of Jesus and became remarkably proficient in the use of oral and interlocutory methods. So large a place did this work of teaching occupy in the mind of the Christian Church during the first centuries that, in spite of the fact that there were no missionary societies, no missionary institutions, no organized efforts at missionary propaganda in the Ante-Nicene age, nevertheless, "in less than three hundred years from the death of Saint John the whole population of the Roman empire, which then represented the civilized world, was nominally Christianized."

In the endeavor, however, to reduce the message of Jesus to a body of definite teaching which should be free from admixture with alien elements, that message was unduly narrowed and constrained. In the effort to standardize the organization and the worship of the church it was inevitable that its life should become externalized. Only thus was it possible to introduce into the life and thinking of mankind the leaven of the Christian message; but once introduced, it possessed within itself inherent qualities which in due time should set men fully free. In spite of all defects, Christianity was still an ethical religion, universal in its appeal, and anchored in the historic facts connected with the life and death of Jesus Christ.

The very success of the church during the first centuries had so alarmed the Roman emperors that they threatened its existence. There seemed to the leaders no alternative but to make terms with the empire and establish the church as a part of the empire, but, as Haslett remarks,[1] "in its attempt to Christianize the Roman empire, the church was Romanized by the empire, and did not recover from this secularization for a thousand years."

Such as remained of the older intellectual life was taken up into the doctrines of the church. So far as it was realized that great stores of knowledge had disappeared, men consoled themselves with the thought that its value had been only temporal, while the duty of the church was

---

[1] Haslett, The Pedagogical Bible School, p. 33.

to educate for eternal life. Great thinkers, among whom Augustine was preeminent, gave themselves to the task of elaborating this body of spiritual knowledge into a system. This devotion to theology was associated with a spirit of asceticism and other-worldliness, which led to the founding of many monasteries. From the seventh to the thirteenth century these were the chief centers of intellectual life and education, though even here the instruction was meager enough, including generally reading, writing, singing, and calculating the church calendar.

As the sphere of the church's influence widened and the demand for learning increased, schools multiplied. The monastic schools, at first designed to train novitiates, received also lay pupils. Their course of study was also enlarged and a graded system introduced, covering a period of seven years. Charlemagne opened the cloisters for the benefit of the people and attempted to introduce a system of compulsory education—a plan which failed of fruition for lack of teachers. Schools were established in connection with the cathedrals, primarily to train candidates for the clergy, but open also to lay youth. And there were guild schools and chantry schools, in charge of priests whose primary responsibility was that of a chaplain but whose spare time was available for teaching.

Between the eleventh and the fifteenth centuries occurred the series of movements known as the crusades. The very antithesis of Christianity in many respects, they nevertheless exerted a tremendous influence upon civilization. These successive waves of migration, extending over a period of more than two centuries, brought together the peoples of Europe in new acquaintanceship. The rude tribes of the North were refined by association with races whose manners were superior to their own. Trade was stimulated, and men's minds were broadened by contact with the older art and learning. The impulse to travel was quickened by the discovery of the mariner's compass. This created a demand for more and larger ships. New cities sprang into prominence as centers of wealth and of influence. About the middle of the fifteenth century Copernicus published his great work, De Revolutionibus Orbium, which lent a new romance to voyages of adventure and discovery. In 1492 the New World was discovered.

This broadening of horizon gave a new sense of power and created new interests. There was a demand for knowledge and for books which the invention of printing soon enabled men to satisfy. Groups of students congregated in the larger centers, attracted by the personality of great scholars like Abelard. Universities sprang up all over Europe. Migratory students and mendicant friars carried the new learning into remote villages, and discussion developed great dialectical skill. Men grew more tolerant and became skeptical of tradition and restive under authority, while the introduction of gunpowder placed in the hands of the humbler elements of society the means for the overthrow of feudalism and the assertion of their rights.

Meanwhile lines of cleavage were opening between ecclesiastical and state authority, between "profane" and Christian learning, between the spirit of imperialism and the spirit of freedom, between elaborate and formal worship—which was often found in association with the most corrupt morals—and a sincere and simple-hearted piety.

The followers of Peter Waldo, expelled from Lyons because of their criticism of the corrupt clergy, traveled through southern France preaching and teaching, distributing translations of the Bible as they went. Scholars, like Erasmus, whose fame as a classical scholar was unprecedented, clearly recognized the need of a spiritual revival and believed that this could be brought through instruction, especially in the Scriptures. He advocated a return to the Greek and Hebrew and published the first critical edition of the New Testament. He found fault with the clergy for inattention to their duties, interest in secular matters, voluptuous habits, laziness, ignorance, and superstition. Wycliffe challenged the doctrines of the Catholic Church and devoted himself to translating the Bible into the vernacular. In Bohemia, John Huss attacked the church upon practical as well as doctrinal grounds, for which he finally suffered martyrdom. The Brethren of the Common Life, of whom Thomas à Kempis was one of the earliest leaders, carried on a work of education among the poorer classes, living a simple communistic life, like that of the primitive church. Thus, in the midst of an expanding knowledge there was a groping after a simpler type of religious faith and worship, a more immediate approach to God, a more intimate acquaintance with the Scriptures, a more genuine life, and a truer freedom.

When Martin Luther nailed his ninety-five theses upon the church door at Wittenberg he could hardly have realized how tremendous would be the upheaval which was to follow that act. Himself an Augustinian monk, intensely religious and weighed down by a deep sense of guilt, he had given himself to the study of the writings of Augustine and came to the conclusion that salvation and the assurance of forgiveness were to be obtained only through faith, through the direct approach of the individual to God. This repudiation of sacerdotalism and reassertion of the primitive Christian conception of individual privilege and responsibility in religion involved not only radical readjustments in the conduct of the church; it involved also a system of popular education, to enable every man intelligently to assume and faithfully to discharge his full responsibility. Luther perceived this necessity and often touched upon the subject in his writings. He gave himself with indefatigable energy to the translation of the Bible into the common speech, in order that it might be accessible to all. The publishing of this translation and of controversial literature stimulated an interest in reading and created a demand for schools. Luther believed, however, that the scope of education should be broadened to include the classics, Hebrew and Greek, and also history, mathematics, physical exercises, singing, and the practical arts.

The Reformation movement was aimed at the abolition of ecclesiastical authority. Luther, therefore, advocated that the responsibility for popular education be laid upon the state. His argument is based upon the fact that education is essential to the public welfare: the welfare of the state "does not depend alone on its treasures, its beautiful buildings, and its military equipment, but upon its having many polished, learned, intelligent, honorable and well-bred citizens, who, when they have become all this, may then get wealth and put it to good use. . . . The world has need of educated men and women, to the end that the men may govern the country properly, and that the women may properly bring up their children, care for their domestics, and direct the affairs of their households." It was this vital concern in education which justified the state in exerting its authority to compel its children to attend school. "I hold it to be incumbent on those in authority to command their subjects to keep their children at school. If they have the right to command their subjects, the able-bodied among them, in time of war, to handle musket and pike, to mount the walls, or to do whatever else the exigency may require, with how much more reason ought they to compel the people to keep their children at school."

Neither was Luther blind to the responsibility of the

home and the church for providing religious instruction. He prepared two catechisms, a larger and a smaller, as helps to religious teaching. He believed that parents were responsible for the training of their children in habits of reverence and respect and in Christian conduct. He felt that teaching ability and experience should also be a prerequisite to the holding of the office of preacher or bishop.

The actual working out of his plan for popular education was left to his friend, Melanchthon, who drew up, in 1528, the "Saxony School Plan," the first step toward a school system under control of the state. Melanchthon has been called the preceptor of Germany, and it is said at his death there was scarcely a city in all Germany which had not modified its schools according to his direct advice, and scarcely a school of any importance which did not number among its teachers some pupil of his. Like his master, Melanchthon labored at the University of Wittenberg, which was founded in 1502 as the first university of the new learning and became the center of Protestantism. Other universities in Germany threw off all allegiance to the pope and became disseminators of Protestant influence. Marburg, Königsberg, Jena, Helstadt, Dorpat, were all added during the century. On the other hand, seven Roman Catholic universities were founded within the German states and exerted a reactionary influence. Thus did the controversialists of the Reformation period seek to perpetuate their doctrines, through the teaching of the schools and universities, for the Jesuits had already undertaken to combat the influence of the Reformation by its own methods and had established large numbers of elementary schools for the propagation of Roman Catholic doctrines. Two things, however, had become firmly impressed upon the minds of men by Luther and his followers: the right of the individual to freedom in religion, and the right of every child to education, with the implication that the responsibility for providing such education rests with the state.

Attention has been called to the two convictions established in the thinking of the American people: first, the children of the nation must be educated by the nation; and, second, this education must proceed in such manner as not to interfere with freedom in religion. These two cardinal principles are our direct inheritance from the Reformation. Whatever differences are apparent between the systems of popular education in America and Germany to-day may be attributed in part to the divergent trend in the development of democracy and of religion in the United States.

CHAPTER V

SOME PROPHETS OF MODERN DEMOCRACY AND THE NEW EDUCATION

FORCES were released by the Reformation which gave new impulse to the movement for democracy and changed radically the aim and methods of education. The interests which now commanded attention were all liberating interests. Scholasticism was deductive, analytical, logical. Nevertheless, it cultivated the powers of memory, developed skill in argument and accuracy of statement, and awakened an appreciation of learning. The Renaissance was a movement toward individualism, emphasizing the Greek idea of culture and the importance of knowledge as a means to freedom. Men everywhere grew restive against authority and restraint. In the north of Europe this spirit, finding expression in the exaltation of individual judgment and the defiance of the authority of the church, inaugurated the Reformation.

Through travel and the observation of nature the field of knowledge broadened. Kepler, Galileo, and Harvey all lived in the latter part of the sixteenth and the beginning of the seventeenth centuries. Newton worked out the law of gravitation soon after. At about the same time Francis Bacon was urging men to lay aside their presuppositions and to make real contributions to knowledge by the observation of facts and inductive reasoning. The human mind was beginning to assert itself, and those in authority were thrown upon the defensive.

While the Catholics and Protestants were engaged in the Thirty Years' War, Comenius, a Moravian, banished from his native country by the Catholic Austrians, was quietly elaborating a new theory of education. His attempt at an encyclopedic organization of all knowledge in The Great Didactic stimulated an interest in research. Comenius sought to annex to religion the other recently explored fields of knowledge and to utilize them in securing the mastery of natural forces. He held that "man is naturally required: (1) to be acquainted with all things; (2) to be endowed with power over all things and over himself; (3) to refer himself and all things to God, the source of all." Thus the aim of education became, to his mind, the complete development of man as a rational creature; and he argued that elementary education should therefore be made universal and compulsory. His was a far broader conception than the one then generally current, that education was necessary in order that one might be able to read the Bible. The center of gravity had shifted from subject-matter to personality, while religion still occupied the central place in the development of the person.

Comenius also made distinct contribution to the organization of education. His great principle was that of adaptation; education should be adapted at each stage to the age and capacities of the child. Not only was it the purpose of education to develop personality, but four distinct stages of childhood were recognized in his scheme: infancy, childhood, boyhood, and youth. To meet the needs of different ages he would have graded textbooks, present subjects concretely, use objects illustratively, and would have the pupils memorize only what had been explained. Comenius tried to economize time by encouraging regularity of attendance, the setting apart of the best part of the day for teaching, and the substitution of class for individual instruction. Gentleness he would substitute for force, abolish corporal punishment, and appeal to the natural interests of the pupil. The theories of Comenius did not produce any great immediate change in educational practice, although his textbooks proved widely popular.

John Locke rendered a great service at this time by applying the methods of observation to the processes of the mind and thus laying a basis for the science of psychology. Believing that knowledge is derived through reflection upon experience, and that the elements of thought are sensations arising from contact with physical forces or stimuli, he argued against accepting statements at face value, merely upon authority. This principle he applied in the fields of government, religion, and education. The English Revolution of 1688 overthrew in England the theory of the divine right of kings and established a representative Parliament. Locke justified the Revolution, and at that time of bitter sectarian jealousies pleaded for a more liberal spirit in religion.

Locke's theories on education were mainly set forth in two of his works, Some Thoughts Concerning Education, and The Conduct of the Understanding. Locke conceived of the human mind as a blank to begin with. Development comes through discipline, the thwarting of natural instincts and tendencies, and the building up of habits. The ideal, "a sound mind in a sound body," is to be attained through physical, moral, and mental discipline, which are to secure vigor of body, virtue, and knowledge. While he laid especial emphasis upon the importance of virtue, he also affirmed that religious instruction is the foundation of virtue. He made a clear distinction between instruction and education, defining instruction as the method of education. Locke considered learning the least part of education. The purpose of intellectual education, he declared, is not primarily to acquire knowledge, but to train the mind in certain habits. He discerned in particular subjects of study characteristic

44

values. Notwithstanding his conception of education as discipline, Locke would not make it irksome. He believed in utilizing the child's natural activities, especially the play tendency, and would have study a sport and recreation, not a task. According to Locke, therefore, education is not to be valued primarily as a means of religious propaganda, nor because of its *content*—least of all for its inculcation of theological doctrines—but because of the disciplinary nature of the *process* in its effect upon the moral character of the individual.

During the eighteenth century religion as represented in the Roman Catholic Church in France had developed an elaborate ceremonial, but had ceased to exert a strong influence in the life of the people. Many of the priesthood were immersed in secular affairs and led lives of open immorality. The opposition of the church to important discoveries and its failure to keep pace with the development of science alienated the educated classes and brought religion into contempt. The court life under Louis XIV had become formal and artificial. The centralized government was in the hands of an absolute king, who had destroyed the powers of the nobles and reduced them to a body of parasites whose actions toward each other were governed by an elaborate system of rules of etiquette. "The dancing master was the most important factor in the whole educational situation. His function was to make little children into young ladies and gentlemen as expeditiously as possible."[1] It was a kind of life "in which everything that was spontaneous, emotional, natural, childlike, was eliminated in favor of indifference, artificiality, and polite formality." These ideals prevailed, not only at the French court, but also in the life of the well-to-do, in the middle class, and even among artisans. They were widely copied in all parts of Europe, especially

[1] Parker, The History of Modern Elementary Education p. 170.

in Russia, Germany, England, and, to a certain extent, were affected also in America.

The reaction against this extreme formalism came partly through the movement commonly known as the Enlightenment, of which Voltaire was a brilliant exponent. This movement was opposed to all forms of tyranny, superstition, and hypocrisy, and sought to secure individual freedom through the emancipation of the intellect. There was a profound belief in the right of the individual to exercise his own judgment, unhampered by the beliefs and superstitions of the church and the traditions of society. An overemphasis upon this right, however, led to social anarchism, atheism, and indiscriminate attack upon the very foundations of all institutions through which authority is exercised. Moreover, the leaders of the movement were selfish and contemptuous of the lower classes, whom they believed incapable of being educated, and hence not amenable to reason. It was believed that society might be brought under the control of reason, through the culture of the few. Thus the movement tended to become aristocratic, substituting a new aristocracy of reason for the older one of family and official position.

Against the dead formalism in church and state, on the one hand, and this cold rationalism with its unconcern for the masses, on the other, Rousseau hurled his passionate protest. Born in Geneva eight years after the death of Locke, indulged in childhood, he developed into a weak, sentimental, highly emotional nature, utterly undisciplined and with strongly vagabond tendencies. His character has been described as "an extraordinary combination of strength and weakness, of truth and falsity, of that which is attractive with that which is repulsive."[1] Nevertheless, he exerted an immediate and far-reaching

[1] Monroe, A Short History of Education.

influence, due in part to his deep, reverential love for nature and his sincere sympathy with the common people, but also to his ability to clothe his ideas in forceful and popular language. Assuming that "everything is good as it comes from the hands of the Author of nature, but everything degenerates in the hands of man," Rousseau elaborated his doctrine that nature is to be studied and followed. He would have society get back to nature and live the simple life.

His ideas on education, set forth in the form of a romance in the philosophical essay, Emile, turned the attention toward child-study. While his contemporaries were treating little children like miniature men and women, Rousseau asserted the right of the child to be understood. He argued that the point of view of education should be determined by the nature of the child's instincts and capacities. Nature is to be allowed to develop a pure character. The child will learn from experience what things are wise and good, and will learn economy through his own failures or successes. Rousseau distinguished four distinct periods in child development; from birth to five years, from five to twelve, from twelve to fifteen, and from fifteen to twenty. The first period is to be devoted to physical development and is to be spent in the open air, free of all restraint. The second period is to be devoted mainly to sense-training, and to discovery of natural laws through experience. During the next three years the emphasis is to be upon intellectual training, to be carried on in closest contact with nature, and to be limited to those things only which are useful. Rousseau recognized the significance of the social instincts appearing in adolescence and urged that at fifteen the pupil be placed for the first time in direct contact with man, in order to expand the horizon of his interests and to develop his moral and religious nature.

In spite of much that is extravagant and contradictory, certain things stand out clearly in the thinking of Rousseau. There is, in the first place, a certain reverence for the personality of the child; the teacher is to come to the child as a learner, not as an autocrat; he is to discover in the child the purpose and intent of nature and become a fellow worker with nature in accomplishing that purpose. The teacher must discern and follow the order of development in the child, must provide appropriate activities, must utilize curiosity and interest as motives, must direct the powers of observation and reasoning, and connect these processes with motor activity. The attitude of the teacher toward the child throughout is that of a friend and a guide. The child's judgment is to be trained through exercise and is not to be vitiated or perverted by premature memorizing of words and symbols. He is to be taught scientific investigation at first hand and encouraged to self-expression through drawings. Rousseau believed religion to be an affair of the inner life, expressed in inward worship and in love to fellow man, but the theological aspects of religion he regarded as unsuited to children.

Among those who came under the spell of Rousseau was the Swiss reformer, Pestalozzi. Living at a time (1746-1826) when revolution was the frequent remedy for social ill, Pestalozzi was profoundly convinced that social and political reforms were to be brought about by education—not the current education, but an education new in purpose, based upon new principles, conducted in a new spirit and according to new methods. It was he who first compelled the public to appreciate the position that education is to be considered from the point of view of the developing mind of the child, and that the true basis for education must be experimentation rather than tradition. Many of his own ideas and suggestions are the result of experimentation. Probably Monroe[1] is right in thinking that this is the reason why "this man who did not begin to teach until fifty years of age, and who, from a practical point of view, failed in every enterprise he undertook in his long life, after all has had more influence than any other one person in the educational progress of the nineteenth century."

Pestalozzi's warm human sympathy and deeply religious spirit pervade his statements regarding the work of the teacher:

In the newborn child are hidden those faculties which are to unfold during life. The individual and separate organs of his being form themselves gradually into unison, and build up humanity in the image of God. The education of man is a purely moral result. It is not the educator who puts new powers and faculties into man and imparts to him breath and life. He only takes care that no untoward influence shall disturb nature's march of development. The moral, intellectual, and practical powers of man must be nurtured within himself and not from artificial substitutes. Thus, faith must be cultivated by our own act of believing, not by reasoning about faith; love, by our own act of loving, not by fine words about love; thought, by our own act of thinking, not by merely appropriating the thoughts of other men; and knowledge, by our own investigation, not by endless talk about the result of art and science.

Pestalozzi felt that he had in the new education a means of elevating the common people out of their ignorance, squalor, and misery into the full enjoyment of their privileges, the full exercise of their powers—a status to which all should rightfully attain. He believed that it was the business of true education to develop the elements of power which God had implanted in each individual by furnishing, in carefully selected and appropriate order, the elements of experience needed for their natural exercise.

---

[1] A Short History of Education.

RELIGIOUS EDUCATION AND DEMOCRACY

This idea of education as organic development led to the more careful analysis of subject-matter and to the endeavor to present first the more simple elements, proceeding inductively toward a mastery of the more complex. It brought a new spirit into education, for Pestalozzi conceived of the schoolroom as a transformed home, similar to that in its relationships and purpose, and pervaded by an atmosphere of sympathy. And it gave new promise to the movement for universal education as a means of uplifting society and promoting human welfare.

Pestalozzi, however, lacked the ability to formulate a clear and logical philosophical basis for his ideas. Herbart succeeded to this task, and found that basis in a unified mental life and development. Agreeing with Locke in making virtue the chief end in education, he believed that this end will best be realized by keeping in mind the Greek ideal of a liberal education as a many-sided development. This he set forth in his doctrine of interest, which, according to Herbart, denotes that kind of mental activity which it is the business of instruction to arouse, and which becomes a permanent result of education.

Interest means self-activity. The demand for many-sided interest is, therefore, a demand for many-sided activity. But not all self-activity, only the right degree of the right kind, is desirable; else lively children might very well be left to themselves. There would be no need of educating or even governing them. It is the purpose of instruction to give right direction to their thoughts and impulses, to incline these toward the morally good and true. Children are thus in a measure passive. But this passivity should by no means involve a suppression of self-activity. It should, on the contrary, imply a stimulation of all that is best in the child.[1]

This theory of interest led, first, to an analysis of sub-

---

[1] Herbart, Outlines of Educational Doctrine. See Parker, Modern Elementary Education, p. 389.

ject-matter and to its classification in terms of interests. As a consequence, Herbart restored to the curriculum historical and language studies, which Rousseau and Pestalozzi would displace with science. Again, Herbart developed more fully the principles of method in teaching, emphasizing especially the use of interest as a means of gaining and holding attention, the necessity of adapting instruction to the pupil's past experience and present frame of mind, the methodical treatment of facts in the presentation of the subject-matter of instruction, and the interrelating of subjects in such a way as to influence the pupil's behavior. Thus he gave precision and definiteness to Pestalozzi's idea of education as a means of securing a better type of conduct, although he lacked the emotional qualities and intense human sympathy which gave to the work of Pestalozzi such a strong social appeal.

It was Friedrich Froebel, a contemporary of Herbart and an enthusiastic follower of Pestalozzi, following in the footsteps of Rousseau, who organized his school training around a series of activities, though he differed from Rousseau in making these social from the beginning. Of a deeply mystical, religious nature, he held that "in all things there lives and reigns an eternal law" and that "this all-controlling law is necessarily based on an all-pervading, energetic, living, self-conscious, and hence eternal unity. . . . This unity is God. All things have come from this divine unity, God. . . . In all things there lives and reigns the divine unity, God. . . . The divine influence that lives in each thing is the essence of each thing."[1]

To Froebel, everything in nature was an expression of this unity, and all objects symbolic of the Deity. His love for nature and his interest in the analogies between

---

[1] Friedrich Froebel, The Education of Man. See Parker, Modern Elementary Education, p. 433.

physical and spiritual phenomena led him to make large use of symbols in his teaching. His life was devoted to the teaching of very small children, for whom he founded the kindergarten, based upon the child's instinctive love of play, and seeking through the guidance of the play instinct to develop in the child the ability to construct, to invent, to speak, and to be thoughtful for others. In the work of Froebel the vision of Rousseau and of Pestalozzi was realized. In his hands the schoolroom became a home, pervaded by an atmosphere of gentleness and love, a place not of harsh repression but of joyous activity, spontaneity, and continual discovery. Here teachers are not taskmasters but companions and friends, and all alike are children of God, reverently seeking a deeper knowledge of him and his ways in all his works and striving to express his will toward one another.

All these men were prophets, catching visions of a new day, in which the individual should not only be free to develop and express his personality, to find and to worship God in his own way, but should also find himself surrounded and supported by his fellow men, helping him to appreciate and appropriate all the heritage of thought and learning and idealism from the past and uniting with him in the discovery of still other truth with which to enrich life in the future. The Great Didactic of Comenius, Locke's theory of discipline and virtue, Voltaire's exaltation of the reason, Rousseau's cry "Back to nature," Pestalozzi's faith in the educability of the common people, Herbart's doctrine of interest, and Froebel's discovery of the value of play—all these were waymarks of progress toward a real democracy in which the state should stand as the expression of a common sense of responsibility while education became synonymous with opportunity, with the Christian Church as an inspiring force behind them both. It was not until the nineteenth century, however, that their dreams began to take shape in carefully constructed systems of education on a national scale. The way needed to be prepared through revolution and the overthrow of feudalism and absolutism for modern democracy and the new education. The English Revolution in 1688, the American Revolution in 1776, the French Revolution in 1789, are all milestones in this progress. Some of the characteristic forms of educational organization as created by modern democracy, especially as they reveal those tendencies which concern religion and the relation of the church to education, may now invite our attention.

CHAPTER VI

TYPICAL SYSTEMS OF STATE EDUCATION

1. GERMANY

In view of the efforts of Luther and Melanchthon to promote popular education under the auspices of the state, it is not strange that Germany was, in fact, the first country to establish a state system of compulsory education. In the early part of the eighteenth century, though the energies of the nation were depleted by war, Frederick William I, by his own personal efforts, secured the establishment of over a thousand elementary schools in rural districts, and in 1717 passed a decree making attendance compulsory wherever schools existed.

These policies were continued during the reign of his son, Frederick the Great, under whom religious toleration and freedom of thought and speech were promoted. Actively interested in the advancement of science, he surrounded himself with the foremost scientists of Europe, among whom Voltaire was a brilliant example. Rousseau's influence also was felt in Germany through such educators as Basedow and Salzmann. In 1763 he issued the General Code of Regulations for Rural Schools, from which it is customary to date the Prussian elementary school system. This code required the attendance of all children between the ages of five and thirteen or fourteen, prescribed the course of instruction, including the principles of Christianity, reading, and writing, made provision for examinations and the orderly withdrawal from school, specified the hours of the school session, tuition fees, qualifications for teachers and officers of inspection. The

54

execution of the law, however, was still left with the representatives of the church.

Shortly after the death of Frederick the Great in 1787, the control of the schools was transferred from the church to a national Council of Education. The policy of state control became still more explicit in the Fundamental Legal Code of Prussia, adopted in 1794, in which a chapter was devoted to education. By this code all public schools and educational institutions were brought under the supervision of the state and made subject to its inspection, and such institutions might not thereafter be founded except with the knowledge and consent of the state. Attendance was made compulsory, and school support became a matter of general contribution. Religious instruction was provided, but children were not to be compelled to receive such instruction against the will of their parents. It was recognized that Lutherans and Roman Catholics have equal rights, but no religious obstacle was interposed against school attendance. The principles set forth in the Legal Code have become constant and characteristic features of the German school system: state control, popular support, compulsory attendance, with religion as an integral part of the curriculum, yet with due regard for religious freedom.

After the defeat of Prussia in the battle of Jena in 1806, it became evident that a complete social reorganization was necessary. Accordingly, by royal decree, the feudal aristocracy lost its social and legal prerogatives, and reforms were introduced securing to every individual the full degree of prosperity which he was capable of attaining. A new system of compulsory military service was established, with promotions based on merit, and every effort made to promote industry and commerce. Under these measures wealth rapidly increased, the efficiency of the army was so greatly improved that within a few years

Germany was able to render substantial assistance in the final overthrow of Napoleon, and the spirit of the people rose correspondingly. The middle classes became more and more influential. In 1848 constitutional government was established for the empire and parliamentary representation was granted to the people. During the latter half of the nineteenth century the extraordinary industrial development of Germany has been accompanied by a growth of democratic feeling which has found expression through the social democratic party. During this time also there has been a steady development of national sentiment and self-consciousness, more intense, perhaps, than in the other countries of Europe. This nationalism has been evident in the increase of militarism, in the repudiation of foreign influences in language and general culture, and in the movement for national efficiency. These are the outward signs of a deep-seated conviction that Germany has been intrusted with a precious heritage of learning and ideals, and that the state is the institution through which these are to be safeguarded, transmitted, and advanced. In the eyes of the German people the strongly paternalistic and autocratic attitude of the government was considered to be justified, on the ground that the government is the agency responsible for securing the highest efficiency of all the people, for preserving to them their dearest possessions, and for protecting against exploitations the socially inferior, the weak, and the disabled. Thus Germany, although maintaining a monarchical form of government, might perhaps be said to possess the spirit of democracy in the sense in which Dewey defines democracy, as primarily "a mode of associated living, of conjoint communicated experience" where the individuals of the nation consciously and intelligently participate in a great common interest. It is a democracy, however, which differs from the American type of democracy in being of the socialistic, rather than the individualistic type.

Out of this spirit of nationalism, this "participation in a common interest," this regard for German *Kultur,* sprang the motive for popular education, the idea being that the state, as the external organization of the national life, should provide all members of the nation with the facilities for their moral and intellectual training. Paulsen distinguishes three periods in the history of German education during the nineteenth century. The first, an era of organization lasting for a generation, during which the system was perfected from the university down to the primary schools. This was followed by a period of stagnation coincident with the years of reaction and political revolution about the middle of the century. The last period has witnessed a restoration of confidence between government and people and a renewed enthusiasm for education, "every increase of the intellectual and moral powers of the individual being regarded as a gain to the whole community."

The German system of education comprises three types of school: the *Volkschule,* extending through the twelfth or thirteenth year; the secondary school, or *Gymnasium,* covering about nine years; and the university, with its varied opportunity for graduate and professional work. Prior to 1648 the primary school was an adjunct of the church; between that date and 1800 it was still largely under the direction of the church, though the state exercised its authority in the matter of attendance and gradually extended its scope of influence. Since 1800 the development has been marked and rapid. The *Gymnasium* also is a product of the nineteenth century, and the universities have assumed their present character during the same period.

In the years of depression following the Prussian defeat

at Jena in 1807, the philosopher Fichte attempted to inspire the people to a new patriotism, declaring that the hope of the nation lay in the establishment of popular education according to the methods of Pestalozzi, whom he had learned to know and admire in Zurich. As a result the government sent seventeen teachers to be trained in the school of the great Swiss educator. Paulsen attributes to Pestalozzi the determining of the aim of the elementary school, "the raising of each human being to the level of a free personality, intellectually as well as morally independent," and the finding of a way to attain this freedom, namely, through the exercise of the individual's natural powers. The departure from mechanical methods of memorizing and repetition, and the substitution of methods designed to awaken and stimulate the mental powers and provide opportunity for their exercise, particularly the exercise of judgment and choice, was directly in line with Pestalozzi's doctrine. It was this development of a sense of freedom in choice, and of responsibility as constituting the essence of independence, which was the chief concern of the German people in the days following the French Revolution, as it was the main purpose of Pestalozzi to rouse the masses from their indolence and servility into free, self-respecting citizens.

The influence of Herbart is evident in the later development of the schools, particularly in the selection and arrangement of studies in the curriculum and in the methods of treatment and presentation. At first the work of the schools had been mainly confined to a study of the Bible, the memorization of hymns and Scripture passages, and the learning of the catechism. To this end reading and writing were taught. Arithmetic, grammar, and geography followed. A new interest in historical studies and in nature-study began to develop early in the nineteenth century. After the death of Herbart a movement began which was designed to apply his theories more thoroughly to the work of the primary schools. The studies were classified as to their character-making value for different ages, their appeal to the interests of children and adaptability to their experience, and the sequence of studies was determined upon the basis of their relation to each other in the process of learning. The plan of a course in biblical history, parallel to the course in German history, as worked out in the practice school at Jena, will illustrate this tendency. The course began in the third year and proceeded as follows:

	SACRED HISTORY	GERMAN HISTORY
3d yr.	Patriarchs and Moses.	Legends of Thuringia.
4th yr.	Judges and Kings.	Niebelungen Tales.
5th yr.	Life of Christ.	Charlemagne, etc.
6th yr.	Life of Christ.	Middle Ages.
7th yr.	Apostle Paul.	Reformation.
8th yr.	Luther, Catechism.	Frederick the Great, Napoleonic Wars, etc.

A comparison of these two courses indicates also the progress in content from the more concrete, simple, external, and physical to the more abstract, complex, and spiritual, and in form from the more vivid, dramatic story to the more reflective and argumentative style.

The *Gymnasium* reflects in its very name the interest in classical studies which prevailed in the sixteenth century and afterward. The main subjects at first were Latin, Greek, and Hebrew. As greater emphasis began to be placed upon the vernacular, German and French were added. Mathematics, natural science, history, and geography came soon after. During the nineteenth century a new curriculum was drawn up, in which four principal subjects, Latin, Greek, German, and mathematics, were assigned places of equal honor.

The attempt to provide for all types of student led to

an overcrowding of the curriculum, and there soon arose another type of school devoted to the requirements of modern life, with instruction in modern languages, natural science, and history. This institution was called the *Realschule,* and agitation commenced for recognition upon the same basis with the *Gymnasia.* A third type of school also developed, known as the *Ober-Realschule,* which developed out of an earlier trade-school and offered a course without Latin. Since 1900 the instruction provided by each of these three types has been regarded as of equal value, it being stipulated, however, that each shall provide a nine years' course, and the right being accorded to the different faculties in the universities to specify which type of school shall be recognized as furnishing the proper basis for a particular profession. As a further illustration of this principle of supplying differing types of school to suit varying needs, and as a result of the movement toward the elevation of womanhood, there has arisen a similar school for girls, the *Hoehere Maedchen-schule,* offering a ten years' course.

In all these schools, both primary and secondary, religious instruction occupies an essential place. In the program of the secondary schools announced in 1824 the Minister of Education includes the following note: "Especially must the teacher of religious instruction not lose sight of the fact that he is, in behalf of the state, to educate his pupils to become true Christians; not to teach a kind of ethereal morality robbed of all deep significance, but he must develop a God-fearing moral sentiment, which rests upon faith in Jesus Christ and on the well-founded knowledge of the truths of the Christian redemption." The same requirement appears in school schedules as recently as 1903 and 1907, it being distinctly stated that religion is an indispensible element in the character and training of every citizen, and that instruction in the Word of God is essential to a symmetrical development. It is further suggested that such instruction is to manifest itself by confession, by an active interest in the life of the church, and by exerting a wholesome influence upon society.

While the Scriptures are declared to be the center of instruction, it is stipulated that Bible stories shall be taught in the lower grades, and the memorizing of texts, hymns, and of the catechism shall be grouped about these. In the middle classes stress is laid upon history, biography, and ethical teaching. The New Testament and church history are the principal subjects in the higher grades. As a result of this instruction the pupil becomes familiar with the leading events, persons, and teachings of the Bible, and gains an idea of the church, its history, and the great leaders who played an important part in its development. Again, he becomes acquainted with a wide range of literature of the finest type, committing to memory its choicest passages and appropriating its lofty ideals.[1]

In Germany, as in America, religious freedom is a fundamental principle. This is provided for in Germany by permitting the religious instruction to be given by teachers of different faiths, Protestant, Roman Catholic, or Jewish, to suit the preference of the parent. The teacher must, however, in each case satisfy the state, through examination, of his scholarly and teaching ability and of his special knowledge of the history and teachings of Christianity. The ecclesiastical authorities concur with the state authorities in the appointment of the teachers of religion, and representatives of the church have the right to inspect the instruction and make recommendations to the official provincial board.

This plan of providing religious instruction in state

---

[1] For Curriculum, see Part II, p. 153.

schools is not altogether satisfactory, even to the Germans themselves. While there has been a remarkable development of the curriculum and a thoroughgoing application of scientific method to the other subjects studied, in the case of the Bible and religious instruction the charge is made that traditional methods have been adhered to and traditional interpretations insisted upon which are out of harmony with views held and taught in the other parts of the curriculum. This results sometimes in a perfunctory attitude on the part of the teacher, or in serious perplexity on the part of the pupil. Furthermore, the insistence upon memoriter and catechetical methods often obscures the meaning and beauty of the material studied. The tendency is to make the teaching formal and doctrinal rather than fresh and concrete and vital. Interest is dulled by too frequent review of the same period of history and by too minute division of the instruction into subordinate parts. And while the great aim of education, as conceived by the state, consists in the development of the character and personality of the individual, the aim of religious instruction, as disclosed in the methods in use, seems to be to convey a certain amount of Bible knowledge and secure assent to abstract statements of doctrine. Thus, it is argued, the religious instruction as given at present tends toward artificiality and insincerity and religious indifference.

At the same time sentiment does not yet favor taking religious instruction out of the schools. The conviction is strong that the splendid literature in the Bible and the lofty ideals of Christianity are a part of the birthright of every individual. There is a tendency, however, toward a clearer definition of the real function of church and state in the nurture of the religious life. On the part of the school it is urged that more care be taken to secure as instructors persons who have character and personality and enthusiasm for religion, and that the instructor be left free to develop his instruction in harmony with his own convictions and ideas. On the part of the church, it is seen to be embarrassing for the church to require instructors to present church doctrines. This use of the authority of the state by the church to secure its own ends is held to be pernicious. But it is proposed that the more formal and dogmatic material be given over to the church to handle in its own way, and to hold the church responsible for the development of the pupil's personal religious life.

Education in Germany during the last century has become thoroughly democratized. The influence of the universities has been wholly in this direction. Probably there is no country in the world where intellectual freedom is more highly prized and less interfered with than it is in Germany, especially in university circles. University students and professors are not only permitted but expected, to hold diverse and often conflicting views, the only condition being that the holder shall be ready at all times to defend his views in forceful and logical argument. In the search for truth no criterion is imposed other than the human reason, and since the founding of the University of Berlin in 1810 the ideal of all German universities has been to provide a place and facilities for free investigation into all fields of knowledge.

The church, on the other hand, is still more or less autocratic in Germany; the Roman Catholic Church, on principle. The various branches of the Lutheran Church, which avowedly owe their origin to the protest against autocracy in religion, are nevertheless themselves largely bound by tradition. While there is freedom of theological research in the universities, in the teaching of religion the same methods and the same formulations of doctrine largely prevail which were current in the sixteenth century. It is this contrast in the whole spirit and method of education, between literalness and dogmatism and discipline on the one hand, and freedom, adaptation, and interest on the other, which to-day negatives very largely the efforts put forth in religious instruction in the state schools of Germany.

2. FRANCE

Germany is an autocratic state with a democratic system of education. France has a republican form of government and a system of education that is autocratic. The German system makes for intellectual freedom, even though the state discourages and restricts the exercise of individual initiative. The French system is administered with a military precision which is also unfavorable to the development of individuality through education. In Germany, and particularly in Prussia, a very large proportion of the population is Protestant, but opportunity is given to Protestant and Roman Catholic alike to supply the religious element in education. In France three fourths of the population is Catholic, but so great has been the distrust of the attitude of the church toward the republic that since 1882 the teaching of religion in the public schools has been prohibited, and since 1886 it has been required that all teachers in schools receiving aid from the state should be laymen. By the law which went into effect in 1902 many religious associations were obliged to abolish their schools altogether, under the provision that all associations must be authorized by the government, any deemed detrimental to be dissolved. Thus it appears that while France as well as Germany provides for popular education that is compulsory and free, the forms of educational organization in the two countries are very dissimilar.

The educational system of France is the product of a

very recent and rapid development, but is extraordinarily complete. The impulse toward this development came with the humiliating defeat in the Franco-Prussian war. The republic has felt it to be of the first importance to secure an enlightened citizenship, and has labored perhaps with more zeal than any other European nation for a wide diffusion of intelligence. In 1881-82 laws were passed making attendance compulsory and abolishing tuition fees. As a result the proportion of illiteracy was reduced in seventeen years from 14.4 per cent to 5.1 per cent. Every grade of education has been revolutionized, and the schools from the lowest grade, or mother-school, to the university have been closely articulated into a system directed by a strongly organized central power.

The type of educational organization in France is quite different from that familiar in the United States. In France, primary and secondary education do not form one continuous and progressive series but, rather, two distinct and parallel types of schools. The primary instruction extends over the period between the ages of six and thirteen, but this period may be extended below by the "maternal schools"—a composite of kindergarten and day nursery—and above by extension courses, upper primary schools, and manual training and apprentice schools. In this way the period covered by the system of "primary" instruction may extend from three to sixteen years of age. "Secondary" education, on the other hand, begins at nine years and continues for nine years. This also has a preparatory section, covering the years between seven and nine. That is to say, the primary school in France is not a preparation for the secondary school but is designed to fit pupils for agricultural, industrial, and commercial life. The secondary schools, on the other hand, are intended to prepare for university and professional life. The whole question of education is considered from the national point of view, and the system of education is one of the most highly centralized in the world, under the administration of the minister of education. Separate normal schools are provided for the preparation of teachers, who are all officers of the state and must pledge themselves, as normal students, to teach for at least ten years.

Since 1882 moral and civic instruction has headed the list of required subjects in the elementary schools of France and is as much an integral part of the curriculum as is arithmetic or any other subject. The program of moral instruction is very complete and represents the effort to find an effective and nonsectarian means of developing the ethical side of the child's nature in a system of popular education from which religion has been excluded. The time devoted to such instruction during the elementary and intermediate years, ages seven to eleven, is one hour a week; in the upper courses, eleven to thirteen years, one hour and a half a week. This time is divided into three equal periods and distributed over the week on alternate days, the instruction being given usually at nine o'clock in the morning. Appeal is made to the sense of duty rather than to the religious motive, although duties toward God are mentioned among those obligatory upon the individual. Creeds and catechisms are prohibited.

For the earlier years, seven to nine, the instruction consists in part of familiar conversations between teacher and pupils, in part of precepts, parable, and fables which are designed to build up moral standards in the pupil. In addition to these the teacher directs practical exercises which tend to put morality into action. Effort is constantly made, through observation of the character of the individual pupils, the enforcement of school discipline, appeal to the feelings and moral judgment, and correction of false motives, to stimulate and develop in the pupils a sensitiveness to moral obligations. Aversion to immoral conduct is awakened by encouraging the pupils to bring in from their own observation illustrations of the bad effects of drunkenness, idleness, cruelty, and other forms of vice. On the other hand, it is attempted, through the contemplation of scenes of grandeur in nature, to arouse feelings of admiration and religious reverence.

During the next years, nine to eleven, instruction is made more definite and is concerned with the relations which the pupil sustains to society in its various aspects. Thus the duties of the child toward the members of the family, his duty in school both with respect to his attitude toward his teacher and toward the work assigned; his duty toward his country; his duty toward himself—cleanliness, temperance, and sobriety; his duty as a member of the economic order—thrift, avoidance of debt; his duty toward other men—kindness, charity, justice, fraternity; and his duty toward God and God's laws as revealed in conscience and reason—the duty of obedience and reverence; all these are taken up in order.[1] This instruction is followed, during the eleventh to the thirteenth years, by a still more detailed study of duties toward family, society, and country.

The textbooks in use differ in method of presentation, some containing many quotations from literature illustrating the moral qualities to be taught. Others emphasize definitions or present the teaching in the form of summaries. The method of grading is also diverse, in some instances separate treatment being provided for the elementary and intermediate and highest divisions, following the divisions in the primary schools; in other cases all are combined in one textbook. Some authors provide a handbook for the teacher to accompany the pupil's textbook, suggesting additional material and methods for

[1] See Part II, p. 156.

teaching. In general, there is a greater abundance and variety of textbooks for the intermediate courses than for the elementary or higher courses.

From an examination of the textbooks in general use, one gains the impression that while a large amount of material has been gathered together dealing with moral relations, it has been assembled primarily for reasons which appeal to the adult. Little attempt has been made to consider the interests of the pupil or to select those duties which suit his present need. Much of the material will never have practical value save for a small proportion of the pupils who happen to be engaged in some particular calling. The material is presented with too much of hortatory emphasis, with too little attempt to win the attention and cooperation of the pupil. It is expected that many of the statements and precepts will be memorized, and to this end the compositions and illustrative material will prove helpful. There is almost complete absence, however, of any provision to secure moral training. Indeed, as one has said, "France affords the anomaly of a program of moral instruction suited to a republic, and a school organization adapted to a monarchy. The teacher is expected to instruct his pupils in initiative and self-reliance, but the strongly centralized school system forbids him to exercise either of these admirable qualities. And the discipline maintained prevents pupils from putting this teaching into practice. Personal dignity and self-respect are to be taught, but neither is possible in any high degree to the teacher, whose duties are so minutely prescribed that the minister of education at Paris can tell exactly what is being done at any given instant in every school in France. Both are hostile to the dominant spirit of French life—militarism."[1]

---

[1] Education and National Character, Proceedings of Religious Education Association, 1908, 187-188, Myers, "Moral Instruction in the Public Schools of France."

On the whole, it cannot be said that the results of the French system of moral education are entirely satisfactory. The list of duties prescribed in the official program is comprehensive and the machinery for carrying out the program is elaborate and impressive. The program, however, is defective in that it ignores the stages of child development, with their characteristic interests and needs, and furthermore in its inconsistency with the scheme of organization and administration. The textbooks and methods of presentation are artificial and mechanical and tend to make the teaching perfunctory and lacking in vitality. In consequence, morals as taught in the schools of France may be regarded as a subject of study rather than as a course of training in conduct. This would seem to justify the conclusion that the results "appear pitiably insignificant when compared with the magnitude of machinery and effort which produced them."[1]

France has been at great pains to exclude positive instruction in religion from its system of popular education. The state does not, however, altogether repudiate religion as a factor in education. On the contrary, it recognizes its right to such a place by leaving Thursday afternoons free for the imparting of religious instruction in the churches. The importance of such instruction is thus implicitly admitted, but its nature and scope, its content and method, are left to the church to determine.

3. ENGLAND

Notwithstanding its monarchical form of government, England is often cited as the best illustration of a democracy. It is said that in England there is a disposition to insist upon individual rights, so strong and so widely prevalent as to amount to a national characteristic, and at the same time a sense of obligation to serve the com-

---

[1] There is widespread dissatisfaction and agitation for improvement.

mon welfare that is hardly less prevalent and strong. On the other hand, some of the mental attitudes which accompanied feudalism seem, to the American observer, to have been singularly persistent in English society. The proprietors of large estates, surrounded by a yeomanry more or less dependent upon their generosity and benevolence, have kept alive the distinction between those of "gentle" birth and the "common people," a distinction which is not wholly obliterated even to-day, in spite of the growth of industrialism and the movement of the population toward the city. If this stratification of society into classes circumscribes the area of freedom for a given individual and limits the scope of his initiative, it also safeguards his rights within that area, for any "gentleman" would scorn to exploit a weaker member of society or take unfair advantage for his personal profit.

England has an established church, the Church of England. Here, also, the spirit of individualism finds expression in the High Church, Broad Church, and other less pronounced tendencies. Furthermore, the adherents of the state church only slightly outnumber those of other communions, if at all. Roman Catholics are numerous and the nonconformist bodies include Methodists, Baptists, and Congregationalists, as well as Presbyterians, Friends, Unitarians, and others. The number of Jews is relatively small. As in other countries, education in England was in the hands of the church until very recently.

To the presence of class spirit and the prevalence of a strong religious sentiment has been chiefly due the fact that the history of education in England has been "largely a record of experiments." The movement for popular education was long retarded in England through the apprehension of the upper classes, lest education should turn out to be a dangerous thing. In 1833 the question was under discussion as to whether the House of Commons should make its first grant, of £20,000, "for purposes of education." Cobbett, otherwise regarded as a very progressive man, raised this vigorous objection: "Take two men, one that can plow and make hurdles and be a good shepherd, and one that can plow and read, and the first is the better man." He regarded the proposed grant as a movement "to increase the number of schoolmasters and mistresses, that new class of idlers." And for a long time after that, it was frequently charged that education was responsible for making the rising generation of workmen restless and discontented with their lot in life. Was not the scarcity of agricultural laborers and the decay of agriculture a direct result of the overschooling of laborers' children?

Another curious objection against the public support of popular education was that voiced by Disraeli, in 1839. He argued that "the individual should be strong and the government weak, and that to diminish the duties of the citizens was to imperil the rights of the subjects; that wherever was found what was called paternal government, was found a state education; that it had been discovered that the best way to secure implicit obedience was to commence tyranny in the nursery; that the truth was, where elementary instruction was left to the government the subject became a machine; that if the movers of the measure for a plan of national education persisted and succeeded, they would eventually find that they had revolutionized English character, and when that was effected they could no longer expect English achievements; and that he should oppose to the utmost of his power this rash attempt to centralize instruction." Such utterances from men eminent in English public life indicate the reluctance with which the government came to commit itself to the policy of appropriating money for educational purposes.

71

Objection against a national system of education was also brought by the Church of England, which regarded the movement as a direct attack, not only upon the church as an institution, but upon religion itself. This point of view found expression in statements like the following:

All that is happening in the matter of education is a call to the church to put out her strength and to do valiant battle for her principles in the schools. . . . Our work is to teach children the facts of our religion, the doctrines of our religion, the duties of our religion. We must teach them the facts of our religion that they may be intelligent Christians, not ignorant as heathens; the doctrines, that they may not be Christians only, but churchmen; the duties, that they may not be churchmen only, but communicants. This last, in fact, is the object at which we are uniformly to aim, the training of the young Christian for full communion with the church, and as preliminary to that, a training for confirmation. The whole school time of a child should gradually lead up to this. . . . The time has come when probably the whole fate of the Church of England, humanly speaking, will turn upon the hold she may have upon the rising generation. Political changes are giving more and more power to the people. If the church has the people with her, she will be beyond all danger from adverse legislation. Let her, then, educate the children of the people in her principles.

At the same time the education which the Church of England attempted to provide through its schools, and that which was provided through other agencies of a private and philanthropic nature, was inadequate. In the attempt to meet the existing need, there grew up a system of instruction by older pupil teachers, or "monitors," especially developed by Joseph Lancaster (1778-1838) and called by his name. These Lancasterian schools were rigidly graded and served for a time as a kind of substitute for a national system of schools. They had no conception, however, of the psychological aspects of teaching and no acquaintance with the ideals of education which were developing on the continent. The instruction was largely memoriter, formal and superficial.

When at last the argument for a national system of education could not longer be gainsaid, the movement was still delayed because of the difficulty of providing such education in a manner consistent with English ideas of religious liberty. Denominational sensitiveness would hardly permit the turning over to the state of the whole task of administering education, including instruction in religion, as had been the case in Germany. On the other hand, it was still less possible for England to follow the course of France and exclude religion altogether from a state system of education. England will have nothing to do with an education which is exclusively secular. The difficulty of providing a system of popular education which should include religion and at the same time avoid giving offense to denominational feeling seemed for a time insurmountable, and for many years little was accomplished toward the development of a national organization.

Previous to 1870 England, of all civilized countries, had the most backward and least effective educational organization. Since that date, considerable progress has been made in the extension of school privileges and the raising of educational standards, and the idea of free elementary schools and compulsory attendance is now firmly established in English legislation and practice. The foundation of the present system was laid in the passing of the Elementary Education Act of 1870, which required that each district should provide adequate facilities for elementary instruction. The Education Department was obliged to make a statement of what was demanded in each case. Where provision was not made voluntarily to meet these demands a school board was to be elected in the district, to provide, maintain, and keep efficient the requisite elementary schools. Children attending "board schools" were to pay a weekly fee to be determined by the board, which was, however, to be remitted in cases where parents were regarded as unable to pay. School boards were allowed, if they desired, to require compulsory attendance of all children between the ages of five and thirteen years, who were not receiving instruction elsewhere, unless these children had passed the standards of scholarship fixed by the local authorities, or were exempt under the Factory Acts. In 1876 the age of possible compulsion was raised to fourteen years, and it was enacted that children under ten years should not be employed at labor. In 1880 school boards were required to make attendance compulsory for all children under ten years of age. In 1889 the age was again raised to twelve years, and in 1900 it might be extended to fourteen years. In 1890 the payment of tuition fees in elementary schools was abolished. At about this time the Education Department was replaced by a Board of Education for England and Wales, including in its membership the chancellor of the exchequer.

In addition to the board schools, "voluntary schools" have also been generally maintained. These schools were largely under the control of the Church of England and were supported by voluntary subscriptions. The opposition of the Church of England to the establishment of board schools has already been referred to, and many gave of their time and money for the maintenance of the voluntary schools because of the fear that if these schools should be replaced by board schools, under popular control, the schools would become not only nonsectarian, but "godless." Undoubtedly this attitude has had great influence with the managers of the board schools in securing for these schools constant and systematic religious instruction. The debate upon this question finally resulted in introducing into the Education Act the familiar "conscience clause" from which the following paragraphs are quoted:

It shall not be required, as a condition of any child being admitted into or continuing in the school, that he shall attend or abstain from attending any Sunday school, or any place of religious worship, or that he shall attend any religious observance or any instruction in religious subjects in the school or elsewhere, from which observance or instruction he may be withdrawn by his parent, or that he shall, if withdrawn by his parent, attend the school on any day exclusively set apart for religious observance by the religious body to which his parents belong.

The time or times during which any religious observance is practiced, or instruction in religious subjects is given, at any meeting of the school shall be either at the beginning or the end of such meeting, and shall be inserted in a time-table to be approved by the Education Department, and to be kept permanently and conspicuously affixed in every schoolroom; and any scholar may be withdrawn by his parent from such observance or instruction without forfeiting any of the other benefits of the school.

The school shall be open at all times to the inspection of her Majesty's inspectors, so, however, that it shall be no part of the duties of such inspectors to inquire into any instruction in religious subjects given at such school or to examine any scholar therein in religious knowledge or in any religious subject or book.

No religious catechism or religious formulary which is distinctive of any particular denomination shall be taught in the school.

As the board schools developed, the voluntary schools complained that while they gave instruction to as many, or more, children than were cared for in the board schools, the funds received from subscription were not sufficient to enable them to maintain the standards of the board schools, which were supported by taxation. In response to this complaint, an act was passed in 1902, applying everywhere except in London, which swept away the old school boards and replaced them by education authorities empowered to provide for all the schools in their respective districts out of local taxes. Whatever schools receive such support are under the general supervision of the local education authority, which is the county or borough council. An education committee, whose appointment is regulated by the same authority, has power to determine the secular education to be given in the public elementary schools, and to fix the number and the educational qualifications of the teachers. No school which fails to comply with the requirements of the education committee can receive a government grant. On the other hand, the managers of the denominational schools are allowed to determine the religious instruction given therein and the religious qualifications of the teachers. But a pupil need not attend such instruction against his will, and cannot be excluded from the school for religious reasons.

The Act of 1902 was bitterly assailed by the Nonconformists, who were apprehensive lest the Church of England might exercise an undue influence in educational matters and who were further opposed to the principle of being taxed for the support of instruction which might possibly prove to be sectarian. In reply to this objection it was pointed out that the Established Church had provided practically all the elementary schools prior to 1870 and that an expenditure of £50,000,000 would be involved in creating new facilities for pupils in case the facilities already at hand in the voluntary schools should not be utilized.

By this time, however, another strong argument for the nationalizing of education was advanced. Owing to the growth of the industrial system, the development of commercial interests, and the pressure of competition, an insistent demand had arisen for wider diffusion of knowledge, and especially for industrial and technical education. This situation was made clear in an article by Sir John Gorst, shortly before the passage of the Act of 1902, from which the following extract is taken:

Unless reform is very promptly undertaken, the English nation will be less instructed than the people of European states, of America, and even of our own colonies. . . . If it is true that the international rivalry of the future will be one of commerce and manufactures, the uninstructed nations will have to reconcile themselves to be the menial servants of the rest of the world and to perform the lower and rougher operations of modern industry; while all those which require taste, skill, and invention gradually fall into the hands of people who are better taught. If a race that aspires to exercise imperial influence in the world must possess knowledge as well as courage, and intelligence as well as wealth, the people of England must be content to see the empire decline, unless other citizens of the empire take up the task for which the lack of public instruction renders the people of England unequal. It is therefore no exaggeration to call the state of public instruction in England an emergency. The danger is imminent. There is no time to lose. Teachers and schools cannot be created in a moment by act of Parliament. If all the authorities in England—the people, the parents, the churches, the county and municipal councils, the central government—get to work this day in earnest to improve public instruction, it would be years before the improved machinery could be got into working order and our public instruction brought up to the level of that which has for many years already been possessed by our commercial and industrial rivals.

The benefits anticipated from the nationalizing of education outweighed, in the judgment of Parliament, the dangers urged on sectarian grounds. Nevertheless, the problem of determining the relation between the board school and the voluntary school is but a phase of the larger problem of the relation of state education to religious education, and this larger problem still remains unsettled.

Not only did the Act of 1902 open the way for the unification and improvement of elementary education: one of its main purposes was to assure the support of secondary education out of the public funds. Previous to this time secondary education in England had not been comprehensively dealt with. One of the chief reasons for this delay is ascribed to the fact that a false distinction had been prevalent in the popular mind, primary education having been thought of as being for the poor, who cannot pay for it, while secondary education was for the "middle classes," who can pay. Secondary education was therefore largely left to private institutions, conducted for profit, or to those supported by endowments. "But the new point of view is that it is the business of the state to keep open the ways of intellectual opportunity from the bottom to the top of the national system of education, in order to secure as much as possible of the advantage which accrues to the community from making the best of its great abilities, however humbly born." In accordance with this principle, the Act of 1902 authorized the education authorities to consider within their respective areas the needs of secondary education and to take such steps as seemed to them desirable, after consulting with the Board of Education, to supply or aid in the supply of such instruction, being empowered to raise taxes for the purpose.

With regard to religious instruction, the provisions of the Act of 1902 were similar to those of the earlier act of 1870, providing that the council, in the application of money for school purposes, shall not require that any particular form of religious instruction or worship, or any religious catechism or formulary which is distinctive of any particular denomination shall or shall not be taught in any school *aided* by the council, and, on the other hand, that no pupil, on the ground of his religious belief, shall be excluded from the privileges of the school, or in any wise be discriminated against. Furthermore, it provides that no catechism or formulary distinctive of any particular religious denomination shall be taught in any school *provided* by the council, except where the council may permit, at the request of parents and scholars, the giving of religious instruction in the school otherwise than at the cost of the council. When so given it must be under conditions prescribed by the council and in such manner as to give no unfair advantage to any denomination. The question of religious affiliation or attendance upon religious worship is not to be raised with any pupil as a condition of his being admitted to any school aided by a government grant; and the times for religious worship or instruction are to be conveniently arranged for the withdrawal of any pupil who may not care to attend.[1]

England now accepts the principle that education is a responsibility of the state rather than of the parent or the church, and that the state must provide education, impartially and in all forms, for all its citizens. It still regards religious instruction, however, as an integral and necessary part of education and believes that the essentials of religious instruction can be so imparted as not to offend denominational sensibilities. This part of the program has met with opposition from the Established Church, which has taken the ground that it was in a position officially to determine the nature of religious instruction, and also from Nonconformists, who have objected to the appropriation of public funds for what they regard as denominational or sectarian teaching. The situation is the more complicated in England owing to the fact that the schools are of two classes: those created by the state and supported by the state, and those created by private (church) initiative but now taken over and aided by the state.

---

[1] For typical curricula of England, Australia, and Canada, see Part II, pp. 158, 167.

79

CHAPTER VII

THE AMERICAN PUBLIC SCHOOL SYSTEM IN ITS RELATION TO THE CHURCHES AND DEMOCRACY[1]

THE impulse toward popular education in the United States was first felt in New England, and, as in Germany, it sprang from the desire to make the Bible accessible to all. But while the movement started in each country from the same root-idea, the course of subsequent development in the United States differed in some important respects from that pursued in Germany. These differences are perhaps mainly to be accounted for by the fact that the spirit of the Reformation reached America by way of England and Holland, and brought with it the flavor of Calvinism and the Puritan movement. These acquired characteristics considerably modified the conception of religion, the conception of the state, and the conception of the relation of education to church and state.

In England, the assertion of individualism in religion was perhaps less pronounced than in Germany. There was, indeed, violent opposition to foreign ecclesiastical authority, to monasticism and to formalism in worship. Opinion, however, was sharply divided between those who favored the maintenance of the Roman Catholic Church,

---

[1] Strictly speaking, the term, "American Public School System," is a misnomer. There is no national system of education in the United States in the sense that there is in Germany, France, or England. Although the national government has a Commissioner of Education, it has no direct administrative relation to the public schools, the control and support of which are left to the several State governments. Grants of land have been made for educational purposes to the newer States, some 86,000,000 acres having been devoted to this purpose. These grants have been supplemented in some instances by gifts to the several States from the surplus funds in the National Treasury, but aside from these activities the central government has mainly confined its efforts in behalf of education to the gathering of statistics and the preparation of reports.

those who would have a modified Catholicism suited to English tastes, with services in the English language and directly responsible to the English sovereign, and those who would make a clean sweep of things and introduce thoroughgoing changes in doctrine and in forms of government and worship, to correspond with continental Calvinism. It was the party which advocated the middle course which finally prevailed in England, although Calvinism became dominant in Scotland. Moreover, England had felt the influence of Erasmus and Wycliffe, who, though conscious of the need of effecting moral reforms, were humanists and held that an intimate and appreciative familiarity with the classical authors, the church Fathers and the Scriptures was all that was necessary to bring these about. At all events, education in England remained until very recently largely a function of the church.

The Puritan party, however, including an extreme radical wing, the "Separatists," who held that the organization of the church should be in separate, self-governing congregations, found themselves the victims of discrimination and persecution. Many of them fled to Holland and to America. Between 1628 and 1640 about twenty thousand English Puritans migrated to New England, a homogeneous company of thrifty and capable people, who had been prosperous at home and constituted the sturdiest element in the English nation. The towns where they settled around Massachusetts Bay were modeled after the English parishes and townships. Each town, however, was a perfect illustration of pure democracy, with the church as the center of its life. The church was a self-governing congregation, and the community, likewise, was self-governing through the town meeting. When these townships came to unite under a common government, the model after which the state was patterned was the religious republic of Geneva. It was this Puritan religious commonwealth which set the fashion for democracy in the United States and first gave impulse to the movement for compulsory popular education.

But when the New England colonists perceived the need of more general and adequate education they did not recommend that the state assume the responsibility of providing an educational system and by exercise of its authority compel the attendance of pupils, as Luther had done in Germany. To their mind there was no authority in church or state, except the will of the free citizens as expressed in their democratic assemblies; the same free citizens constituted both church and state, and if any preeminence was to be accorded their acts in one capacity as compared with the other, it belonged to the church rather than the state. Their point of view is clearly reflected in the well-known law, passed by the Massachusetts Bay Colony in 1647 and providing for the establishment of schools at public expense:

It being one chief point of that old deluder, Satan, to keep men from the knowledge of the Scriptures, as in former times by keeping them in an unknown tongue, so in these latter times by persuading from the use of tongues, that so at last the true sense and meaning of the original might be clouded by false glosses of saint-seeming deceivers, that learning might not be buried in the grave of our fathers in church and commonwealth, the Lord assisting our endeavors—It is therefore ordered that every township in this jurisdiction, after the Lord has increased them to the number of fifty householders shall then forthwith appoint one within their town to teach all such children as shall resort to him to write and read, whose wages shall be paid either by the parents or masters of such children, or by the inhabitants in general, by way of supply, as the major part of those that order the prudentials of the town shall appoint; providing those that send their children be not oppressed by paying much more than they can have them taught for in other towns; and it is forthwith ordered that where any town shall increase to the number of one hundred families or householders, they shall set up a grammar school, the master thereof being able to instruct youth so far as they may be fitted for the university, provided that if any town neglect the performance hereof above one year, that every town shall pay £5 to the next school till they shall perform this order.

This law is often referred to as "the corner stone of the American public school system." This statement is justified in the sense that this was the first recognition in the United States of the principle that the responsibility for providing education rests upon the community. In this instance the state acted as the agent of the church; the state has continued to act as the responsible agent in education, although all thought of its connection with the church has long since faded from consciousness.

This use of the authority of the state in the service of the church had not yet become the practice in England and did not win popular acceptance there for many years. In this respect, Massachusetts leaned more toward the usage in Germany, Holland, and Scotland, which countries had already passed laws compelling the establishment of schools. Wherever Protestant influence was dominant, there was to be found an emphasis upon popular education as the means for disseminating a knowledge of the Bible.

The schools in Massachusetts did not enjoy unbroken prosperity. During the latter half of the seventeenth century popular interest in the maintenance of schools rapidly declined. This was due in part to the influx of many new settlers who were adherents of other forms of the Protestant faith—Baptists, Episcopalians, Quakers—whose presence diluted the strength of the Calvinistic sentiment and modified somewhat its intolerant despotism. This weakening of control and introduction of rival elements into the community life gave rise to religious controversy and bred indifference on the school question.

To meet this situation, the fine for failure to maintain a town school was increased in 1701 to £20, which had a stimulating effect upon many communities. Another difficulty arose from the fact that in the earlier days, the settlements were compactly made around the meeting-house as a center, but as time went on the population became more scattered, as the danger from Indians decreased and fertile lands made their appeal to the thrifty farmer. To serve the more sparsely settled communities, "moving schools" were established, holding their sessions in one section of the town for a portion of the year, then moving on to another. Thus arose the custom of providing "district" schools.

Throughout New England the history of education followed a similar course. Connecticut passed a law in 1650 which was practically in verbatim agreement with that passed three years before by Massachusetts. Outside New England there was less interest in establishing State systems of compulsory education.

In 1683 Pennsylvania passed a law requiring that all children should be so taught as to be able to read the Bible and to write, by twelve years of age. Pennsylvania, however, differed from the New England colonies in one important particular. These had been settled by vigorous pioneers of homogeneous Puritan stock, many of whom were themselves graduates of universities in England. Pennsylvania, on the other hand, was much more cosmopolitan, including in its Protestant population Baptists, Quakers, Methodists, Presbyterians, Lutherans, members of the German Reformed Church, Moravians, and others. All held to the Protestant principle, that ability to read the Bible was necessary to salvation, but each had its own school as the agency by which this end was to be attained.

The compulsory education law in Pennsylvania, therefore, soon became a dead letter, school facilities being supplied by voluntary effort and through the cooperation of interested and resourceful families. Neighborhood schools became common in the western part of the State, and together with schools established through direct influence of churches, remained until 1834 the principal available agencies for popular education.

In the United States, as in Germany, France, and England, the public schools were not established upon a firm basis until during the nineteenth century. In Massachusetts a law was passed in 1826 requiring every town to choose a school committee to have general supervision of all the schools of the town, select textbooks, examine teachers, and provide certificates. This was an important step toward setting professional standards. In 1834 a State school fund was set aside, to participate in which the towns were required to raise a tax for each child of school age and make statistical reports. A State Board of Education was created in 1837 to secure information regarding the schools and made recommendations to the Legislature. The first secretary of this board was Horace Mann, who succeeded in arousing public sentiment in the support of the schools and with great skill pointed out existing defects and outlined methods of improvement. Among the tangible results accomplished were the erection of schoolhouses, an increase in the salaries of teachers, a lengthening of the school year, the securing of more effective supervision, and the establishment of normal schools.

The State constitution of Pennsylvania, which was adopted in 1790, provided for the establishment of schools throughout the State "in such manner that the poor may be taught gratis." It was not until 1834 that a law was passed creating a State school system which should provide for all the children. This law was widely and bitterly opposed, partly by churches of various denominations which had maintained their own schools and feared interference with vested interests, and partly also by childless individuals who objected to being taxed for school purposes. In a few years, however, opposition was overcome.

New York was administered by an English governor until the American Revolution. Consequently many of the schools of New York city were maintained by the Society for the Propagation of the Gospel in Foreign Parts, organized in England in 1701. In 1805 New York city was still depending entirely upon private and church schools. In that year the Legislature permitted the incorporation of "The Society for Establishing a Free School in the City of New York," for children not otherwise provided for by any religious society. Aid was granted from funds contributed by the State and by the city, according to a plan not unlike that followed in England with the board schools. Sectarian difficulties also arose in New York similar to those in England, with this difference—that New York had no established church. So bitter did the strife become between Protestants and Catholics over the granting of school funds that the Legislature created in 1842 the New York City Board of Education, to consist of members popularly elected from each ward, and providing for local inspectors and trustees. By this same act of the Legislature it was decided that no portion of the school funds could be granted to any school in which "any religious sectarian doctrine or tenet shall be taught, inculcated or practiced."

. In the earlier part of the nineteenth century, when the problem of finding a sufficient number of competent teachers was more acute, the monitorial system of Lancaster was widely adopted in the United States, but when normal schools became more abundant and efficient this

86

system was soon superseded. During the last fifty years progress has been rapid in all branches of State education, particularly in respect to the expansion of the curriculum and the development of methods of teaching. In this development the influence of the great leaders in Switzerland and Germany has been marked and constant, although their theories have been greatly modified to suit the different conditions in this country.

Pestalozzi should perhaps be named as the one deserving first to be mentioned, not only because he was actually one of the earliest in order of time, but because there is much that still abides which is directly traceable to him. Introduced into the United States through one of his associates, Naef, who came to teach in Philadelphia in 1806, the theories of Pestalozzi became widely disseminated in periodical literature, and his methods were gradually adopted into individual schools and normal schools. In 1860 an active propaganda known as the Oswego Movement was undertaken, largely as the result of successful experiments in England and Canada in connection with the industrial education of juvenile delinquents. The application of the principle of manual labor was not limited, however, in the United States to its original Pestalozzian purpose of moral redemption, but it was utilized in providing the possibility of self-support for needy students. In the latter part of the century it began to be generally adopted here as the basis of organization for juvenile reformatory institutions. Pestalozzi's influence is perhaps best illustrated in the application of his principles to the methods of instruction in language, elementary science, home geography, and primary arithmetic. Colburn's arithmetic, which was in general use for nearly forty years, is the most conspicuous example of a textbook constructed in accordance with Pestalozzi's theories, the distinctive feature of which was the inductive procedure from simple, concrete, known objects to more complex and abstract ideas.

In the early nineties a movement began in America for popularizing the teachings of Herbart, Charles DeGarmo, and the brothers, Frank and Charles McMurry, being the most vigorous apostles of the movement. The effects have been seen in an expansion of the curriculum to include especially a larger proportion of historical studies, and in the interpretation of history so as to disclose its broader and more vital social meanings. The appreciation of literature, and particularly the study of complete classics, has received a stimulus from the Herbartian movement. Another result is seen in the more recent attempts to estimate the cultural values in different studies and to arrange the subjects in the curriculum so that their effect shall be unified and cumulative. This principle of concentration was especially elaborated in the school work of Colonel Parker in Chicago. Herbart's influence is perhaps most generally apparent in its application to teaching method. The doctrine of "interest" and the "five formal steps" in teaching have become familiar commonplaces.

The first American kindergarten was opened by Miss Elizabeth Peabody in Boston in 1860, and the first American school for training kindergarten teachers in the same city eight years later. In the last two decades of the nineteenth century the kindergarten movement rapidly spread throughout the United States, kindergartens being maintained in many communities by kindergarten associations, and in others becoming established as a part of the regular public school system.

The influence of the kindergarten extended upward through all the grades, appearing in the increased use of constructive and expressive activities for educational purposes. Its wider application is to be seen in the manual training movement, designed to aid the pupil in "making the hand the obedient servant of the brain." Between the years 1880 and 1890 manual training was adopted in the high schools of nearly forty cities, and by 1905 was taught in about two hundred cities. Since then the demand for less formal exercises, and especially for special forms of industrial and vocational training, has operated to check somewhat the growth of the movement. Broadly speaking, the principle of self-expression, and in particular, of motor expression, so strongly advocated by Froebel, is now universally recognized as one of the first essentials of educational method. The late William James was perhaps the most influential expounder of this principle.

Thus, in the United States as in England and upon the continent of Europe, the nineteenth century has been a time of great activity in education. Accepting the principle that the State is responsible for the education of all its children, the Legislatures of all the States have worked out their own independent systems, some of the newer States taking advantage of the experience of the others by incorporating in their State constitutions provision for a complete system of popular education from primary school to university.

Following these preliminary steps of organization and extension there have come successive waves of intensive development, with their emphasis upon object teaching and illustration, scientific observation, curriculum expansion, adaptation and correlation, self-expression, manual training, sense and motor training, industrial and vocational training. Rousseau's plea that education should be suited to the needs of the child, and Comenius' suggestion that it follow the order of child development, have at last been heard. One element, however, is still lacking from the system of popular education in the United States—the element of religion.

However much we may deplore the exclusion of religion from the subjects taught in the public school curriculum, this fact should not and does not blind the American people to the value of the public school as a democratizing agency. Its influence in this respect has been often remarked, especially as it concerns the newer Americans, large numbers of whom came to these shores too late in life to learn to speak a new language with any fluency and will always carry about with them an old-world attitude toward government and citizenship. With these, democracy may never be anything else than something vague and shadowy. But their children generally become much more truly democratic, the great agency in this transformation being, of course, the public school.

Here are assembled all ages and types, and all are surrounded by the same atmosphere, all subjected to the same requirements. Here, for the first time in many cases, is it possible for the child of the man who happens to be at the bottom of the social scale to prove his right to recognition on equal terms with the child of one who may regard himself as belonging among the favored few. In this friendly competition it is by no means universal that the child who has had the more favorable environment wins the laurels over the other. Moreover, the very participation of all the children in a common program of work and of play is promotive of a deeper sympathy, understanding, and respect between the different elements of the community life. The public school is itself a democracy in miniature, and through the wise efforts of educators in introducing measures of self-government among the pupils themselves it is providing more and more not only the atmosphere, but actual training in the practice of democracy.

No institution stands closer to the people, being immediately related to the local community. It is supported by direct taxation; it has won the interest, respect, and cordial support of practically all elements of the population; it has been comparatively free from political interference and is peculiarly responsive to public opinion. It has been remarkably effective in reaching the children of all the people and in promoting a wide diffusion of intelligence. It is neither strange nor unreasonable that the American people should regard the public school as perhaps their most characteristic and altogether hopeful achievement and as a peculiarly valuable social asset.

The impulse which gave rise to the movement for popular education in all countries has been traced back to the Reformation. During all this period since the Reformation there has been a constant tendency toward intellectual freedom and real democracy. The development of the reasoning powers, the recovery of the stores of classic learning, the enthusiasm for discovery, and the promise of new knowledge to be obtained through observation of facts and phenomena in nature, the study of the mind and its processes, the protest against the authority of tradition and all restraints of arbitrary formality, the new faith in the educability of all men, the new hope for society to be realized through education, the new conception of the teacher's work, the attempt to analyze and classify all knowledge with reference to its use in teaching and its value to life, the development of methods of teaching based upon the facts of child development and in accordance with the laws of growth—all these indicate an increasing appreciation of the value of the individual, a growing reverence for personality, and a determination to secure more and more for each individual the opportunity for self-improvement and self-expression; that is, to realize democracy.

It is customary to characterize this movement as a movement toward the secularization of education. If by this is meant the tendency to popularize education and make it available for all men, the determination to take the responsibility for the support and direction of education out of the hands of ecclesiastical organizations and place it upon the shoulders of all the people, the change in the conception of the aims of education from the assumption that it was a means of acquainting children with the teachings of the church, or of enabling them to read the Bible upon which those teachings were based, to the idea that the curriculum of study should include a wide range of subjects many of which cannot be classified under the term "religion"—if this be the meaning of secularization then there is ground for interpreting the movement as a secular movement. The word "secular," however, should not mislead us into thinking of the modern movement toward popular education as in any sense anti-Christian or even non-Christian or as opposed to the work of the Christian Church. Though some of the philosophers who have uttered themselves with reference to education have been skeptical in their attitude, and some few have been called atheists, secularization, as applied to education, really means emancipation, freedom—intellectual freedom, moral freedom, religious freedom—and those who sometimes seem most jealous against permitting the church any share in the direction of public education are not necessarily expressing a lack of sympathy with religion or Christianity, but, rather, a distrust of the spirit of sectarianism and an anxiety lest the freedom which has been so dearly won may be impaired.

At the same time the fact remains that the enormous intensive development which has taken place in American education, however valuable as a preparation for democracy, has not only taken place without reference to an inclusion of the religious element, but has actually preoccupied in large measure the place in the life of the child which might otherwise be utilized by the churches for religious instruction, were they prepared to provide it. This overcrowding of program is more noticeable in the United States than in Germany, where religion already has its allotted place in the curriculum and where different types of education are provided in distinct types of school. It operates peculiarly to the disadvantage of Protestants, since the Roman Catholics maintain parochial schools in which they control the entire program, while the Jews, observing the seventh day as a day of worship, are in a better position to utilize Sunday for a vigorous educational program, if desired. The time has arrived for the Protestant churches to assume together the responsibility of providing this needed religious element in popular education and thus make their civic contribution to the cause of democracy. The development of their own educational agencies on the one hand, and recent educational experiments on the other, have already paved the way for such an effective organization of Protestant forces.

CHAPTER VIII

THE DEVELOPMENT OF EDUCATIONAL AGENCIES WITHIN THE PROTESTANT CHURCHES

THE first law establishing schools at public expense was intended, as we have seen, to extend the knowledge of the Bible. What was self-evident and to be expected in a homogeneous Puritan commonwealth was, however, beset with difficulty where Protestant and Romanist ideals come into collision, as later in New York city, over the equitable distribution of school funds. In a sense, it was the old Reformation controversy over the right to exercise private judgment in the interpretation of the Scriptures, transferred to the field of education in a free republic, since the exercise of this right is conditioned upon the ability to read. For many years the controversy has continued in the United States, becoming more complicated as denominations of every name have grown more and more sensitive to the possibility of encouraging sectarian teaching under the guise of instruction in the Bible.

In a few States even the reading of the Bible in the public schools is officially discountenanced. In Illinois the State Supreme Court has ruled against it; in California, Minnesota, Missouri, and Washington similar action has been taken by the attorney-general of the State; while in Arizona, Montana, and New York the State Superintendent of Education has acted unfavorably. Wisconsin and Nebraska have forbidden a *sectarian* use of the Bible, the reading of extracts being expressly permitted in Wisconsin. Despite these official pronouncements, the Bible is still read in all these States, wherever

individual teachers desire to do so and community sentiment is not distinctly adverse. In two States, Massachusetts and Pennsylvania, Bible reading is required by
law for the whole State. The National Reform Association is authority for the statement that "so far from being
banished from nearly all American public schools, as
many have supposed, it is habitually read in three fourths
of them."

"The Bible in the schools question" has passed through
various vicissitudes, partisans often taking the view that
the decision of the question as to whether or not the Bible
shall be read daily in a school devotional exercise will
determine also the classification of the school as "religious" or "godless." But we have seen that, in the case
of Germany at least, the mere fact of Bible reading, or
even of Bible *study* by the pupils, does not of itself necessarily count for very much in their religious life. It all
depends upon *how* it is taught: upon the spirit and atmosphere in which the teaching is conducted. The same
principles we have also seen illustrated in connection with
the teaching of morals in France. In other words, for
effective instruction in religion and morals, there is need
for the same kind of skill in the use of teaching methods,
the same kind of interest and mastery and freedom of
initiative on the part of the teacher, as in any other kind
of teaching.

This principle has grown constantly clearer through the
history of the controversy over the teaching of the Bible
in the schools, and all religious bodies have not only
tacitly accepted it, but have acted upon it, each one developing its own denominational organization for the
purpose of providing religious teaching in its own way
for its own constituency. Thus, the Jews have developed
their own religious schools, the Roman Catholics have
established parochial schools, while the various branches

of Protestants have depended mainly upon the Sunday school. In this way there has grown up in the United States what is really a dual system of popular education; that provided in the public schools for all children, and that provided in the religious schools and Sunday schools for the children of the respective faiths. The two parts of the system have developed along parallel lines, though not always at the same rate of progress. In each case the development has taken place almost wholly within the nineteenth century.

The Sunday school movement received its first impulse through the Society for Promoting Sunday Schools through the British Dominions, which was created to extend the type of school originated by Robert Raikes. Schools of this type were primarily intended for the children of the poor, and, although held on Sunday, provided instruction in the common branches and employed paid teachers. At the death of the founder, in 1811, the number of pupils in the British Dominions and in the United States had reached 250,000.

In 1791 there was organized in Philadelphia the "First Day or Sunday School Society," which carried on in this country a propaganda similar to that which had previously been promoted in England. It is interesting to note that the three leading spirits in the formation of this society were Bishop White, an Episcopalian; Matthew Carey, a Roman Catholic; and Dr. Benjamin Rush, a Universalist. They were actuated by a sense of civic responsibility, as is evident from the preamble to the constitution adopted by the society:

Whereas, The good education of youth is of first importance to society, and numbers of children, the offspring of indigent parents, have not proper opportunities of instruction previous to their being apprenticed to trades; and

Whereas, Among the youth of every large city various instances occur of the first day of the week, called Sunday—a day which ought to be devoted to religious improvement—being employed to the worst of purposes, the depravity of morals and manners;

It is therefore the opinion of sundry persons that the establishment of Sunday schools in this city would be of essential advantage to the rising generations; and for effecting that benevolent purpose they have formed themselves into a Society.

It is noteworthy also that the instruction proposed was confined to "reading and writing from the Bible and such other moral and religious books as the Society may from time to time direct." The same motive and the same conception of the aim of education were influential here which were operative in the Massachusetts Bay Colony in the passage of the Act of 1647, providing for public schools; and, indeed, the society petitioned the Legislature to establish Sunday schools as free schools, but without success.

Other unions sprang up, among which was the Evangelical Society, organized in Philadelphia in 1808 to promote locally the establishment of Sunday evening schools. The Pittsburgh Union was formed in 1809, the Boston Society for the Moral and Religious Instruction of the Poor, in 1816, and the New York Sunday School Union the same year. A fresh impetus was given the Sunday school movement by the Rev. Robert Way, of London, who stopped at Philadelphia in 1811, on his way as a missionary to India. In 1824 the American Sunday School Union was organized, in which were embraced a number of the earlier organizations. It set for itself a threefold purpose: the disseminating of information through publication; the selection and preparation of lesson material; and the "endeavor to plant a Sunday school wherever there is a population." The activities of this organization extended throughout the newer States of the West and South, and were so effectively carried on that in some States not a community remained in which there was not a Sunday school.

As Sunday schools were organized, the teachers of contiguous localities met together for mutual counsel. Out of these grew informal organizations, and finally larger Sunday school conventions. Several national conventions were held at intervals, in which such men as J. H. Vincent, Edward Eggleston, H. Clay Trumbull, and B. F. Jacobs were conspicuous as leaders. These conventions greatly stimulated the schools in perfecting their methods of organization and teaching.

A demand sprang up for lesson material, and denominational boards were established for the printing and distribution of Sunday school lessons. A great impetus was given to this work by the adoption in 1870 of the uniform lesson system, the effect of which was to make generally available the results of biblical scholarship, and to make more universal the custom of providing biblical instruction through the medium of the Sunday school.

The National Convention gradually extended its organization geographically, until a complete system was established, bringing together into fraternal and cooperative relations the Sunday school forces of the various townships, uniting these in State Sunday school associations, and finally federating them into a national and international organization. The outstanding characteristic of this movement is the fact that it has been promoted by the initiative of laymen, rather than by the official leaders of denominations. It was born in the desire for cooperation between all workers and agencies in order to attain the largest efficiency with the least possible disturbance of local autonomy. It has grown from a single general meeting to an organization holding thousands of conferences annually, and requiring for its work a large force of paid workers with a triennial budget of $70,000. Its service has been that of a vast promoting agency developing around the uniform lesson system.

Such had been the development of popular education under the auspices of the state that by the beginning of this century the public schools had progressed in efficiency far beyond the point reached by the Sunday schools. So marked was the contrast between the two types of education, and so strong the conviction among educators as well as church workers that some radical improvements should be made, that there was formed in 1903 the Religious Education Association. The object of this association was to unite in one comprehensive organization the workers in all ecclesiastical, adult, cultural, and social organizations desiring fellowship, exchange of thought, information, and experience for cooperation in religious education. Its methods have been those of agitation, through conventions, conferences, and addresses; group organizations, local and departmental; and publication of books, magazines, and pamphlets. It has refrained, however, from attempting interference with the administration of educational forces and programs. Its aim has been "to inspire the religious forces with the educational ideal, and educational forces with the religious ideal."

At length the demand for a better type of lesson material became so insistent that it found emphatic utterance in the international Sunday school conventions; first at Denver in 1902, again at Toronto in 1905, and finally at Louisville in 1908, which passed the unanimous vote:

That this convention authorize its Lesson Committee also to continue the preparation of a thoroughly graded course of lessons, which may be used by any Sunday school which desires it, whether in whole or in part.

The passage of this vote opened the way for incorporating in the teaching of the Sunday school all those principles which already had found acceptance in public school instruction: the principle of adaptation of material and method to the interests and needs of the child at successive ages; the principle of self-activity and self-expression; the principle of correlation between studies; the principle of coordination with other teaching agencies. These principles have all entered as controlling influences into the preparation of the completely graded courses of study for the entire curriculum. Since 1908 an entire series of annually graded lesson courses has been issued in various editions by different denominations. Independent publishing houses have also issued similar series of graded lessons, so that the Sunday schools are at present abundantly supplied with lesson material of high educational value.

This development of educational material has necessitated more precise methods of teaching, and has made imperative some provision for the training of teachers. Thus arose the teachers' training movement, which has been promoted both by the International Sunday School Association and by denominational agencies. Courses of study have been prepared for teachers, local conferences and institutes have been widely held, summer schools have been organized, colleges have introduced into their curricula subjects bearing upon religious education, and theological seminaries have added new departments for the purpose of training leaders in the new branch of education.

So long as the uniform lessons occupied the whole time of the Sunday school it was necessary to resort to "supplemental lessons," "mission bands," "bands of mercy," and similar agencies, in order to present the complete round of interests concerning which the churches felt that information should be provided their children and youth. The Young People's Missionary Movement, which had arisen in order to press home upon young people their personal responsibility for the missionary enterprise, saw in the new order of things the opportunity to make missionary instruction an integral part of religious education, and, accordingly, changed its name to the more significant one, Missionary Education Movement. This organization has been actively associated with the denominational agencies in the preparation of the new graded courses of study.

These developments have stimulated the denominations to strengthen their official boards in order to provide more adequate denominational leadership. Educational secretaries have been appointed in several denominations to cooperate with editors and missionary superintendents, and to emphasize the educational ideals. As a further step toward denominational effectiveness, the Sunday School Council was organized in Philadelphia in 1910, the immediate occasion being the necessity of closer cooperation between the denominations in the work of training teachers. It was found, moreover, that the denominations had many problems in common whose solution would be hastened by a closer affiliation. Some thirty denominations are thus represented in this Council. One of the immediate results which followed this action was the reorganization of the International Sunday School Lesson Committee to include a larger number of denominational representatives and a larger proportion of those directly concerned in the actual construction of the lessons. Another form of association is the Commission on Christian Education of the Federal Council of the Churches of Christ in America, which was formed in 1912, after the analogy of the other commissions of the Federal Council.

Thus the Sunday school movement has proceeded through the following stages: first, extension, as promoted by the Sunday School Union and denominational agencies, until practically every church now has its Sunday school; second, lesson promotion, most actively prosecuted in connection with the uniform lesson system; third, organization, which has been greatly stimulated by the International Sunday School Association; fourth, the setting of higher ideals, for which the impulse was given by the Religious Education Association; fifth, intensive development and the training of teachers in which all agencies have cooperated; sixth, the movement toward closer official cooperation and federation.

While this movement was progressing other specialized movements have also been taking place, particularly those having to do with the education of young people. The establishment of Young Men's and Young Women's Christian Associations in practically all cities and many rural communities has been a notable illustration of interdenominational cooperation. Through the efforts of these associations, broad education plans have been put into operation, based upon careful study of the special needs of these ages. At a time also when colleges and higher institutions of learning were seeking release from ecclesiastical control, the college department of the Young Men's and Young Women's Christian Associations has quietly maintained religious influence in these institutions without emphasizing sectarian or denominational differences.

More recently the denominations themselves, realizing the importance of developing well trained leaders in religious education, as well as securing recruits for the ministry, have taken steps to provide official boards charged with this responsibility. These boards are now federated in the Council of Church Boards, which is analogous to the Sunday School Council, though working in a specialized field.

A movement began in the eighties which led to the organization of young people within the local churches specifically for training in the expression of a devotional life and in forms of service and church work. This young people's movement has assumed national proportions, although the interdenominational affiliations have never been so strong as those between Sunday schools. In addition to these are many smaller organizations, such as the Boy Scouts, the Camp Fire Girls, and the like, some of them national in scope, devoted to the training of children and youth along special lines of service or at special periods in their growth.

From the standpoint of organization and material, the Protestant churches already have at hand sufficient resources to serve as a basis for a system of popular instruction in religion on a national scale. Starting with much the same motive which gave rise to the public schools, the desire to extend the knowledge of the Bible, the Sunday school movement, like the movement for popular education in general, has appropriated the aims and methods which experiment and experience have proved effective. Thus the Sunday schools, no less truly than the public schools, now recognize, at least in theory, that the primary aim of religious education, as of other forms of education, is complete self-realization; that it is necessary, to this end, to select, prepare, and present the material of study with reference to the immediate interests and needs of the pupil, and that those pupils who are at a similar stage of development must be taught together in grades, in order to meet individual needs; that not only the Bible, but other subjects as well—nature, missionary narrative, the inspiring chapters from church history, and the story of contemporary life—all are fruitful as media through which to impart a knowledge of Christian truth; that clubs, classes, choirs, and young people's organizations are convenient means through which to give expression to the enthusiasms which have been aroused; that all these need to be bound together under a unified administration in the local church and denominationally, in order to insure the largest effectiveness; that skill in teaching and administration, as well as completeness and convenience of equipment, are essential factors in the teaching process; and that all phases of the teaching work of the church should be placed upon a scientific basis, with careful records of the progress of each pupil at each stage of the teaching process.

The Protestant Sunday school movement is greatly hampered at present by the tradition that the work must all be done at one time, on one day, and, for the most part, at one session, and even in one large group. This custom began when schools, like those of Robert Raikes and their successors in Philadelphia, were formed as a philanthropic agency and were held on Sunday because of the demoralizing influence of idleness upon children and youth. At that time education was comparatively a simple matter, and Sunday a day devoted chiefly to religion. Now all life has become much more complex, education—even in religion—is a much more exacting task, and Sunday has become very generally a day for rest and recreation. The very development, therefore, of the church's educational resources within recent years has made more apparent than ever the inadequacy of the time allowed and the necessity of providing more time and some better plan for making such instruction thoroughly effective. That the need for some larger provision is keenly felt is evident, not only from the recent developments within the churches themselves and the movements toward closer federation, but also from certain significant experiments within the ranks of the public school forces which look toward a closer alliance between those in charge of the public school system and those who are interested in the educational work of the churches.

CHAPTER IX

SOME RECENT EXPERIMENTS IN RELIGIOUS EDUCATION[1]

It is a significant fact that professional educators are taking the initiative in devising plans for religious education, the execution of which involves the cooperation of the churches. In some instances they frankly express the conviction that the churches are not only responsible for providing the religious element in popular education, but that they must be stimulated toward the attainment of such standards as are maintained in the public schools. Three of the experiments to be described concern high school pupils. The others apply to pupils of all grades. The last two experiments are interesting as illustrations of cooperative work between different denominations, on their own initiative. All the plans alike involve interdenominational cooperation for the most effective results, while all seek to conserve the principle of religious liberty and denominational initiative.

1. The North Dakota Plan[2]

This experiment was devised in 1912 by Professor Vernon P. Squiers, of the University of North Dakota, and is intended for pupils of high school age. Its appeal is based upon the statement that "a knowledge of the Bible is an essential in a good education," and the plan proposes to provide an opportunity for young people to become familiar with the Bible as history and literature. The argument urges that this is necessary to any intelligent

---

[1] For an elaborate discussion of State credit, see Wood, School and College Credit for Outside Bible Study.
[2] For syllabus of North Dakota Plan, see Part II, pp. 173f.

105

appreciation of English literature, but that the average young person to-day lacks this knowledge, such ignorance being even a matter of common jest.

Any intention to engage in a religious propaganda is emphatically disclaimed. The plan as proposed by Professor Squiers "was recommended by the State Educational Association, unanimously indorsed by the Conference of City Superintendents and High School Principals, and adopted by the State Board of Education as a purely educational measure." Any quickening of interest in religion which might follow is only incidental to the main purpose. There is no thought of interfering in any way with the prerogatives of the church, nor of disregarding the accepted status of church and state as separate institutions. It is simply assumed that the state, being charged with the responsibility of educating its youth, is at liberty to include in its program whatever it believes to be essential. The scope of the state's activities is confined to such aspects of the educational process as win universal approval.

The plan is embodied in an outline or syllabus of Bible study prepared by the five members of the State Board of Education. This syllabus determines the ground to be covered in the study, and the nature and range of facts to be considered. The only textbook prescribed is the Bible itself, of which any recognized version is acceptable. At the completion of the course the State offers a credit of one half unit toward the fifteen or sixteen required for graduation, upon condition that the candidate pass an examination, this credit being equivalent to that regularly allowed to a study taken five times a week for eighteen weeks. It is understood that no public funds are used for promotion, all expenses being borne by the State Sunday School Association. No public buildings or teachers are required for the work of instruction, since the instruction is provided voluntarily by the churches of the various denominations. Syllabus, examination, and credit constitute the features of the plan in which the State participates, and here its responsibility ends.

The voluntary nature of the entire instruction is emphasized. No pupil is required to take the study. Individual teachers are free to emphasize as much as they will the religious values of the literature, or to assign additional readings in textbooks and reference works. The study may be conducted on Sunday or week-day, at the Sunday school, in the young people's society, or at home—all these are matters of indifference to the State, which is concerned simply in securing an objective study of Bible facts and in ascertaining how completely the pupil has gained a knowledge of these facts.

The requirements embrace studies in biblical geography, acquaintance with fifty Old Testament narratives, an outline of Hebrew history before Christ, the books of the Old Testament, and five memory passages.

The plan has met with a hearty response from churches of all denominations, both Protestant and Roman Catholic, the largest number of examination papers being submitted in one year by a Catholic teacher using the Douai version, every paper of which was approved by the examiner and awarded credit. Sunday school workers have felt the stimulus of having Bible study standardized, pupils have come to the study with a new interest because of the incentive provided in the half-credit, and day school teachers have been more willing to participate in the work of the Sunday schools. No criticism of the plan is reported from within the State.

Fifteen young people attempted the examination at the first opportunity, in January, 1913. Of these, eleven were successful. In June of that year 112 papers from thirty-two communities were sent in, ninety-eight receiving credit. In June, 1916, 166 papers were received from fifty-four towns, of which 156 were given credit.

Incidentally, the plan has reacted upon the Sunday schools, inspiring them to higher efficiency in all their departments. Teachers realize that their work is being brought into comparison with that in the day school. This, in turn, has created a demand for training classes and has raised the quality of the teaching. Through this cooperative relationship between home, school, and church, the real unity of their common task has been emphasized.

The North Dakota plan has created wide interest and initial steps have been taken in Indiana, Washington, Oregon, California, Iowa, and West Virginia toward putting a similar plan in operation. Individual high schools have also adopted the plan in towns in Missouri, Alabama, and possibly in other States.[1]

2. The Colorado Plan[2]

Another experiment, slightly earlier in its beginnings than the North Dakota plan, though a little slower to secure full adoption, had its origin in Greeley, Colorado, in 1910. The plan, as at first proposed, was designed to provide elective courses in Bible study for the students at the State Teachers' College and proved so popular that two hundred and fifty students elected the course in 1911, sixty of the number being members of the Roman Catholic Church. It was decided to extend the scope of the plan to make it applicable to the high schools, and in November of that year the Educational Council of the State Teachers' Association appointed a committee of three to consider the plan and to cooperate with a similar com-

[1] For description of adaptations in various States, see Wood, *op. cit.*, chas. v-x.
[2] For syllabus of the Colorado Plan, see Part II, p. 185.

mittee of the State Sunday School Association in working out a course for the high schools of Colorado.

While this committee was at work it learned of the program already independently inaugurated in North Dakota. In November, 1913, it presented to the State Teachers' Association the following resolutions, which were unanimously adopted:

1. The religious education of the boys and girls who are in our public schools is a matter of unquestioned importance, and should be emphasized and furthered in every legitimate way.

2. The Sunday school is a historic institution, backed by strong religious organizations, and exercising a wide religious influence over young people. Up to a recent date, however, but little serious effort seems to have been made to set up acceptable standards of teaching in its work, or to secure on the part of the pupils any real preparation of assigned lessons. If such improvements can be made, the Sunday school is entitled to an honorable place among our educational forces.

3. We believe that a closer cooperation between the public schools and the Sunday school would be of mutual advantage, and might assist the latter in becoming a more efficient agency of religious education, and that such cooperation is possible without transgressing our fundamental principles of religious liberty.

4. We therefore recommend that this association approve of the strong effort now being made by the churches, the denominational educational departments, and the Colorado State Sunday School Association, to elevate the standards of teaching in Sunday schools, to improve their courses of study, and to secure on the part of the pupils the same grade of lesson preparation as is demanded in public school work; that, with this object in view, it commend to the Sunday schools for classes of high school grade the recognized standards of the North Central Association of Secondary Schools and Colleges; that, when these standards have been attained, it recommend that high schools give credit for Bible study of corresponding grade in the Sunday schools, to an extent not to exceed one fourth unit for each year's work, and that this body appoint a permanent committee to cooperate in prudent and legitimate ways for all the foregoing purposes with a similar committee from the Colorado State Sunday School Association.

The distinctive features of the Colorado plan as compared with the North Dakota plan are, therefore, its frank recognition of the Sunday schools as a correlative educational agency, its pledge of active and helpful cooperation, and its clearly defined purpose to standardize the Sunday school teaching as a condition of granting credit to the pupil.

This plan provides a four years' elective course for high school students, to be adapted to their unfolding life and correlated with the curriculum of the high schools. The course, in outline, is as follows:

Course I. Heroes and Leaders of Israel—Ready in detail, September, 1914.

Course II. 1st semester: The Friends and Followers of Jesus. 2d semester: The Life and Labors of Jesus. Both ready in detail September, 1915.

Course III. 1st semester: Bible History. 2d semester: Biblical Literature. Both ready in detail September, 1916.

Course IV. Social Institutions: The Social Application of Bible Teaching: To be ready in detail September, 1917.

As in the case of the North Dakota plan, no State funds are to be devoted to this purpose, no State or school building to be used, no public school teachers to give instruction during school hours. The work is to be done in the various churches during Sunday school hours, each denomination being free to impart instruction in its own way. If, however, credit is to be asked, the teachers must conform to the recognized standards for high school, namely, "The minimum scholastic attainment of high school teachers shall be equivalent to graduation from a college belonging to the North Central Association of Colleges and Secondary Schools, including special training in the subjects they teach."

Furthermore, the State Sunday School Association is called upon to maintain and conduct annually training-schools in order that the teachers may become properly qualified for meeting the standard.

The instruction must comprise forty recitations of forty-five minutes, each year for four years, and the pupil must meet all high school requirements, as to attendance, deportment, general attitude, and character of work done. And the churches, on their part, must provide separate rooms, free from interruption during the lesson period, suitable desks or table-room for each pupil, a blackboard, maps, Bible dictionary, and other needed reference works. In estimating the work for credit, examination counts one half and recitations or thesis work one half.

In 1915 856 high school pupils were enrolled throughout the State, of whom about 200 were of the Roman Catholic faith. The number was considerably larger the following year. Many more were included in the classes who were not enrolled for credit.

The Colorado plan has also been favorably considered in other States. At the Kansas State Teachers' Association in 1914, a resolution was passed embodying virtually the same features which appear in Colorado, including the standardization of the teacher and the equipment.

3. The Lakewood, Ohio, Plan

The superintendent of the high school in Lakewood, a residential suburb of Cleveland, Ohio, was also a member of the Educational Committee of the Federated Churches of Greater Cleveland. In response to a request from that body, and with the sympathetic concurrence of the Lakewood Board of Education, steps were taken to introduce biblical history and literature directly into the high school curriculum.

As a preliminary step, the department of biblical history and literature in Western Reserve University was induced to accept the course as leading to one of the regular entrance credits of the university. The plan of the course is as follows:

1. The course to be elective, open to juniors and seniors; the juniors choosing it in place of history, and the seniors in place of English.
2. The recitations to come five times a week in a regular period, as any subject.
3. To be taught by a member of the faculty, a college graduate who has majored in that subject or has done graduate work in that field.
4. To be taught as history and literature with a view to acquainting the students with the Bible as a book of literary, historical, and ethical value; aiming not to be dogmatic or sectarian.
5. Any version of the Bible to be permitted.

After some difficulty in procuring a suitable textbook, a selection was finally made and a reference library and maps were installed. The course was conducted according to methods followed in similar high school courses in history and literature, and the average standing attained in the examination was 86.8 per cent for the half-year. Great interest was manifested on the part of the students, who expressed warm appreciation of the opportunity thus afforded.

4. THE GARY PLAN[1]

This experiment in education has been widely advertised. The features which concern instruction in religion are purely incidental to the larger educational scheme, which, briefly considered, is based upon the theory that the public school is but one of the many educational agencies operative upon the life of a child.

The home is another important factor, and so are the church, the public library, the public playgrounds, and the shop where he learns his trade. These may be regarded

[1] For sample denominational curricula at Gary, see Part II, pp. 207f.

as constructive educational agencies. Over against these are the destructive agencies: among these may be reckoned, in some instances, the moving picture show, the poolroom, the saloon, the back alley. If we would know how a child is being educated, we must take all these into consideration, for education is the resultant of all these forces. The importance of this statement will appear if we attempt to follow through one day's program in the life of an ordinary boy. Allowing eight hours for sleep, two hours for meals, six hours for school, there yet remain eight hours of the day to be accounted for. Often it is during these eight hours that he is being most effectively taught, for then he is apt to be doing things on his own initiative, without oversight or restraint or direction, and things, too, which are absorbingly interesting. Moreover, this teaching often runs directly counter to that which the home and the school attempt to supply, thus neutralizing in some measure their effort. Add to this the long vacation, when in many instances the boy is left to himself, without any suggested program, and we have at hand an explanation of the demoralized condition frequently commented upon by teachers at the opening of the school year.

The superintendent of the Gary Schools, Mr. William A. Wirt, believes it to be the duty of society to prepare a program for the entire life of the child in which due recognition shall be made of all these educational forces, bringing together into cooperative relationship those which are constructive, and eliminating, so far as possible, those which are destructive. It is his theory, furthermore, that the time of the child does not belong to the school, but to the parent; the school acts simply as the agent of the parent in arranging the program and supplying those influences which the home cannot supply, unaided.

RELIGIOUS EDUCATION AND DEMOCRACY

With this view of education Mr. Wirt found in the town of Gary a unique field for experimentation. The United States Steel Corporation had just selected, on a sandy shore of Lake Michigan, a site for the building of a great new industrial plant. A city sprang into being as if by magic. Its population consisted largely of foreigners, needing adequate education in the fundamentals of American citizenship; needing also training in the industrial trades. The first problem which faced the new superintendent was the problem of providing school buildings fast enough to meet the demand. To meet this emergency he devised the plan of conducting four simultaneous educational programs, or practically four schools at a time, in connection with one school building. Incidentally, he incorporated in this scheme not only the school itself but the other educational agencies as well. The curriculum is divided into four parts: mental discipline—such as is ordinarily given in the schools—vocational training, auditorium work, and outside activities. "While one division is at study, another is in the vocational shops, the third is in the auditorium, and the fourth at outside activities, such as playground, gymnasium, public library, or church." This is all made possible by lengthening the school day, the school week, and the school year. The advantage of it to the community lies not only in the fact that more work can be carried on with the same investment in school buildings, but all, parents and pupils alike, are kept face to face with the fact that many things in life have educational value. Thus an added respect is given to the home, the library, the church, as educational institutions.

The bearing of this upon the problem of the church and the Sunday school is this: the public school does not attempt to provide religious education, nor to interfere in any way with those who do. It simply makes the place

114

for such instruction in the program, releasing the child from other school duties, upon request of the parents, in order to be taught the Bible and religion at the church of their choice. That this opportunity is appreciated may be seen from the fact that eight denominations responded, some of them providing salaried teachers, others undertaking the work with voluntary teachers and upon their own resources. About 2,000 children have thus been brought under week day instruction in religion, among whom are to be numbered Jews as well as Christians.

As compared with the North Dakota and Colorado plans, the Gary plan exhibits the following differences:

1. The Gary plan is not limited, in its provisions, to high school students.

2. It does not offer credit.

3. It therefore attempts no specifications as to the nature of the course, its duration, the conditions under which teaching shall be done, or any other matters pertaining to standardization.

4. It assumes no responsibility whatever for the pupil's attendance upon the church school or for his record while there. It takes the ground that such responsibility belongs to the parent.

5. It encourages religious instruction in the church school in that it recognizes the church as one among many educational agencies, and hence as entitled to a portion of the child's time, so far as this can be arranged in a manner not to conflict with his school program. The lengthened school day and school year make possible the use of a larger amount of time apart from the school program than might otherwise be the case.

5. THE GARY AND THE ETTINGER PLANS IN NEW YORK CITY

In order to meet the great demand upon its public school system, New York city has been compelled to resort to various expedients. In some cases it has been possible to serve the children with part-time schedules only. For the last two years the Ettinger plan has been in operation in certain schools, according to which a schedule of interlocking hours is arranged so that groups A and B will alternate at various periods between 8:30 and 4:30. Some 90,000 children are affected by this plan, half of whom are free up to 10:30 in the morning and the other half free after 2:30. In the fall of 1914 the Gary plan was introduced into one school in Brooklyn, and in February, 1915, into another school in the Bronx. Under this plan in New York city, as in Gary, the pupils will follow a schedule in which four different types of activity will be proceeding simultaneously, and which will permit children during the "auditorium period" to go to the churches for religious instruction.

Out of the 1,000,000 children of school age in New York city, it is estimated that approximately 500,000 are receiving no religious instruction whatever, and, inasmuch as many of these children, on account of part-time programs, or through the provisions of the Ettinger or Gary plans, may be available to the churches for religious instruction, it was evident that the churches of New York city were confronted by an emergency which might by proper enterprise and wise planning be turned into an opportunity. This fact was particularly emphasized by the vote of the Board of Education determining to extend the Gary plan to twelve schools in the Bronx as soon as the buildings could be reconstructed. This will release 35,000 children for religious instruction under church auspices.

In view of this situation a conference was called at Columbia University, May 20, 1915, upon the initiative of the Demonstration School Committee of the Episcopal Church which was attended by one hundred representatives from the various religious bodies of the city. Mr. William A. Wirt, superintendent of the Gary Schools, outlined the possibilities of religious instruction in connection with the Gary plan. At this conference a temporary committee was appointed to organize a permanent official interdenominational committee to take advantage of the opportunity for week-day religious instruction. The report of the committee contained the following resolution:

Resolved, That we will endeavor to persuade our various ministerial associations to plan for a city-wide revival of religious education. To this end we will recommend:

1. That a permanent interdenominational committee on religious education be created;

2. That the City Sunday School Association, together with the Committee on Religious Education of the Federation of Churches, be requested to prepare and submit a plan of specific measures for advance in both the home and the church school;

3. That the permanent committee, after approval of such plans, take steps for a simultaneous proclamation and propaganda within all the churches, and for paying the necessary expenses.

The plans of the committee so far as outlined contemplate cooperation with school programs in securing week-day religious instruction and in providing teachers and places at convenient locations where, through denominational or united effort, as local congregations desire, there is no thought of making religious education compulsory. Appeal will be made for the cooperation of parents and for voluntary and missionary service on the part of the church itself. The aim will be to make the instruction broadly religious and ethical rather than sectarian. There will be, of course, no direct connection between the church and the public school, the church merely utilizing such time as is not under control of the Board of Education. The only condition imposed by the interdenominational committee is that the time used by the church is not needed by the school for academic training, it being assumed that five hours a day for five days of the week may properly be claimed by the school.

Steps have been taken to organize in Manhattanville a district council composed of twenty-five clergymen and school authorities responsible for the welfare of the children of the neighborhood. Upon this council are representatives of the Dutch Reformed, Episcopal, Jewish, Methodist, Lutheran, Reformed, Presbyterian, and Roman Catholic Churches. A census of the district was authorized to ascertain the exact number and location of children not affiliated with any religious body. Upon the basis of this census it is proposed to enlist the cooperation of parents in securing for their children systematic weekday religious instruction.

The effect of the plan already has been to stimulate in the churches a consciousness of their community responsibility, and for the first time to bring together into agreement all the religious bodies of New York in working out a program of religious instruction for every school child "in which all sectarian difficulties shall be laid aside and all shall stand upon the broad platform of the child's right to be taught the Fatherhood of God and the brotherhood of man."

6. THE RELIGIOUS DAY SCHOOL[1]

This institution originated in Wisconsin in 1898, the first schools being organized in rural communities by the Rev. H. R. Vaughn, a Congregational pastor at Elk Mound. Realizing the inadequacy of Sunday school instruction in Protestant churches, and observing that the German and Scandinavian Lutheran bodies conduct schools regularly in their own languages in vacation time, a part of the program being devoted to the study of the catechism and Bible history, it had occurred to him that this free time might also be utilized by the English-speaking Protestant churches for providing a program of systematic religious instruction.

---

[1] For curricula of the Religious Day School, see Part II, p. 220.

From modest beginnings the plan developed during the years between 1900 and 1910. Emphasis was wisely laid at first upon work in the teachers' training institute at Elk Mound, whose system included demonstration of methods and practice teaching. No effort has been made to carry on a propaganda, but the plan has been allowed to develop in a natural manner and experimentally. The demand has grown so strong that printed directions have been prepared for organizing such schools and constructing the curriculum.

The schools are held for two or three weeks during the summer. The sessions last from nine until twelve o'clock. The children are graded as in public school, although two grades may be combined where the numbers are too few to constitute a profitable class. These two-grade groups may be recognized the next year, the pupils using the lower grade material the first year and taking the upper grade material the second year, thus providing each grade with a graded course of study. Six teachers are required: a kindergartner, four teachers for the two-grade groups, and one teacher for the high school group, or, still more, if the school is larger. The teachers are paid a moderate salary, and preference is given to those who have been trained for public school work. A supervising principal is also necessary to train the teachers in the characteristic methods of the schools.

The session is divided into four forty-five-minute periods. Three regular courses of instruction are provided for each group except the kindergarten. During the first, second, and fourth periods, the classes are taught separately; in the third period there is a ten-minute recess, after which a half-hour is spent together in joint assembly.

In all grades one period is devoted to instruction through carefully graded Bible stories, oral, and without homiletical comment or specific personal application. By this story-telling method, the pupils, in the course of eight seasons, acquire the mastery of nearly one hundred distinct Bible stories. Another period is likewise devoted to missionary stories for all grades, taught after a similar manner. The work in both these courses is supplemented by maps, pictures, and notebook features. Miscellaneous activities occupy another period, such as study, notebook work, memory work, and Bible drill, and instruction in personal religion. The remaining period is used for worship, in the program of which the prayers, Scripture selections, and hymns already memorized find a place. This is regarded as the climax of the entire session.

The following noteworthy considerations are suggested by the promoters of these schools:

1. The utilization of a few weeks during the long vacation period, which might otherwise be wasted, or worse than wasted.

2. The high educational value of concentrating the attention daily during this school period upon the finest religious and ethical material, in an atmosphere pervaded by the spirit of worship. By this means it is often possible to make a much stronger impression during these three weeks of systematic, daily instruction than during an entire year of ordinary, once-a-week, Sunday school attendance.

3. The possibility of securing at this season of the year the services of expert teachers.

4. The necessity of interdenominational cooperation. The schools are managed by a strong local committee and receive financial support from the local churches, acting in a federated capacity. One dollar per family is usually charged for tuition, the balance being provided by church appropriations or private subscription.

These schools have become established in a dozen or more of the smaller towns and villages in Wisconsin as well as in some larger places like Eau Claire, Madison, Beaver Dam, and Rockford, Illinois.

7. Daily Vacation Bible School[1]

Another similar experiment, inspired by the fact that time for religious instruction is available during the vacation period, has been devised for meeting the needs of children in the cities. Of the 22,000,000 boys and girls of school age, from whom school oversight is withdrawn more than two months during the summer, it is estimated that one third are enrolled in the elementary schools of the fifty cities which exceed 100,000 in population. About one half of these spend the summer upon the streets, exposed to all kinds of demoralizing influences.

In 1901, Mr. Robert G. Boville attempted to meet this need in New York by organizing daily vacation Bible schools in five church buildings. It occurred to him that "idle children, idle churches, and idle students of the colleges" might be brought together for community welfare. The schools were so successful that the experiment was repeated the following year and the schools introduced in churches of seven different denominations.

In 1907, the call for the organization of similar schools in other cities led to the formation of the National Vacation Bible School Committee, which was incorporated in 1911 as the Daily Vacation Bible School Association.

The plan, briefly described, is as follows:

(a) To promote the community use of church buildings in cities and rural districts, for child welfare on broad, non-sectarian lines, especially when public schools are closed in summer. The Daily Vacation Bible School Association is the only national organization which has this for its mission. Church buildings represent a vast investment of wealth and they should be used for community welfare.

(b) To promote the social welfare of children, irrespective of race or creed, by giving them competent leaders and teachers, suitable and happy occupations, sympathetic oversight of games,

---

[1] For Daily Program, see Part II, p. 223.

good songs, and above all to combine with this program religious training, which is the supreme need of childhood.

(c) To employ in this field of service college men and women who are filled with the vision of Christlike social service and who are fitted to be efficient leaders of children in worship, work, and play. It is an educational and economic benefit to enable these educated young men and women to utilize their vacation months for social service.

The instruction includes not only Bible stories, hymns, and memory passages from the Bible, but also net-making and basket-weaving. It is customary to hold an exhibit at the close of the period when parents and friends may have opportunity to observe the more tangible results of the school. Some three hundred schools have been conducted in a single season, at a cost of about eighty-five cents for each child.

SOME CONCLUSIONS SUGGESTED BY THE FOREGOING EXPERIMENTS

These experiments are symptomatic. They indicate a widespread conviction that more religious instruction is needed, that such instruction should be of a higher grade than is now generally available, that the churches are the proper agencies for providing it, and that cooperation between denominations is necessary in order to accomplish the task. The experiments also indicate the points where weaknesses are thought to exist, and suggest how these may be remedied. Among these weaknesses the following may be mentioned:

1. Lack of incentive or motive: In the minds of the pupils, Sunday school study does not appear to "count" among the requirements for a liberal education. Credits are therefore proposed as providing the necessary motive. This credit is a feature of the North Dakota and Colorado plans.

2. Lack of definite standards: Indefiniteness as to the number and length of recitation periods and uncertainty as to the ground

to be covered breed carelessness in the pupil. Both the North
Dakota and Colorado plans include a syllabus in which these
matters are clearly set forth.

3. Lack of competent teachers and of precise statements as to
the qualifications of teachers: The Colorado plan is particularly
definite in its specifications regarding the teacher's preparation.

4. Lack of proper equipment: The Colorado plan makes it clear
that private classrooms, freedom from interruption, suitable
tables, chairs, blackboards, maps, and reference books, are not
to be regarded as luxuries, but as essentials of good teaching. By
making the attainment of these standards a condition for granting credit, a motive is provided the churches for supplying these
necessities.

5. Lack of community consciousness that the Sunday school is,
in fact, an educational agency: The very proposal that the public
schools grant credit for work done in Sunday schools is itself a
tacit reminder of the fact that, in the popular mind, the Sunday
school has no educational standing.

6. Lack of sufficient time at the disposal of the churches at
present for accomplishing what is really needed in religious instruction: The Gary plan is interesting as suggesting a method
whereby the status of the churches as educational agencies of the
community may be recognized and time secured in which to do
their legitimate work.

One may infer from these experiments that educators
are growing impatient with the attitude of the churches
toward their educational task, and are disposed to take
matters into their own hands, if this can be done without
encroaching upon the principle of religious freedom. The
granting of credit, involving as it does standardization
of the curriculum, equipment, and teaching methods, the
adjustment of time schedules, and even the absorption
of biblical instruction into the high-school curriculum—
all these are measures seriously advocated and actually
in operation.

While appreciating the spirit in which these experiments have been made and rejoicing at this evidence of a
popular interest in Bible study, the Protestant churches

should, however, realize the full import of the tendencies which are here revealed. Among these the following are especially deserving of mention:

The turning over to the state of the right to determine for the churches the content of religious instruction, which is practically what happens when the state issues a syllabus as the basis of certification. Any church or denomination may, indeed, make additions to the syllabus, or interpret in its own way its religious values; nevertheless, it is the syllabus which, in the eyes of the pupil, and, indeed, of the teacher, will assume importance, while the qualifying interpretations, not counting for credit, will be, by implication, unimportant.

Again, while it is urged that credit be confined to the knowledge of historical and literary facts, the natural effect of this is to put a premium upon memory work and apparently to discriminate against those other activities and responses of the pupil which are vital to independent thinking and to training in responsibility.

Probably few communities are ready to turn over to the high school the instruction in biblical history and literature, even as an elective course, as has been done in the Lakewood High School. Yet the tendency in the North Dakota and Colorado plans is strongly and logically in this direction. If, however, the instruction is to be given in the high school and the teachers are to confine themselves strictly to the teaching of the facts of history and to the pointing out of literary qualities, this will tend to make the study purely formal and objective. On the other hand, any attempt to interpret the history sympathetically will expose the teacher to criticism on the ground of sectarianism.

In the light of history, both in this country and in Europe, the proposal to grant state credit for work done in the Sunday schools looks like a step backward. Such credit involves a certain measure of state control of religious instruction. Wherever such control has been in the hands of the state it has resulted either in making religious instruction formal and academic, as in Germany, or else friction between state and church has arisen, as in England.

Even the time schedules fixed by the Gary schools, which seem at first thought to afford opportunity for week-day instruction in religion by the churches, have been found inconvenient in practice. Where churches are at a distance from the school much time is lost to the pupil in passing to and from the church, while the complicated nature of the schedules, and their frequent change, renders difficult, if not impossible, any careful grading of the pupils in the church schools. Similar difficulties are involved where the state assumes to determine the basis and method of correlation of religious instruction with so-called "secular" instruction.

On the other hand, the experiments originating with the churches working cooperatively, as in the case of the religious day school and the daily vacation Bible school, as well as the experience of the Roman Catholic, Jewish, and Lutheran Churches, seem to show that it is possible for the churches themselves to secure many, if not all, of these desired results, without relying upon public school credit. Indeed, the much-coveted state authority, which is supposed to be so essential to the success of the public school system, is nothing else than the force of public opinion. This support the Protestant churches may have whenever they come to the point where they can give united and emphatic expression to their common conviction.

However one may hesitate to advocate the general adoption of some of these experiments, taken together they all add cumulative weight to the body of evidence indicating a growing sentiment in favor of raising the standards of religious instruction, of relating it more closely to the work of the public schools, and of seeking a basis for more effective cooperation between the churches and the public schools in their common educational task. It remains now to consider some proposals outlining the possibilities of such cooperation and to offer some suggestions regarding a common program.

CHAPTER X

THE MUTUAL RELATIONS OF CHURCH AND
STATE IN PROVIDING EDUCATION
FOR DEMOCRACY

It is a significant fact, as we have seen, that several
suggestive educational experiments involving cooperation
between the churches and the public schools have recently
been set in operation by educators in the public schools.
It is also significant that from similar sources has come
the demand that the popular notion of education must
be broadened so as to include several other important
agencies in the local community besides the public school.
Mr. Wirt has emphasized this idea in his advocacy of the
Gary system. This suggestion has been recently still further elaborated into an interesting theory as to the relation of religion to the general educational program.

In 1915 the National Education Association offered a
prize of one thousand dollars for the best essay on "The
Essential Place of Religion in Education—with an Outline of a Plan for Introducing Religious Teaching into
the Public Schools."[1] The Association stipulated that
those competing for the prize should define religion in a
broad way so as not to run counter to the creeds of
Protestant, Roman Catholic, or Jew. In response to this
offer 1,381 competitors entered the contest, representing
every State in the Union but one. Four hundred and
thirty-two essays were submitted. Of these, four, in
addition to the prize essay written by Professor Charles

[1] For outline of Curriculum, see Part II, p. 240.

RELIGIOUS EDUCATION AND DEMOCRACY

E. Rugh, of California, were regarded by the judges as of sufficient merit to include in the printed pamphlet.

The writer of the prize essay takes the ground that there is a divine order into which the child is born, just as there is a physical order or a social order, and that education consists in providing proper stimuli to enable the child to make appropriate response to his surroundings. This conception of education may be embodied in a series of life formulas.

1. Physical life—response of the body to physical things. Examples: lungs to air; alimentary canal to food; ear to sound; eye to light.

2. Mental life—response of mind to mental things. Examples: language impulses to language; art impulses to music, painting, and literature.

3. Moral life—response of person to social order. Examples: personal response to manners, customs, fashions, standards of conduct and behavior.

4. Spiritual life—response of the will to an ideal order. Examples: a person trying to realize ideals; planning to be rather than to have.

5. Religious life—response of the soul to God. Examples: the response of the whole being to the universal order; the attempt to find and found the life on eternal and universal personal principles.

He distinguishes the following elements in the problem of religious education:

Are there in a normal child native impulses that are essentially religious, or that may be associated or identified with religious principles? Has society produced religious achievements and forms that ought to be grafted upon the religious impulses in order to favor the individual development and social progress? How is this teaching process to be accomplished? Should it be done in the public schools?

With reference to the first two he makes an affirmative answer and proceeds in the remainder of the essay to outline a program for carrying out these principles through

128

the public schools. In this program he recognizes that three institutions are concerned—the home, the school, and the church. Each of these has definite responsibilities with reference to the religious development of the child, and all must cooperate in the solution of their common problem. Any program, therefore, must include three divisions—a school plan, a plan for correlated and cooperative home instruction, and a similar plan, correlated and cooperative, for the church.

The plan for the schools likewise consists of three parts:

1. The attempt to make the teacher fully conscious of the religious implications and responsibilities of the public schools as now constituted.

2. The vitalizing of the public schools by reorganized curricula so as to make the schools more nearly conformed to the new demands of the present social order and to bring out into clearer relief religious motives and ideals.

3. Specific and definite plans for religious instruction and training.

The underlying principle is that "the religious life of the child can be nourished only by the inner religious vitality of the social life in which the child lives. Religious teaching cannot be thrust into the schools by an instruction program. The program will come when the development of the social life prepares the way and demands it. The general scheme is presented in the form of a diagram:

I. School Plan.
  1. Subjects:
    A. Religious material in present curriculum.
    B. Additional material of religious nature.
    C. Specific religious instruction and training.
  2. Discipline.
    D. School government—democratic—developing institutional
       loyalty.

E. Punishment religious—restoring broken spiritual unity by inducing—
    (1) Repentance.
    (2) Confession.
    (3) Consecration to the right.
       (Example: Prodigal Son.)
F. Philanthropic enterprises.

II. Correlation and Coordination with the Home.
  A. Bringing home experiences into the school.
  B. Sending vital school work into home, both subject-matter and discipline.
  C. Fellowship through parents' days, exhibits, and other social gatherings.

III. Correlation and Coordination with the Church.
    For the present mostly a church problem: The Sunday school and young people's societies can use some of the material of school for their work; some essays, debates, music. Church schools may come to conform in plan and organization to the best public school. Pastors must come to know more about the schools.

This plan, the author believes, fulfills the necessary requirements. It is "psychologically sound. . . . It assumes no unknown elements or processes: . . . demands no esoteric or special privileges, principles, or practices: . . . is based upon the nature of human consciousness and the laws of its development as now known." Again, it is democratic in that it makes for the progress of all; "requires the identification of all interests; . . . proposes the leadership of the wisest and the best" and permits "each person to elect and freely employ any special or denominational practice." According to this plan, "the universal and unifying aspect of religion will be developed in a nation's public school while the private, personal, and denominational forms will be developed without breaking school children into groups"; finally, the plan is religious, being "based primarily upon the principle that religious development consists essentially in

130

the development of religious impulses into the full con-sciousness of the personal kinship with a heavenly Father." "This sense of kinship will give to life integrity and whole-hearted love of God and service of man." The end of education and life thus becomes a progressive idealism leading to perfect adjustment to the universe, and thus achieving immortality. The chief value of the plan, as the author conceives it, is that it "dignifies and glorifies teaching, so that the religious teacher is inspired and guided by the consciousness that he is cooperating with a heavenly Father in bringing to perfection the finest fruits of creation—a true, beautiful, and good human life."

The points advanced in this prize essay are significant in that

1. They represent the standpoint of the public school educator and not primarily that of the churches.

2. They recognize that all education has religious implications from which no part of it can be safely divorced.

3. They emphasize the coordinate importance of school, home, and church, in education.

4. They disclose the religious possibilities of the public schools, even as at present conducted.

5. They suggest steps of further development on the part of the public schools in order more perfectly to realize their possibilities as agencies in the development of religion.

6. They outline possible modifications of procedure on the part of the home and the church in order that these may each fulfill more perfectly their respective functions.

7. They propose methods of closer coordination and cooperation between all these agencies.

As it was the main purpose of the author of the essay to consider the question of instruction in religion, par-ticularly with reference to its bearing upon the public school curriculum, it did not fall within the scope of the essay to undertake a detailed statement of the curriculum, or program of religious instruction and training in the church and in the home. Accepting his fundamental contention as correct, that all education has its religious implications which may not be ignored by any teacher, and that there are three great coordinate agencies of education—the home, the school, and the church—it remains to work out for home and church a systematic plan of education, analogous to the one suggested for the school. Suggestive material for such a plan is to be found in the other essays which accompany the prize essay of Professor Rugh. Other material may be supplied from the textbooks of the various graded systems of Sunday school lessons. It is a somewhat difficult, but by no means impossible task to complete the program for the church and to correlate it properly with the program of the school. The program for the home is as yet hardly formulated at all. The practical question in any local community is the question as to how best to proceed in constructing such a program and in putting it into operation. As preliminary to such procedure, a careful study of the principles formulated at the Convention of the Religious Education Association at Chicago in March, 1916, will be rewarding. These are the expression of the consensus of opinion between representative educators and representatives of the churches. They constitute the "findings" of the convention, which had been devoted to the study and discussion of Week-day Education in Religion in all its various aspects:

1. The church and the state are to be regarded as distinct institutions, which as far as possible cooperate through the agency of their common constituents in their capacity as individual citizens.

2. All children are entitled to an organic program of education which shall include adequate facilities not only for general but for religious instruction and training.

3. Such a division of the child's time as will allow opportunity and strength for religious education should be reached by con-

sultation between parents and public school authorities without formal agreement between the state and the churches as institutions.

4. The work of religious instruction and training should be done by such institutions as the home, the church, and the private school and not by the public school nor in official connection with the public school.

5. The work of religious education must depend for dignity, interest, and stimulus upon the recognition of its worth, not merely by public school authorities but by the people themselves as represented in the homes, the churches, private schools and colleges, and industries.

6. The success of a program of religious education depends:

(1) Upon the adoption of a schedule which shall include the systematic use of week days as well as Sundays for religious instruction and training.

(2) Upon more adequate provision for training in the experience of public and private worship and for the use of worship as an educational force.

(3) Upon the degree to which the materials and methods employed express both sound educational theory and the ideals of the religious community in a systematic plan for instruction and training, which shall include all the educational work of the local church.

(4) Upon the degree to which professional standards and a comprehensive plan are made the basis of the preparation of teachers for work in religious education.

(5) Upon the degree to which parents awake to the unparalleled opportunity for the religious education of our children and youth, the profound need for sympathetic cooperation among all citizens of whatever faith, and the call for sacrifice in time and thought, in effort and money consecrated to the children of the kingdom.

(6) Upon the degree to which the churches awake to their responsibility for the instruction and training of the world's children in the religious life, and take up with intelligence and devotion their common task.

CHAPTER XI

STEPS OF PROCEDURE TOWARD A SYSTEM OF RELIGIOUS EDUCATION BY THE CHURCHES

THE problem of providing an adequate system of religious education is a community problem. It will be solved primarily in individual communities. As preliminary to this, the first step will be to introduce the utmost economy into the educational work at present being conducted in the churches. Many agencies are already available but are wastefully employed.

1. The logical place to begin is in the Sunday school, for this is the one agency of the Protestant churches which touches all ages. For the improvement of *instruction* there needs to be a more definite formulation of the aim of the Sunday school. There is confusion at present as to its purpose. In the minds of some it exists primarily to impart a knowledge of the Bible; others regard it as an agency for replenishing church membership; in some instances it has a missionary and evangelistic purpose, while the more progressive Sunday schools are attempting to meet completely the child's religious needs.

There should be a more careful grading of pupils. While many schools call themselves graded schools, there are comparatively few in which the pupils are graded with care and precision. Many considerations of expediency interfere with the thoroughgoing application of this principle. A clear statement of the basis of grading and promotion needs to be formulated for each school and constantly adhered to.

Graded lessons should be more widely introduced

134

throughout the whole Sunday school. Such lessons should not only be adapted to the needs of each age, but should include nature material, such subjects as church history, national and church organization, and church doctrine. These lessons should then be brought together into the closely knit curriculum of instruction, it being understood that upon the completion of this curriculum a suitable diploma will be granted.

The organization of the Sunday school needs to be more carefully adjusted. At present there is too much waste. Much time is wasted by the pupils because of tardiness and irregular attendance. Time is wasted in the program through lack of definiteness and precise definition of duties for the various officers. With so brief a time at disposal it is imperative that all waste should be eliminated so far as possible.

For effective instruction more adequate buildings and equipment are necessary. Each class requires a separate room, free from interruption and provided with all customary facilities for instruction; suitable furniture, maps, reference books, and illustrative material. Many schools do not use their present building and equipment to the best advantage, feeling themselves under the necessity of having all departments of the school meet at the same time. A rearrangement of the program allowing the departments to meet successively instead of simultaneously would double or treble the utility of present facilities.

The most imperative need is for well-trained teachers. Sunday schools are still too few which provide training for prospective teachers. It is too generally the custom to wait until a teacher is needed before taking steps to provide one. Every school should formulate definite qualifications for its teachers and should have its normal department to enable them to meet these qualifications.

There is need of closer supervision of instruction. This is quite distinct from the function of organization which is more general. At present individual teachers are left too largely to act upon their own responsibility. The result is too little variety of method; too little appreciation of the peculiar needs of each class of pupils; too little unity in the school as a whole.

The Sunday school needs to make provision, however, not only for instruction, but for *training*. For this there should be a clearer conception of the relation between instruction and training and a sharper differentiation in the actual program; for example, the period devoted to worship is at present filled with a variety of "exercises" consisting of memory drills, announcements, hymn practice, instruction on missions, sermonettes, with devotion interspersed. This program needs to be more intelligently formulated. Instruction in the use of liturgical material should not be confused with actual worship. Still less should memory drills and announcements be conceived of as worship. If these things all have a place in the departmental or general session, each should be kept within its proper limits so that the impression upon the mind of the child may not be that of disorder and confusion. If there is to be a place for real worship, it should be such as to make of this the climax of the whole session.

There needs to be training, not only in worship, but in service, and for this more definite organization is necessary. Children need to be made familiar with the objects of service; they need to be inspired to serve and give of their means to missionary and philanthropic purposes; but they need also to have opportunity for practice in living the truths taught them in the period of instruction and in expressing their religious enthusiasms in actual deeds of individual and social service. Each Sunday school should, therefore, have its program for training in service, and all classes in the Sunday school, certainly above the ages of twelve and thirteen, should be organized for service.

The program of service and of worship, when fully formulated, will constitute a curriculum of training parallel to and correlated with the curriculum of instruction.

2. While the Sunday school is in process of reconstruction, it will become evident that the same principles need to be applied to other agencies and organizations within the church. The young people's society will demand attention if it is to serve a specific purpose for a certain period of youth. The nature of that service should be more clearly defined and the age limits of the period more exactly fixed. The program or curriculum should then be worked out with the greatest care and should include certain constant factors of which all young people should be expected to avail themselves during this period. Among these may be named the first-hand study of the local church and the local community by the young people themselves, as well as a study of the history and principles of the denomination to which the local church belongs. The great classic hymns and prayers should be made the possession of young people at this period, and they should know something of the struggles and sacrifices out of which have come the great Christian and Protestant doctrines. This does not mean that the young people's society shall not be free to relate itself to the discussion of current problems in citizenship or to participate in common interdenominational movements. It does mean, however, that its program should be under the direct oversight of the local church and definitely related to the local situation rather than formulated for the country as a whole.

Similar principles apply to the organizations of Boy Scouts and Camp Fire Girls and various other boys' and girls' clubs which are to be found in most churches. The aims of all these need to be carefully defined, the programs of all need to be formulated with immediate reference to the accomplishment of these aims, and the work of all needs to be correlated under unified direction with the work of the Sunday school.

When these aims and programs have thus been formulated and compared with the Sunday school curriculum of instruction and of training, there may be further opportunities for economy as instances appear where the work of one organization overlaps that of another; or of increased effectiveness where an existing need is not at present met by any organization. For this work of unification every church needs an educational director analogous to the superintendent of schools and a committee of the local church on religious education analogous to the local school committee. When all these educational activities are thus unified the local church will discover that it has not merely a Sunday school and various other independent educational agencies, but that it has a church school in which are comprehended all agencies, each with its definite part to perform. Moreover, it will be found that no small part of the work of this church school is already being accomplished in week-day sessions. When all these various programs have been unified and the part which each agency is to perform clearly indicated, this unified program will then constitute the curriculum of the church school.

3. The needs of the local community cannot be fully met, however, by any single church or denomination unless that happens to be the only one in the community. For the complete solution of the local problem there must be a strengthening of cooperative relationship

between the churches. One of the most natural forms of such cooperation is in the community teacher-training institute. This may be at first simply a more or less informal gathering of the teachers in the different church schools or the holding of an occasional conference or institute of several days' duration. Ultimately, however, there should be provided, especially in communities of some size, a permanent normal school for the training of teachers of religion.

Again, the Young Men's Christian Association and the Young Women's Christian Association are agencies already existing in many communities whose purpose is educational and whose work is somewhat highly specialized. Their experience, equipment, and program should be brought more definitely into relation with the educational program of the local churches. In many instances, if properly correlated, the program of the Christian Associations may be regarded as indeed a part of the program of each participating local church, and to facilitate this correlation there may well be included in the boards of directors of the Christian Associations members officially appointed by the churches who are familiar with the educational programs of their respective churches.

The different denominations of the community may undertake to accomplish their educational task through more direct cooperative effort in charge of a special interdenominational committee. The joint conduct of a religious day school or of a daily vacation Bible school will often be easily possible for several churches unitedly, either of the same or of different denominations, where it will be quite impossible for any single church.

4. All this looks toward the realization of complete interdenominational cooperation in the local community. The example of this has been set in the city of New York in the appointment of an Interdenominational Committee

on Week-day Religious Instruction. The principles underlying the work of this committee are two:

1. The development of the child's life should be a unitary process in the light of modern psychology and education, and that development should include in proper correlation the physical, mental, and religious training of child life.

2. The American principle of the separation of church and state is reaffirmed. The committee, representing, so far as possible, all religious bodies, has set for itself the task of stimulating, unifying, and promoting week-day religious instruction in such wise as to conserve religious liberty and maintain every possible safeguard against proselyting.

In cooperation with denominational committees, and with the local churches and synagogues, it seeks to have week-day schools for religious instruction established in different parts of the city to demonstrate:

1. Ways by which all school programs can be taken advantage of without infringing upon the sectarian neutrality of the public schools;

2. Ways by which individual churches can organize their educational work so as to include therein week-day religious instruction;

3. Ways by which churches of several denominations can cooperate in the management of a community school; and

4. Ways by which religious instruction can ultimately be provided on week days for all children of any community.

Such a committee will undertake:

1. A thorough community survey to determine the existing needs of the community. It will include in this survey a tabulation of the organizations and agencies influencing favorably or unfavorably the lives of the children and youth.

2. It will make a careful study of the educational agencies of the community, such as school, library, playgrounds, and the homes themselves, investigating their curricula and, so far as possible, estimating the influence of each one.

Upon the basis of these ascertained facts, this joint

committee will apportion to each religious denomination or group of denominations its appropriate part in the common task.

At this point the Protestant churches may well combine in the establishment of a community school of religion, to be conducted cooperatively. For such a school there will need to be a carefully selected school committee of the participating churches, and probably a paid director or superintendent, the financial support being provided by a voluntary association, similar in type to the kindergarten associations.[1] This school will be conducted on week days, the hours and schedules to be arranged in conference with, though not necessarily in official connection with the school authorities. The aims of this school will be carefully formulated with reference to the work of all the other educational agencies operating in the same field. A curriculum will be constructed to be closely related with the curricula of other existing agencies. A suitable place will need to be determined upon and equipped for the work of teaching; textbooks must be selected and teachers engaged, definite requirements set for the pupils and clear statement made of conditions for credit, promotion, and graduation. Thus at length the Protestant churches may provide in the local community their own system of religious education parallel to the public school system, but independent of it, resting upon its own merits, and, by reason of its high standards, commanding the respect of the whole community. This system of religious education provided in the community school of religion, and the public school system, will be in a kind of friendly competition with each other, each seeking to stimulate the other to greater effectiveness, but both cooperating to provide a complete system of popular education.

---

[1] See the Malden Plan, Part II, pp. 263f.

141

Such interdenominational cooperation is far from being impossible or impracticable. The various denominations have already gone a long way toward the realization of this ideal. Nearly all Protestant denominations to-day are using the same curriculum of religious instruction in their Sunday schools, a curriculum which is practically identical, at least through the elementary grades. Moreover, many denominations are using the same lesson material and textbooks and are employing the same type of organization for training, so that from the standpoint of content, method, and organization there are no insuperable obstacles to be overcome.

Perhaps the greatest present need is the need of intelligent and consistent leadership.[1] That there is a desire for a more complete system of religious education, both on the part of educators and of denominational leaders, is evident. The membership of the churches, however, in the local communities, as well as the citizens generally, need to be aroused to a keener appreciation of the present need and to a deeper sense of responsibility. Moreover, the multiplicity of national organizations in the field of religious education is at present a serious obstacle to progress. There are no less than a dozen such organizations, interdenominational in membership, national in scope, but with programs somewhat divergent and with overlapping fields of influence. Among these may be mentioned: the American Sunday School Union, the International Sunday School Association, the Young Men's Christian Association, and the Young Women's Christian Association, are all unofficially interdenominational and under lay direction; the Young People's Society for Christian Endeavor is an organization started in a single denomination which has become national in scope and has branches in other

---

[1] As an illustration of such denominational leadership, see the suggestions of the Committee on Religious Education of the Baptist Convention, Part II, pp. 253f.

142

denominations; the Boy Scouts and the Camp Fire Girls are nondenominational organizations national in scope, which are often utilized as church educational agencies; the Sunday School Council and the Council of Church Boards are organizations made up of the official representatives of different denominations; the Federal Council Commission on Christian Education includes upon the membership of its executive committee official representatives of various denominations; the Religious Education Association is a nonadministrative body composed of representatives of all denominations, including Jews and Roman Catholics. The lack of a clear definition of function and, to a certain degree, a competitive relationship greatly retards progress. There is no more immediate and imperative need than that these various organizations should become federated and their programs coordinated and unified.

CHAPTER XII

THE COMMUNITY TASK OF THE CHURCHES

A WORLD crisis is upon us, in which the interests of all humanity are involved. These interests are summed up in the word democracy, and democracy is the modern expression of the spirit of Jesus. The purpose of Jesus was to secure for all men the fullness of life; life for the individual in which his consciousness of God should be complete, his access to God immediate, his attitude toward God filial, his communion with God unbroken; and a common life, pervaded by the sense of interdependence and brotherhood. The ideal of democracy is self-realization through self-sacrifice, the finding of the individual self through its submergence in the larger social self. Democracy involves the harmonizing of antagonistic forces within the individual, the maintaining of a nice adjustment or balance between deep-seated instincts which impel the individual to seek selfish advantage at the expense of his fellows, and the higher impulses which urge him to seek the common good. Democracy is a resultant of forces essentially religious and spiritual; it is the product of Christian faith.

The Great War has been a titanic struggle between nationalism—which is individualism on a national scale —and internationalism—which is the application to the relations between nations of those principles of democracy which have already found acceptance between individuals. It is an effort to think democracy in world terms. In this crisis the United States occupies a peculiar position. It is its task as a nation to embody and exemplify, in its

144

dealing with all other nations, the spirit of international brotherhood. The demand for such high service has revealed to this nation as never before its own shortcomings. While priding itself upon its spirit of freedom, its opulent resources, its varied opportunity for individual achievement, and its generous hospitality as a nation, for a time it seemed to stand before the world callous to its suffering, sordidly selfish, and lacking in the spirit of sacrifice.

The modern movement for democracy had its rise in the Reformation. The Protestant churches have been the inspiration of democracy, but in the midst of this world crisis they find themselves still in the early stages of recovery from almost hopeless individualism.

The spirit of the Reformation also gave birth to the modern movement for popular education, as the effective method of propagating democratic ideas and ideals. Democracy, under the guise of the state, has appropriated to itself the educational movement, has determined its aims, developed its organization, and formulated its methods. The church, having relinquished this agency, has made such terms as it could with the state, to insure the inclusion of religion within the state system of education. Every such plan of cooperation at present must be regarded as more or less of a makeshift and unsatisfactory. The relationship is tangential rather than organic. The gigantic forces released in the present world crisis are a tribute to the efficiency of state education, while their employment for destructive ends is an indictment of the inefficiency of religious education.

In Germany religious education lags far behind the rest of education. In France religious education is supplied by the Roman Catholic Church, is uncoordinated with the state system of education, is undemocratic in spirit, while the state system of moral education is bereft of its religious sanctions. The result is artificiality in moral instruction, superficiality and formalism in religion, and mutual distrust between church and state. In England, the connection between church and state has greatly retarded the progress of education in general, and recent development of state education has been attended by bitter controversy between the religious forces.

In the United States, where democracy and education both had their beginnings in the Puritan commonwealth, the Protestant churches have relinquished entirely all connection with the state system of popular education. In both state and church the *rights* of the individual have been emphasized out of all proportion to his *duties* to society. One result of this overemphasis has been a serious weakening of Protestant influence and ineffectiveness of religious instruction. To-day, in the United States, less time is devoted to religious instruction provided by Protestants than is allotted to such instruction in any other first-class civilized country in the world.

Speaking in general terms, the Protestant churches in the United States now rely mainly upon the Sunday school for supplying the religious element in popular education. The Sunday school, an institution at first intended as a philanthropic and reformatory agency for work among delinquents, has been naturalized by the church and compelled to undertake its entire educational task. It is impossible to accomplish that task in the brief time allotted to it. If Wednesday afternoons were devoted to religious instruction in the churches, as some have proposed, the amount of time thus set apart for moral and religious instruction in the United States would still equal only about eight per cent of school time, as compared with between twelve and fifteen per cent in some of the countries of Europe. Nor do the churches succeed in reaching all the children and youth. It has been estimated that nearly ten millions are untouched by religious

146

instruction of any kind—certainly a large and inviting field for missionary endeavor.

Confronted by such a task, it is encouraging to see the leaders in popular education approaching the representatives of the churches with the request for religious instruction in larger amount and of higher quality; to have them proposing to provide the necessary incentives for such instruction, offering to assist in formulating standards, in adjusting school schedules so as to afford more time, and in various ways inviting the serious cooperation of the churches.

Moreover, it is well for the churches to realize that here in America we have been grappling with a new problem in its twofold aspects; the problem of providing compulsory education for all children and, at the same time, of preserving religious freedom. The course of development has been rapid. A complete system of state education has been developed within the last century. During the same period the Protestant churches have been developing somewhat more slowly a parallel system of religious education. Within the last decade remarkable progress has been made in applying to the curriculum and methods of the Sunday school the principles which have found acceptance in the day school.

This very development has made still more apparent the weakness of the Sunday school. The infrequency of its sessions, the disinclination of pupils to undertake serious study on a day devoted to rest, the failure of the home to support an educational program or even to adjust the home life to such a program, the brevity of the period of instruction, the lack of proper equipment, the small proportion of trained teachers—these are some of the weaknesses of the Sunday school as an educational institution. The Sunday school may possibly serve as the nucleus of the system of religious education which is to be. But if so, it needs to be strengthened by the perfecting of its organization, the elimination of waste, the extension of its program, and the correlation of its curriculum with that of the day school and the home.

But in any event the responsibility for taking the initiative in a movement for a wider religious education rests primarily with the churches, especially those of the Protestant faith. Originally the home was the primary agency of education. In course of time the church assumed a part of the responsibility, and again, in turn, delegated a part of its responsibility to the state. At present, in the United States, it is state education that is most highly developed, church education much less developed, while the program for home education is almost entirely lacking. The state begins to realize that it cannot accomplish the whole task, and is stimulating the church to do its distinctive part. The church, on its part, together with the school, must stimulate and guide the home in developing the plan for home religious instruction and training.

The history of the public school points to the conclusion that the further development of religious education will best be accomplished by the working out of these details experimentally and cooperatively in local communities. When the problem has been solved, or partially solved, in one place, other places will be quick to appropriate the results of successful experiment.

The spirit of democracy is astir in the world as never before. Ancient limitations and restraints are being cast aside, dynasties and autocracies overthrown. The way is opening for a new world in which social justice and cooperation and brotherhood shall take the place of individualism and self-seeking and exploitation. But the new world will demand a new spirit, the spirit of self-control, idealism, responsibility, and service. It is this new power which society must somehow develop through religion and education, working hand in hand.

The Protestant churches of America must not fail the cause of democracy in this hour of the world's history. Upon them rests, primarily, as we have seen, the responsibility for taking the initiative in this great task. The task is difficult, because it is so nearly new. But the churches will not hesitate on this account. They will not be so unpatriotic as to ignore their country's need, nor so selfish as to think mainly of their own denominational upbuilding or of merely national prestige. It is an hour of supreme opportunity for the churches to render a world service.

PART TWO

SUGGESTED PLANS AND PROGRAMS OF WEEK-DAY RELIGIOUS INSTRUCTION

CHAPTER I

TYPICAL CURRICULA OF MORAL AND RELIGIOUS IN-STRUCTION IN STATE SYSTEMS OF EDUCATION

I. THE GERMAN SYSTEM OF RELIGIOUS INSTRUCTION

THE following curriculum of religious instruction is the one in use in the Reform-gymnasium, Hohenzollernschule, Schoenberg, Berlin, Germany.[1] The material to be covered during the summer and winter terms, respectively, is designated by the letters S and W.

Preparatory Grades (Elementary)

First Year. (Two hours per week.)
Simple Bible Stories from Old and New Testaments: S. Abraham and Lot; Joseph and His Brothers. W. The Birth of Jesus; The Boy Jesus at Twelve; Jesus the Friend of Children; Stilling the Storm; During each half year several Bible verses, morning, evening and table prayers are memorized.

Second Year. (Two hours.)
S. Old Testament Stories: Cain and Abel; The Joseph stories to his exaltation in Egypt; Moses's Birth. W. Stories of Jesus; The Wise Men; The Wedding at Cana; The Good Samaritan; The stories of the death, resurrection and ascension of Jesus. Selected Scripture verses, and stanzas of hymns memorized.

Third Year. (Two hours.)
S. Bible Stories from the Old and New Testaments. Garden of Eden; The Flood; David and Goliath. Memory work: Commandments 1 to 5; Selected Proverbs and paragraphs from church hymns. W. New Testament Stories: Feeding the Five Thousand; Ten Lepers; The Death of Jesus; Resurrection, Ascension. Memory work: Commandments 6 to 10; Selected Proverbs and hymns as in summer.

---

[1] Supplied by Rev. H. H. Meyer, D.D.

153

RELIGIOUS EDUCATION AND DEMOCRACY

Grammar and High School Grades (Gymnasium)

First Year (Sexta). (Three hours.)

Old Testament narratives from a selected textbook; New Testament narratives grouped around the principal feasts of the church year; Exposition of Luther's Catechism, first chapter; four selected church hymns; other memory passages.

Second Year (Quinta). (Two hours.)

New Testament narratives from a textbook. (Fifty lessons.) Review of Catechism, first chapter. Exposition of the second chapter; four additional church hymns and other selected memory material.

Third Year (Quarta). (Two hours.)

Division and order of the books of the Bible; Drill in finding Bible passages; Review of Bible narratives of previous years. S. Reading and exposition of important Old Testament passages. W. Survey of the life of Jesus based on Mark supplemented by narratives from Matthew, Luke and Acts; Review of Catechism, chapters 1 and 2; Exposition of chapter 3. Memorization: Psalms 1 and 23. Additional church hymns.

Fourth Year (Untertertia). (Two hours.)

The Kingdom of God in the Old Testament; Related passages from historical books, Psalms, Proverbs, and Prophets. Book of Job; Survey of the history of Israel and the Messianic prophecies; Exposition and memorization of Catechism, chapters 4 and 5; Review of the preceding chapters Proverbs, Psalms, and hymns. Memorize Psalms 8 and 90; Three new hymns; Explanation of the church year and ritual.

Fifth Year (Obertertia). Two hours.)

S. The Kingdom of God in the New Testament; Exposition of the Parables and the Sermon on the Mount. Memorization: Psalms 103. 1-13; 121; 139. 1-12; Catechism, chapter 5 completed; Review of memory material, Proverbs, Psalms, Hymns, with a brief survey of Protestant hymnology, church year and ordinances.

Sixth Year (Untersekunda). (Two hours.)

S. Old Testament prophecy; selected studies from Prophets

154

and Psalms; History of Judaism in the New Testament period. W. The life of Jesus according to Matthew from the Synoptic Gospels; Review of memory material, Catechism, etc.

Seventh Year (Obersekunda). (Two hours.)

Acts of the Apostles; First Corinthians and selected passages from other epistles of Paul, studied from the Greek text; Life Sketches of the Apostles; Jewish and Gentile Christianity compared; The Conquest of the Roman Empire by Christianity; Systematic review of memory material, Psalms, hymns, Catechism.

Eighth Year (Unterprima). (Two hours.)

Gospel of John from the Greek text; Church History to the Reformation; Review of Proverbs, Psalms, hymns.

Ninth Year (Oberprima). (Two hours.)

The Creed and Christian Ethics in conjunction with New Testament passages; Church History from the Reformation to the Present Time; Selected Readings from Romans and Galatians from the Greek text; Teachings of Jesus according to the Gospels; Explanation of the Augustinian Creed; A survey of Protestantism in its Principal Denominations; General review.

2. THE FRENCH SYSTEM OF MORAL INSTRUCTION

A Sample Page from Textbook on Morals[1]

One of the most popular textbooks designed for children from nine to eleven years of age is entitled The First Year of Moral and Civic Instruction. Its thirteen chapters are devoted to the following topics:

1. Duties of the Child in the Family, in the School and in Apprenticeship.
2. Duties toward Self.
3. Duties toward Society.
4. Work, Order, Association, etc.
5. Employers and Employed.
6. The Farmer.
7. The Merchant.
8. Service of the State.
9. The Head of the Family.
10. Civil Rights.
11. The State.
12. The Administration.
13. Rights and Duties of Citizens.

The method of lesson treatment is seen from the following sample page, setting forth duties in the family:

1. You ought to love your parents, who love you, nurture you, and educate you.
2. You ought to respect them. Do not be familiar with them, as with your companions.
3. You ought to obey them. Do not dispute with them. One disputes with equals, not with father and mother.
4. The law makes sacred the authority of parents in giving them the right to punish. (A quotation follows, giving the laws of the Republic bearing on the authority of parents over their children.)

---

[1] From Meyer's "Moral Instruction in the Public Schools of France," in Proceedings of the Religious Education Association, 1908, pp. 189-190.

5. You ought to be grateful to your parents for all the care which they give you.

Thus, as it appears, the body of the lesson consists of precepts, interspersed with explanations. These are followed, at the bottom of the page, with questions:

1, 2, 3. State the principal duties of children toward their parents.

4. How does the law make sacred the authority of parents over their children?

5. Why ought you to be grateful to your parents?

At the close of the first chapter the teaching is summarized in a series of resolutions which the pupil is to commit to memory:

1. I shall love my father and my mother. I shall respect and obey them.

2. I shall be grateful to them. I shall render them in old age the care they have given me.

3. I shall love all the members of my family.

4. I shall do honor to the name I bear.

5. At school, I shall work with all my might. I shall put all my attention and all my intelligence into everything I do.

6. I shall love my teacher. I shall obey him, respect him, and be grateful to him.

7. I shall form good habits, and shall choose well my friends. I shall avoid evil companions.

8. During my period of apprenticeship, I shall work hard and be teachable and honest. I shall carefully guard the good habits of my childhood.

For additional information the pupil is frequently referred to a supplement where technical terms are defined and quotations made from the laws. Where such references are given the pupil is expected to look up and copy down the explanations.

157

3. THE ENGLISH PLAN OF RELIGIOUS INSTRUCTION

SYLLABUS OF RELIGIOUS INSTRUCTION, LEEDS (ENGLAND) COUNCIL SCHOOLS, 1904-14[1]

(In this syllabus the word "infant" applies to pupils up to seven years of age. A separate syllabus is prepared for Jewish pupils on the Old Testament only, which they are taught separately. It has not seemed a good reason why Christian and Jewish children should both be deprived of moral education on the only effective basis, the Bible, because there must be some adaptation of the teaching to their differences.)

1. The Bible shall be read in the schools, and there shall be given such instruction therefrom, and such explanations, as are suited to the capacities of the children; provided always that in all the religious teaching and exercises, the provisions of the Education Act, 1870, in Sections VII and XIV are to be strictly complied with, both in letter and spirit, and no attempt is to be made in any way to attach children to any particular denomination.

2. In regard to any particular school, the Education Committee shall consider and determine upon any application made by parents, or by ratepayers of the district, with a view of showing special cause for exception of the school from the operation of this regulation, in whole or in part.

3. In all cases where children are withdrawn from the religious teaching by parents or guardians, suitable and adequate arrangements shall be made for their instruction in secular subjects.

4. The first half-hour of each day shall be devoted to religious instruction. The schools shall be opened by the singing of a hymn from the hymn book provided by the Education Committee, and by offering the Lord's Prayer, and the prayers for opening of school contained in the Committee's syllabus of religious instruction. The door of the schoolroom is to be closed promptly at nine o'clock, and no child admitted until after prayers and the marking of the registers. The door is then to be opened for late scholars, and from that time until 9:30 religious instruction is

---

[1] From Crafts, Bible in Schools Plans of Many Lands, pp. 115-119.

to be given in accordance with the Committee's syllabus, which must be strictly adhered to. The teaching will be in the main oral; but the Bible must be read by the children in the higher standards.

(In infants' schools the head teachers may use the whole or any portion of the prayers.)

5. The head teacher will arrange that each teacher (with the exception of pupil teachers) shall give religious instruction to the class for which he or she is responsible with regard to secular instruction. The head teacher should, however, from time to time, take part in the actual instruction of the several classes.

6. By special permission of the Education Committee, two small Standards (Classes in Infants' Departments) may be grouped for instruction, in which case the Syllabus for the two Standards (or Classes) shall be taken in alternate years.

7. The Council's inspectors will visit the schools from time to time during the hours set apart for religious instruction, to test and report upon the character of the instruction.

8. The pupil teachers shall receive not less than thirty minutes' religious instruction weekly at the pupil teachers' classes in accordance with the Education Committee's scheme of religious instruction for pupil teachers, and an examination conducted by the Council's inspectors shall be held annually, in addition to the term examinations conducted by the pupil teachers' instructor. Any pupil teacher will be excused from these examinations on written application from parent or guardian.

RESOLUTION ADOPTED BY THE EDUCATION COMMITTEE
SEPTEMBER 28, 1904.

"That the local education authority for Leeds will regard attendance at a place of worship during the time given to religious instruction on certain occasions, not exceeding twelve in any year, to be previously notified to the local authority by the school managers, as attendance at school in compliance with its by-laws."

MORNING PRAYERS

Almighty and most merciful Father, who hast safely brought us to the beginning of this day, keep us in the same by thy mighty power; watch over us for good; preserve us in our going out and coming in, and may all our ways be pleasing in thy sight. Amen. ———

O merciful Father, forgive, we pray thee, our past sins and negligence, and grant us the grace of the Holy Spirit to renew our hearts, that we may amend our lives according to thy Holy Word, through Jesus Christ our Lord. Amen.

———

O God, the Fountain of all wisdom, teach us to know thee in the days of our youth; and may we be made wise unto salvation. Amen. ———

Bless, O Lord, in mercy all our dear parents, relations, teachers, school fellows, and friends; may we be kind one to another, and so live together in this life that in the world to come we may have life everlasting. We ask all in the name of Jesus Christ our Lord, who hath taught us when we pray to say "Our Father," etc.

———

The grace of our Lord Jesus Christ, and the love of God, and the fellowship of the Holy Ghost, be with us all evermore. Amen.

EVENING PRAYERS

O heavenly Father, we thank thee for all thy mercies during this day, and all our lives hitherto; we bless thee for our food and clothing, our health and strength, our kind friends and teachers, and all the benefits of thy hand; but above all, for thy Holy Word and the knowledge of thy grace and mercy in our Saviour Jesus Christ. May we praise thee both with our lips and in our lives, and serve thee better day by day. Amen.

———

Preserve us, O Lord, during the coming night from all harm to our bodies, and from all evil thoughts which may hurt our souls. Be thou ever our Shield and Defender. Amen.

———

We commend to thy kind care all whom we love, and pray thee to take us all into thy holy and safe-keeping, through Jesus Christ our Lord, who hath taught us to pray, saying "Our Father," etc.

———

The Lord bless and keep us; the Lord lift up the light of his countenance upon us and give us peace, now and for evermore. Amen.

TYPICAL CURRICULA IN STATE SYSTEMS

Candidates: Book of Genesis.

First Year: Books of Exodus, Joshua, and Judges.

Second Year: First and Second Books of Samuel and St. Luke's Gospel.

Third Year: First and Second Books of Kings and Acts of the Apostles.

SYLLABUS FOR INFANTS
FIRST CLASS

Period of School Year	REPETITION	INSTRUCTION
1st	The Lord's Prayer.	Story of the Garden of Eden; Story of Cain and Abel.
2nd	"Depart from evil and do good" (Psa. 34. 14). "Whoso putteth his trust in the Lord shall be safe" (Prov. 29. 25). "The Lord is nigh unto all them that call upon Him" (Psa. 145. 18).	Story of Noah and the Flood; Story of Daniel and the Lions.
3rd	"Children, obey your parents" (Eph. 6. 1). "Let brotherly love continue" (Heb. 13. 1). "Keep thy tongue from evil, and thy lips from speaking guile" (Psa. 34. 13).	Story of the Offering of Isaac; Story of Jacob and Esau.
4th	"Be ye kind one to another, tender-hearted, forgiving one another" (Eph. 4. 32). "Be not overcome of evil, but overcome evil with good" (Rom. 12. 21). "Let us not be weary in well-doing; for in due season we shall reap, if we faint not" (Gal. 6. 9).	Story of Joseph and His Brethren; Story of the Early Life of Moses.
5th	"Suffer little children to come unto me, and forbid them not" (Luke 18. 16). "I love them that love me; and those that seek me early shall find me" (Prov. 8. 17). "A soft answer turneth away wrath" (Prov. 15. 1).	Story of Jesus: His Birth—In the Temple—Blessing the Children—Feeding the Multitude.

SYLLABUS FOR INFANTS
SECOND CLASS

Period of School Year	REPETITION	INSTRUCTION
1st	Repeat and sing a verse of a hymn.	Story of the Garden of Eden.
2nd	Repeat and sing another verse of a hymn	Story of the Flood.
3rd	Repeat and sing another verse of a hymn.	Story of Joseph and His Brethren.
4th	Repeat and sing another verse or two of a hymn.	Story of David and Goliath.
5th	Repeat and sing another verse or two of a hymn.	The Call of Samuel.
6th	Repeat and sing another verse or two of a hymn.	Story of the Birth of Jesus, and Visit of the Wise Men.
7th	"Bear ye one another's burdens" (Gal. 6. 2). "The Lord is my Shepherd, I shall not want" (Psa. 23. 1). "Enter not into the path of the wicked, and go not in the way of evil men" (Prov. 4. 14).	Story of the Good Samaritan; Story of the Lost Sheep; Story of the Prodigal Son.

TYPICAL CURRICULA IN STATE SYSTEMS

SYLLABUS FOR INFANTS
Third Class

Period of School Year	Repetition	Instruction
1st	Repeat and sing a verse of a hymn.	Story of the Garden of Eden.
2nd	Repeat and sing another verse of a hymn.	Story of the Flood.
3rd	Repeat and sing another verse of a hymn.	Story of Joseph and His Brethren.
4th	Repeat and sing another verse of a hymn.	Story of David and Goliath.
5th	Repeat and sing another verse of a hymn.	Story of the Birth of Jesus, and the Visit of the Wise Men.
6th	Repeat and sing another verse of a hymn.	Re-tell the Stories of the previous Periods.

N. B.—The Hymns are to be selected from the Hymn Book provided by the Education Committee, and should be such as are suitable for very young children. Before being committed to memory the hymns should be explained in simple language. Two or more verses may be taken from the same hymn.

The teachers should see that the children are not only able to repeat the texts, but that they have an intelligent apprehension of their meaning.

SYLLABUS FOR OLDER SCHOLARS
Standard I

Period of School Year	Repetition	Instruction
1st	The Lord's Prayer and the first three commandments.	Examples from Scripture of the observance and breach of these commandments.
2nd	The Ten Commandments, with examples of their observance and breach.	The Creation; The Garden of Eden; Cain and Abel (Gen. 1 to 4).
3rd	Psa. 23.	The Flood, and the Tower of Babel (Gen. 6 to 9. 19; 11. 1–9).
4th	Matt. 5. 3–9.	Preaching of John, and Baptism of Jesus (Mark 1. 1–11); Jesus at Capernaum (Mark 1. 21–28); Cleansing the Leper (Mark 1. 40–45); Healing the Palsy (Mark 2. 1–12); Parable of the Sower (Mark 4. 1–20).
5th	Matt. 11. 28–30.	Stilling the Tempest (Mark 4. 35–41); Raising of Jairus's Daughter, and Healing of Woman (Mark 5. 21–43); Feeding the Multitudes (Mark 6. 32–44; 8. 1–9); Jesus Walking on the Sea (Mark 6. 45–56); Healing of Blind Bartimæus (Mark 10. 46–52).
6th	Matt. 19. 13, 14; 22. 37–39.	Gethsemane and the Betrayal (Mark 14. 26–49); Jesus Before the High Priest—Peter's Denial (Mark 14. 53–72); Trial Before Pilate (Mark 15. 1–15); The Crucifixion (Mark 15. 16–41); Burial and Resurrection (Mark 15. 42 to 16. 20).

	SYLLABUS FOR OLDER SCHOLARS STANDARD II			SYLLABUS FOR OLDER SCHOLARS STANDARD III	
Period of School Year	REPETITION	INSTRUCTION	Period of School Year	REPETITION	INSTRUCTION
1st	The Lord's Prayer and Ten Commandments. Revise passages learned in Standard I.	History of Abraham (Gen. 15; 21. 1–21; 22. 1–19; 24).	1st	The Lord's Prayer and the Ten Commandments. Revise the passages learned in Standard I.	History of Joseph (early portion); (Gen. 37; 39. 1–6; 39. 20–23; 40).
2nd	Psa. 1.	History of Isaac, Rebekah, and Esau (Gen. 24; 25. 27–34; 27).	2nd	Revise the passages learned in Standard II.	History of Joseph (middle portion); (Gen. 41 to 45. 15).
3rd	Psa. 15.	History of Jacob (Gen. 27 to 29. 20; 31 to 33).	3rd	Psa. 8.	History of Joseph (later portion) (Gen. 45. 16 to Gen. 50).
4th	John 4. 24; 14. 1–3.	Birth of Jesus and Visit of Wise Men (Matt. 1. 18–25; 2. 1–12); Massacre of the Children and Flight into Egypt (Matt. 2. 13–23); John the Baptist—Baptism of Jesus (Matt. 3); Death of John (Matt. 14. 1–13); Healing the Centurion's Servant (Matt. 8. 5–13); Feeding the Multitudes (Matt. 14. 14–21; 15. 32–38).	4th	Psa. 103. 8–18.	Birth of Jesus and Visit of the Shepherds (Luke 2. 1–20); Jesus in the Temple (Luke 2. 14–52); Preaching of the Baptist—Baptism of Jesus (Luke 3. 1–22); The Temptation (Luke 4. 1–13); Preaching and Miracles at Capernaum (Luke 4. 16–44); Calling of Peter, James, and John (Luke 5. 1–11).
5th	Luke 15. 3–7.	Parable of the Sower (Matt. 13. 1–23); Parable of the Mustard Seed (Matt. 13. 31, 32); Parable of the Unforgiving Servant (Matt. 18. 21–35); Parable of the Ten Virgins (Matt. 25. 1–13); Parable of the Talents (Matt. 25. 14–30).	5th	Luke 15. 11–16.	Healing on the Sabbath (Luke 6. 6–11; 13. 10–17; 14. 1–6); Raising the Widow's Son (Luke 7. 11–17); Martha and Mary (Luke 10. 38–42); Healing of the Ten Lepers (Luke 17. 11–19); The Rich Young Ruler (Luke 18. 18–23); Zaccheus (Luke 19. 1–10).
6th	Luke 10. 27, 30–37.	Entry into Jerusalem (Matt. 21. 1–17); The Last Supper (Matt. 26. 17–30); Judas (Matt. 26. 14–16, 47–50; 27. 3–10); Gethsemane (Matt. 26. 31–46, 51–56); Jesus Before the High Priest (Matt. 26. 57–75); Trial Before Pilate (Matt. 27. 1, 2, 11–26); The Crucifixion (Matt. 27. 27–56); The Burial and Resurrection (Matt. 27. 57–66; 28).	6th	Luke 15. 11–24.	Entry into Jerusalem (Luke 19. 28–48); The Widow's Mite (Luke 21. 1–4); The Last Supper (Luke 22. 1–34); Gethsemane and the Betrayal (Luke 22. 39–54); Jesus Before the High Priest—Peter's Denial (Luke 22. 55–71); Trial Before Pilate and Herod (Luke 23. 1–25); The Crucifixion and Burial (Luke 23. 26–56); The Resurrection and Ascension (Luke 24).

TYPICAL CURRICULA IN STATE SYSTEMS

SYLLABUS FOR OLDER SCHOLARS
STANDARD IV

SYLLABUS FOR OLDER SCHOLARS
STANDARD V

Period of School Year	REPETITION	INSTRUCTION	Period of School Year	REPETITION	INSTRUCTION
1st	The Lord's Prayer and Ten Commandments. Revise the passages learned in Standards I and II.	History of Moses (early portion) (Exod. 1 to 12).	1st	The Lord's Prayer and Ten Commandments. Revise the passages learned in Standard III.	Crossing Jordan (Josh. 3; 4); Fall of Jericho (Josh. 6); Achan (Josh. 7); Division of Palestine, and Death of Joshua (Josh. 24); Deborah (Judg. 4).
2nd	Review the passages learned in Standard III.	History of Moses (middle portion); (Exod. 13 to 20; 32).	2nd	Revise the passages learned in Standard IV.	Gideon (Judg. 6 to 7. 22); Jephthah's Daughter (Judg. 11. 29–40); Samson (Judg. 14 to 16); Ruth (Ruth 1 to 4); Samuel and Eli (1 Sam. 1 to 3).
3rd	Psa. 19. 1–11.	History of Moses (later portion); (Num. 13; 14, 20 to 24; Deut. 34).	3rd	Psa. 121.	Saul Made King (1 Sam. 8 to 10); David and Goliath (1 Sam. 17); David and Jonathan (1 Sam. 18; 20); David and Saul (1 Sam. 24; 31; 2 Sam. 1).
4th	Psa. 19. 1–14 and Luke 7. 40–43.	Baptism by John (John 1. 19–34); Marriage at Cana (John 2. 1–12); Clearing the Temple of the Money-changers (John 2. 13–22); The Woman of Samaria (John 4. 1–42); Healing the Nobleman's Son (John 4. 46–54).	4th	Psa. 34. 1–14.	The Ascension; Choice of an Apostle (Acts 1); Day of Pentecost (Acts 2); Healing of the Lame Man in the Temple (Acts 3. 1–10); Peter and John Before the High Priest (Acts 4. 1–31); Ananias and Sapphira (Acts 4. 32 to 5. 11).
5th	Psa. 119. 9–16.	The Pool of Bethesda (John 5. 1–16); Feeding the Multitude (John 6. 1–15); Walking on the Sea (John 5. 16–21); Healing a Man Born Blind (John 9. 1–38); Raising of Lazarus (John 11. 1–46); Jesus at Bethany; Entry into Jerusalem (John 12. 1–19).	5th	John 15. 1–12.	Peter and John Released from Prison (Acts 5. 17–25); Gamaliel's Advice (Acts 5. 26–42); Stephen (Acts 6 to 7); Simon the Sorcerer (Acts 8. 5–25); Saul's Conversion (Acts 9. 1–31).
6th	Luke 18. 9–14.	The Last Supper (John 13. 1–38); The Betrayal (John 18. 1–14); Peter's Denial (John 18. 15–27); Jesus Before Pilate (John 18. 28 to 19. 16); The Crucifixion (John 19. 17–34); Burial and Resurrection (John 19. 38 to 20. 18); Appearances after the Resurrection (John 20. 19 to 21. 25).	6th	Eph. 6. 1–9.	Peter and Dorcas (Acts 9. 32–43); Peter and Cornelius (Acts 10); Barnabas Sent to Antioch (Acts 11. 19–30); Peter Delivered from Prison (Acts 12).

RELIGIOUS EDUCATION AND DEMOCRACY

Period of School Year	REPETITION	INSTRUCTION
1st	The Lord's Prayer and Ten Commandments. Revise the passages learned in Standard IV.	Absalom (2 Sam. 14. 25 to 15; 17; 18); Solomon (1 Kings 3; 4. 29–34; 5 to 6. 14; 10. 1–10); Rehoboam and Jeroboam (1 Kings 12 to 13. 10).
2nd	Revise the passages learned in Standard V.	Elijah and Ahab (1 Kings 16. 29–33; 17 to 19; 21; 22. 20–38); Elisha (2 Kings 2; 4); Naaman (2 Kings 5).
3rd	Psa. 91. 1–10.	Elisha (2 Kings 6; 7; 13. 14–20; Hezekiah (2 Kings 18. 13 to 20. 11); Josiah (2 Kings 22 to 23. 30); The Captivity (2 Kings 24. 10 to 25. 12).
4th	Psa. 107. 1–8.	Paul and Barnabas and Elymas (Acts 13. 1–12); The Gospel Preached to the Gentiles at Antioch (Acts 13. 14–52); Paul at Iconium and Lystra (Acts 14. 1–22); Dispute of Paul and Barnabas (Acts 15. 36–40); Paul and Silas Preaching in Macedonia (Acts 16. 9–15); Paul and Silas in Prison (Acts 16. 16–40).
5th	Prov. 3. 1–7, 13–17.	Paul at Athens (Acts 17. 16–34); Paul at Corinth (Acts 18. 1–17); Paul at Ephesus (Acts 19. 23–41); Eutychus (Acts 20. 7–12); Paul's Farewell to the Christians of Ephesus (Acts 20. 17–38); Paul at Jerusalem (Acts 21. 15–40).
6th	1 Cor. 13.	Paul's Defense Before His Countrymen (Acts 22. 1–30); Paul Before the Council—Plot to Kill Him (Acts 23); Paul Before Felix (Acts 24); Paul Before Festus and Agrippa (Acts 25; 26); Paul's Voyage to Rome and Shipwreck (Acts 27; 28. 1–15); Paul in Rome (Acts 28. 16–31).

4. THE AUSTRALIAN PLAN[1]

In 1848 the Hon. John Herbert Plunkett, an Irish Roman Catholic, who was chairman of the Commissioners of National Education in New South Wales, caused the Scripture lessons that were taught in public schools in Ireland under its National Educational Board to be introduced in the national schools of New South Wales, where they have been used ever since. The system was enlarged in 1866, when Sir Henry Parkes was premier, and the law has been as follows ever since:

The New South Wales Act, Clauses 7, 17 and 18, provides:

"7. In all schools under this Act the teaching shall be strictly nonsectarian, but the words 'secular instruction' shall be held to include general religious teaching, as distinguished from dogmatical or polemical theology.

"17. Any minister of religion is entitled in school hours, on days to be arranged with the School Committee, to give children of his own denomination, separated from others, an hour's religious instruction.

"18. Any parent may withdraw his child from all religious teaching if he objects to such religious instruction being given."

This New South Wales law was adopted by the State of West Australia in 1893; by Tasmania, 1868; by Norfolk Island, 1906; Queensland (by a State referendum) in 1910, and by South Africa in 1913.

One of the distinctive features of the Australian system is that it always contemplates the use of Bible selections carefully made by some official committee with a view to providing uncontroversial selections of proper length, that are also psychologically adapted to the various grades. This plan removed the objection that some teachers, if allowed to read anything in the Bible, might not make wise selections.

These Bible lessons are not merely read, as in the United States, but taught in an unsectarian way. The comments allowed are not theological, but "grammatical, geographical, and historical." Teachers are unreservedly trusted by the Parliaments, the parents, and the churches to give these lessons, and, although the system is working in four Australian States, and has existed in

---

[1] Condensed from Crafts, *op. cit.*, p. 85ff.

167

RELIGIOUS EDUCATION AND DEMOCRACY

New South Wales for nearly half a century, there is no case on record where a Roman Catholic, a Jewish, a Secularist, or any other teacher has taken an unfair advantage of the lessons to impart or suggest his own particular views.

The whole time occupied under the system usually averages not more than one hour and a half each week, which means three half-hour Bible lessons.

The fact that the withdrawals are so few as to be negligible for statistical purposes is ample testimony of the approval of the system by the parents. The majority of the churches in Australia, including the Anglican, Methodist, Presbyterian, Baptist, Congregational, Lutheran, Church of Christ, and the Salvation Army, are unanimous in support of public education, so long as it includes this system of religious instruction.

By giving religious instruction during school hours, instead of before and after school, children are not punished by being "kept in" as if they had been disobedient or idle.

The Catholics generally oppose the New South Wales Plan in the vote, preferring the "dual system" under which parochial schools, in Quebec, for example, get a certain share of the school fund; but when the New South Wales system is adopted anywhere the result is quietly accepted, as many testimonies prove, by Catholic teachers, parents and pupils.

5. CANADIAN PLANS[1]

(a) *Ontario*

Legislation regarding religious exercises and instruction in public and high schools, approved by Order-in-Council, April 22, 1887.

200. Every public and high school shall be opened with the Lord's Prayer and closed with the reading of the Scriptures and the Lord's Prayer, or the prayer authorized by the Department of Education.

201. The Scriptures shall be read daily and systematically without comment or explanation, and the portions used may be taken from the Book of Selections adopted by the Department for that purpose, or from the Bible, as the trustees, by resolution, may direct.

202. Trustees may also order the reading of the Bible or the authorized Scripture Selections by both pupils and teachers at the opening and closing of the school, and the repeating of the Ten Commandments at least once a week.

203. No pupil shall be required to take part in any religious exercise objected to by his parents or guardians; and in order to the observance of this regulation the teacher, before commencing a religious exercise, is to allow a short interval to elapse, during which the children of Roman Catholics, and of others who have signified their objection, may retire.

204. If, in virtue of the right to be absent from the religious exercises, any pupil does not enter the schoolroom till fifteen minutes after the proper time for opening the school in the forenoon, such absence shall not be treated as an offense against the rules of the school.

205. When a teacher claims to have conscientious scruples in regard to opening or closing the school as herein prescribed, he shall notify the trustees to that effect in writing, and it shall be the duty of the trustees to make such provision in the premises as they may deem expedient.

206. The clergy of any denomination, or their authorized rep-

[1] From Crafts, *op. cit.*, p. 110.

resentatives, shall have the right to give religious instruction to the pupils of their own church in each schoolhouse at least once a week, after the hour of closing the school in the afternoon; and if the clergy of more than one denomination apply to give religious instruction in the same schoolhouse, the board of trustees shall decide on what day of the week the schoolhouse shall be at the disposal of the clergymen of each denomination, at the time above stated. But it shall be lawful for the board of trustees and clergymen of any denomination to agree upon any hour of the day at which a clergyman, or his authorized representative, may give religious instruction to the pupils of his own church, provided it be not during the regular hours of the school.

NOTE.—By Regulation 8 the school hours shall be from nine o'clock in the forenoon till four o'clock in the afternoon; but the trustees, by resolution, may, for the purpose of affording facilities for religious instruction, or for any other proper purpose, prescribe a shorter period.

(b) Saskatchewan[1]

Laws of 1909, amended 1913, sent by Superintendent of Department of Education

136. No religious instruction except as hereinafter provided shall be permitted in the school of any district from the opening of such school until one-half hour previous to its closing in the afternoon, after which time any such instruction permitted or desired by the board may be given.

(2) It shall, however, be permissible for the board of any district to direct that the school be opened by the recitation of the Lord's Prayer. 1901, c. 29, s. 137.

137. Any child shall have the privilege of leaving the schoolroom at the time at which religious instruction is commenced as provided for in the next preceding section or of remaining without taking part in any religious instruction that may be given if the parents or guardians so desire. 1901, c. 29, s. 138.

138. No teacher, school trustee, or inspector shall in any way attempt to deprive such child of any advantage that it might derive from the ordinary education given in such school, and any such action on the part of any school trustee, inspector or teacher shall be held to be a disqualification for and violence of the office held by him. 1901, c. 29, s. 139.

[1]From Crafts, Ibid., p. 113.

134. Ash Wednesday, Good Friday, Easter Monday, Arbor Day (second Friday in May), the birthday of the reigning sovereign, Victoria Day, Dominion Day, Labor Day, Thanksgiving Day, Christmas Day, New Year's Day, and any day specially appointed as a holiday by the Governor General, the Lieutenant Governor of Saskatchewan, the mayor of a city or town or the reeve of a rural municipality shall be holidays; and it shall be at the discretion of the board to permit any other holidays not exceeding one day at a time. 1901, c. 29, s. 135.

SEPARATE SCHOOLS

41. The minority of the ratepayers in any district, whether Protestant or Roman Catholic, may establish a separate school therein; and in such case the ratepayers establishing such Protestant or Roman Catholic separate schools shall be liable only to assessments of such rates as they impose upon themselves in respect thereof. 1901, c. 29, s. 41.

42. The petition for the erection of a separate school district shall be signed by three resident ratepayers of the religious faith indicated in the name of the proposed district; and shall be in the form prescribed by the minister. 1901, c. 29, s. 42.

43. The persons qualified to vote for or against the erection of a separate school district shall be the ratepayers in the district of the same religious faith, Protestant or Roman Catholic, as the petitioners. 1901, c. 29, s. 43.

44a. In case any such district contains within its limits a town or city municipality it shall from the date of its erection be deemed to be a town district, and the board of trustees elected at the first school meeting shall consist of five members, two of whom shall hold office till the date of the first annual election of the district, and three until the date of the second annual election; thereafter all trustees shall be elected and hold office in the manner provided by this Act for town districts. 1912, c. 32, s. 4.

45. After the establishment of a separate school district under the provisions of this Act such separate school district and the board thereof shall possess and exercise all rights, powers, privileges and be subject to the same liabilities and method of government as is herein provided in respect of public school districts.

(2) Any person who is legally assessed or assessable for a public school shall not be liable to assessment for any separate

school established therein; Provided that in the case of any separate school district having heretofore been or hereafter being established within which a separate school is maintained in operation the ratepayers of the religious faith of the minority supporting it shall hereafter be assessable for separate school purposes only, and the ratepayers of the religious faith of the majority constituting the public school district within which such separate school district is established shall be assessable for public school purposes only. 1901, c. 29, s. 45; 1912-13, c. 35, s. 3.

CHAPTER II

OUTLINE OF CURRICULA PROPOSED IN CONNECTION WITH RECENT EXPERIMENTS IN THE UNITED STATES

OFFICIAL SYLLABUS[1] OF BIBLE STUDY FOR HIGH SCHOOL STUDENTS

1. THE NORTH DAKOTA PLAN

Selected and adopted by the High School Board of
North Dakota, August, 1912

INTRODUCTION

A KNOWLEDGE of the Bible is an essential element in a good education. Whether or not one is interested in the Bible as a manual of devotion, it is imperative that he should be familiar with it as a literature and as a history; for no literature and no history have more vitally affected Anglo-Saxon civilization. English literature has been greatly influenced by biblical style and is strewn with allusions to Bible stories and teachings. Shakespeare is said to have over seven hundred such allusions; Tennyson, over four hundred. As Charles Dudley Warner put it: "The Bible is the one book that no intelligent person can afford to be ignorant of. All modern literature and all art are permeated with it. It is not all a question of religion or theology or dogma; it is a question of general intelligence. A boy or girl at college in the presence of the works set for either to master, without a fair knowledge of the Bible is an ignoramus, and is disadvantaged accordingly."

And yet actual experience proves that the average young person has a very imperfect knowledge of this wonderful book. This syllabus has been prepared with the hope that the boys and girls of North Dakota of high school age may be led to a serious study of this great literature. With a Bible containing maps, the dili-

---

[1] Copies may be obtained from the North Dakota Sunday School Association Fargo, North Dakota.

gent student will be adequately equipped, although other helps, if available, may, of course, be used to advantage. The essential thing is to study the Bible itself, to glean its history and the life stories of its great characters, to note the simple beauty of its style, and to grasp its ideas and ideals.

To every high school student who duly passes an examination based on this syllabus, a half-credit will be given on his high school course.

I. Studies in Old Testament Geography

1. Palestine

Palestine is a strip of country at the eastern end of the Mediterranean Sea. It extends east from the sea to the Arabian Desert (on an average about fifty miles), and north from the southeastern corner of the Mediterranean to the river Leontes and Mount Hermon (less than one hundred and fifty miles). If one were to draw a line west from Grand Forks to Petersburg and thence south to the State line, the southeast corner of North Dakota so cut off would approximate the size of Palestine.

Physically, Palestine is divided into four regions or strips running north and south.

1. The first is a plain along the coast from five to twenty-five miles in width and of great fertility. Here were the chief cities of the Philistines and the famous Plain of Sharon.

2. The second is a hilly zone with elevations from three thousand to four thousand feet high in the north but toward the middle flattening out into the Plain of Esraelon, watered by the river Kishon. South of this the surface again breaks into hills and becomes more and more rugged until near Hebron it attains an elevation of over three thousand feet.

3. To the east this hill country slopes rapidly to the deep gorge of the Jordan Valley, the deepest depression on the face of the earth. The Jordan rises on the slopes of Mount Hermon, some distance north of the Sea of Galilee, and descends rapidly until at the Sea of Galilee it is six hundred and eighty-two feet below sea level. It continues to descend through a winding course of nearly two hundred miles (only sixty-five in a straight line) until at the Dead Sea it is twelve hundred and ninety-two feet below sea level. The Jordan Valley varies in width from about four miles in the north to about fourteen in the south. In the north, it is fertile; in the south, alkaline and arid. The Dead

Sea is forty-seven miles long and ten miles wide. South of this lake is the gravelly desert Arabah, gradually rising to a height of six hundred feet above sea level and falling away again toward the Red Sea.

4. To the east of this great cleft of the Jordan and extending to the desert is a pleasant hilly region (Bashan, Gilead, Moab, and Edom) rising to a plateau about two thousand feet in height. This section is well watered and admirably adapted to grazing.

The great variety in the country is conducive to a corresponding diversity in its plants and animals. The authorities mention one hundred and thirteen species of mammals, three hundred and forty-eight of birds, and more than three thousand varieties of flowering plants.

2. The Relation of Palestine to Other Lands

Palestine lay on one of the main routes of travel in the ancient world. To the southwest was Egypt, with its mighty civilization; to the northeast, Mesopotamia, with its powerful empires, across Palestine, between the Nile and the Euphrates swept for many centuries the caravans and armies of the world. There were four main highways corresponding to the four divisions of the country already mentioned. One road followed the coast, leading from Egypt through the Philistine cities (Gaza, Ashdad, etc.) to Phœnicia (Tyre and Sidon) and so on to the north. A second traversed the central range of hills and the Plain of Esraelon, passing through Samaria and Jerusalem and so south to Beersheba where it turned west toward Egypt. On the north it led to Damascus and thence eastward across the desert to Mesopotamia (Assyria, Nineveh, Babylonia, Chaldea, Land of Shinar). A third route followed the Jordan Valley on its eastern side, extending down to Elath on the Red Sea and turning thence to Sinia and beyond. On the north this road also led to Damascus. The fourth highway likewise led from Elath, connecting with caravan routes across the desert to the east and proceeding north through Moab, Ammon and Gilead to the ancient emporium of Damascus. Along these roads and their branches and connections surged the tide of old-world traffic. By the southern routes the Israelites entered the land; by the northern they were, centuries later, led forth into captivity, and in due time returned to reoccupy their ancient home.

NOTE.—Most Bibles nowadays contain maps. The student should carefully study the Old Testament map in connection

175

with the foregoing outline and locate all the places mentioned. He should also locate the chief mountains, as Mount Carmel (near the coast), Mount Tabor, Mount Gilboa, Mount Ebal and Mount Gerizim (near Samaria and Shechem), Mount Pisgah, and Mount Nebo (northeast of Dead Sea), and Mount Sinai or Horeb (to the southwest). He should also locate the important towns and cities, such as Dan or Laish (in the extreme north), Jezreel, Dothan, Samaria, Shiloh, and Bethel (in the central part), and Jericho, Gibeon, Jerusalem, Bethlehem, and Hebron (in the south).

II. The Old Testament Narrative

1. The Creation (Genesis 1).
2. The Garden of Eden (Genesis 2. 8 to 4. 16).
3. The Flood (Genesis 6. 1 to 9. 19).
4. Babel (Genesis 11. 1-9).
5. The Call of Abraham (Genesis 11. 27 to 12. 9).
6. Abraham and Lot (Genesis 13, also 15, also 18. 1 to 19. 28).
7. The Sacrifice of Isaac (Genesis 22).
8. The Marriage of Isaac (Genesis 24).
9. Jacob and Esau (Genesis 27 to 33).
10. Joseph and his Brethren (Genesis 37; also 39 to 47).
11. Early Life of Moses (Exodus 1 and 2).
12. The Call of Moses (Exodus 3 and 4).
13. The Deliverance of Israel (Exodus 5 to 15).
14. Israel in the Wilderness (Exodus 16 and 17).
15. Israel at Sinai (Exodus 19 and 20).
16. The Golden Calf (Exodus 32).
17. The Death of Moses (Deuteronomy 34).
18. The Entrance into Canaan (Joshua 1 to 6).
19. The Great Battle with the Amorites (Joshua 10. 1-15).
20. The Defeat and Death of Sisera (Judges 4 and 5).
21. The Deeds of Gideon (Judges 6 and 7).
22. Jephthah (Judges 11).
23. The Life and Death of Samson (Judges 14 to 16).
24. Ruth, the Faithful Moabitess (Ruth 1 to 4).
25. The Calling of Samuel (1 Samuel 3).
26. The First King of Israel (1 Samuel 8 to 11).
27. The Early Adventures of David (1 Samuel 16 to 18. 9).
28. David and Jonathan (1 Samuel 20).
29. David and Saul (1 Samuel 21 to 24).

CURRICULA IN RECENT EXPERIMENTS

30. The Deaths of Saul and Jonathan (1 Samuel 31 and 2 Samuel 1).
31. David Made King (2 Samuel 5. 1 to 6. 15; also 7 to 9).
32. The Rebellion of Absalom (2 Samuel 14. 25 to 18. 33).
33. Rizpah (2 Samuel 21. 1-14).
34. The Greatness of Solomon (1 Kings 2. 1-12; 3. 1 to 11. 13).
35. The Kingdom Divided (1 Kings 11. 41 to 12. 33; also 14. 21-31).
36. Elijah (1 Kings 16. 29 to 19. 21).
37. Naboth's Vineyard (1 Kings 21; also 22. 29-40; also 2 Kings 9. 30-37).
38. Elijah Translated (2 Kings 2. 1-12).
39. Elijah's Marvelous Achievements (2 Kings 4 to 7).
40. The Wicked Athaliah (2 Kings 11).
41. The Destruction of Sennacherib (2 Kings 18. 13 to 19. 37).
42. The Great Reform under Josiah (2 Kings 22. 1 to 23. 30).
43. The Call of Isaiah (Isaiah 6. 1-8).
44. The Fall of Jerusalem (2 Kings 25. 1-21).
45. Daniel and His Three Friends (Daniel 1 to 2; also 5 and 6).
46. The Return from the Exile in the Time of Cyrus (about B. C. 530—Ezra 1. 1 to 2. 2; 2. 64 to 6. 22).
47. Nehemiah Leads back another Group in Artaxerxes's time (about B. C. 450—Nehemiah 1 to 6).
48. Esther, the Beautiful Queen (Esther 1 to 10).
49. The Test of Job (Job 1 and 2; also 42).
50. Jonah (Jonah 1 to 4).

III. A Brief Outline of Hebrew History Before Christ

The history of the Hebrews as a distinct people begins with their escape from Egypt and their establishment in Palestine, a dozen centuries or more before Christ.

The first great period includes the era of settlement and conquest and extends up to the beginning of the kingdom under Saul (B. C. eleventh century). See Narratives 11-25.

The second great period beginning with the accession of Saul includes the great reigns of David and Solomon, and extends to the division of the kingdom under Rehoboam and Jereboam (B. C. tenth century). See Narratives 26-35.

The third great period includes the reigns of nineteen kings in Israel (northern kingdom) until its overthrow by Sargon, king of Assyria (eighth century) and of twenty kings in Judah (southern kingdom) extending to the fall of Jerusalem and captivity

177

of Judah under Nebuchadnezzar, king of Babylon, in the sixth century. The great characters during this time are Elijah, Elisha, Amos, Hosea, Hezekiah, Isaiah, Micah, Josiah, Jeremiah, Ezekiel. See Narratives 36-44.

The fourth great period includes the captivity of Judah (sixth century), the return and rebuilding of Jerusalem, and the subsequent control of Palestine by the Persians, the Greeks, and the Romans, including the brilliant century of independence under the Maccabees from about the middle of the second century until after the middle of the first century B. C. See Narratives 45-48.

The student would do well to consult a Bible dictionary or an ancient history of the chronology and for the relations existing between the Hebrews and the other great nations of antiquity. It is not always possible to be sure of the exact date of a given event, as the various authorities differ; but the student should grasp the historical periods and be able to assign each great event to its proper century. Any recognized system of chronology will be accepted. Various excellent Hebrew histories are easily obtainable.

IV. The Books of the Old Testament

The thirty-nine books are divided in five groups, as follows:

1. The Pentateuch: Genesis, Exodus, Leviticus, Numbers, Deuteronomy (5 books).
2. The Historical Books: Joshua, Judges, Ruth, First and Second Samuel, First and Second Kings, First and Second Chronicles, Ezra, Nehemiah, Esther (12 books).
3. The Poetical Books: Job, Psalms, Proverbs, Ecclesiastes, The Song of Solomon (5 books).
4. The Major Prophets: Isaiah, Jeremiah, Lamentations, Ezekiel, Daniel (5 books).
5. The Minor Prophets: Hosea, Joel, Amos, Obadiah, Jonah, Micah, Nahum, Habakkuk, Zephaniah, Haggai, Zechariah, Malachi (12 books).

V. Memory Passages from the Old Testament

NOTE.—Learn any five of the following passages. Each of the passages selected should be carefully committed to memory so as to become an abiding possession:

1. The Ten Commandments, Exodus, 20. 3-17.
2. From a speech of Moses, a specimen of Hebrew oratory, Deuteronomy 6. 4-15.

3. The First Psalm.
4. The Twenty-third Psalm.
5. The Forty-sixth Psalm.
6. The One Hundred and Third Psalm.
7. Job, 28. 12-28.
8. Proverbs, Chapter 3. 1-26.
9. Isaiah, 40. 18-31.
10. Isaiah, 55.

VI. Studies in the Life of Christ

A. *Political Divisions in Christ's Time*

The general landscape features in New Testament times are, of course, the same as those already outlined. (See I, above.) But the political divisions were entirely different. These were as follows:

(*a*) To the west of the Jordan:

1. Judæa, corresponding, in the main, to the old kingdom of Judah and including such places as Jerusalem, Jericho, Bethlehem, Bethany, Ephraim, Lydda, and Joppa.

2. Samaria, occupying the central part of the region around the ancient city of Samaria, extending north to the river Kishon, and numbering among its cities Sychar and Cæsarea. Judæa and Samaria were under the proconsul Pontius Pilate.

3. Galilee, lying to the west of the lake of the same name and extending north to Phœnicia (Tyre and Sidon). Among its points of interest were Nazareth, Capernaum, Cana, Chorazin.

(*b*) To the east of the Jordan:

1. Peræa, extending from the river Arnon north somewhat beyond the river Jabbok. This region and Galilee were united under the rule of Herod Antipas, son of Herod the Great.

2. Decapolis, east of Galilee and stretching off to the southeast, a region of flourishing Greek cities.

3. The Tetrarchy of Philip, extending from opposite the Sea of Galilee north to Mount Hermon (the probable scene of the Transfiguration). Among its cities were Bethsaida and Cæsarea Philippi. Its ruler in Christ's time was Philip, another son of Herod the Great.

NOTE.—All these divisions and points of interest should be carefully located on the map.

B. *The Life of Christ*

The four evangelists differ somewhat in their accounts of the

179

RELIGIOUS EDUCATION AND DEMOCRACY

life of Christ. For this there are two causes: (1) John purposely omits mentioning various facts recorded by the earlier writers, intending in his Gospel to give additional information rather than to repeat familiar matter. (Because of their general agreement the first three Gospels are called the "synoptic Gospels"). (2) The synoptic Gospels do not always agree in the order of events; Matthew seems to prefer to treat his matter topically. For example, when recording parables he groups several together, apparently disregarding the exact chronology. See Matthew 13.

It is, therefore, somewhat difficult to determine the exact order of the events in Christ's life. In the outline given below we shall follow, in the main, the order found in Luke; here and there facts not recorded by him are inserted:

OUTLINE

First Period: Childhood and Youth, up to and including the Temptation. Luke 1 to 4. 13. Read also Matthew 2 to 4. Locate places mentioned.

Second Period: The Beginnings of Christ's Active Ministry, or The Year of Obscurity. Read John 2-14.

During this period, after his first miracle in Cana in Galilee, Jesus appears to have worked mainly in Judæa. The event marking the close of this period seems to have been the imprisonment of John the Baptist. See Matthew 4. 12, 13; also Mark 1. 14; also Mark 6. 14-29.

Third Period: The Period of Growing Popularity. Read Luke 4. 14 to 9. 50.

During this period, which probably lasted considerably over a year, Jesus worked mainly in the neighborhood of the Sea of Galilee. Among the chief events to be remembered, in addition to the various miracles and parables, are the following: (1) The choosing of the twelve disciples, in connection with which doubtless occurred the Sermon on the Mount (briefly recorded by Luke in chapter 6. 20-49, and more fully in Matthew 5 to 7, which should be read). (2) Two journeys north for rest and privacy. The first—into Phœnicia—is not mentioned by Luke, but is described in Matthew 15. 21-31; the second is described in Matthew 16. 13-21. Here in Peter's confession was made a definite announcement of Jesus's Messiahship, after which he talked to his disciples of his approaching death. (3) The transfiguration, probably on Mount Hermon.

Fourth Period: The Final Year of Ministry, or Period of Constantly Growing Opposition. Read Luke 9. 51 to 19. 10.

During this period, lasting doubtless for something less than a year, Jesus withdrew from Galilee, but not being welcomed in Samaria journeyed south by a route east of the Jordan (see Mark 10. 1), reaching Jericho shortly before the time of the passover. In this period should also be placed the visit to Bethany and the raising of Lazarus as recorded in John 11. 1-40, and the subsequent sojourn in Ephraim (John 11. 47-54).

Fifth Period: The Passion Week and the Forty Days. Read Luke 19. 11 to 24. 53; also Acts 1. 1-14.

After this triumphal entry into Jerusalem on Sunday, Jesus evidently made his headquarters at Bethany, going each day to Jerusalem to teach in the temple (Luke 21. 37). The bitterness of the hierarchy daily increased. On Thursday evening he celebrated the passover and instituted the Lord's Supper, after which occurred his last extended conversation with his disciples. Read John 14 to 17. Then came the scene in Gethsemane, the arrest, and the trials. The crucifixion followed on Friday and the resurrection on Sunday, after which occurred the various manifestations and the ascension.

VII. Studies in History of the Early Church

Note that the influence of Christianity soon extended beyond Palestine. Study in connection with the following outline a map of the eastern Mediterranean, showing the various voyages of Paul. In the matter of dates there is not absolute agreement among the historians, and so none are given here. The student should, however, adopt some reasonable chronology and follow it consistently.

1. The Progress of the Church at Jerusalem.

Read Acts 1 to 7.

Get clearly in mind the chief events: The manifestation of power on the day of Pentecost; Peter's great sermon and its effect; the enthusiasm and devotion of the church; the incident of Ananias and Sapphira; the beginnings of persecutions; the appointment of the seven deacons and the death of the first martyr, Stephen.

2. The First Missionary Work of the Church. Read Acts 8 to 12.

Note that this work was due largely to scattering of the early Christians by persecution.

Note the work of Philip, the first foreign missionary; the conversion of Saul and his work in Arabia and Damascus (read Galatians 1. 17, 18); also the work of Peter, and his vision at Joppa; the admission to fellowship of Cornelius, the Roman, and the widening vision of the church; the spread of the gospel to Antioch, the chief city of Asia, and the rapid increase of the church in spite of persecution. Locate all places mentioned.

3. The Great Missionary Work of Paul. (1) Paul's First Missionary Journey. Read Acts 13 and 14.

Follow the route of Paul and Barnabas from Antioch across Cyprus and so on to the mainland through Antioch in Pisidia, Iconium, Lystra, and Derbe, and back again by the same route to Attalia, whence they sailed to Antioch. Note carefully their experience in each city and the evidences of their success.

(2) The Great Council at Jerusalem. Read Acts 15. 1-35.

This is very important, as at this time the mother church gave official sanction to the work among the Gentiles, an essential step toward making Christianity a world religion.

(3) The Second Missionary Journey. Read Acts 15. 36 to 18. 22.

Again follow the route of Paul and Silas as they proceeded overland from Antioch by the great Roman road through Tarsus, Paul's early home, and so on across the mountains to the Galatian cities visited on the first journey. Note that instead of going north into Bithynia, as apparently they had planned, they followed the caravan road to Troas, where Paul had the great vision which took him into Europe. Follow his route through Macedonia. Note that his general method of work in each city was to approach the Jews first and then to turn to the natives. Note his varied experiences, especially at Athens and at Corinth, where he remained a year and a half. Recall the friends he made during this trip and follow his return to Antioch via Ephesus and Cæsarea.

(4) The Third Missionary Journey. Read Acts 18. 23 to 21. 16.

Note that as the second journey Paul starts out by visiting Tarsus, Derbe, Iconium, etc., and then follows the great caravan road direct to Ephesus, the chief commercial city on the Ægean, where the gospel had already been preached, somewhat imperfectly, by Apollos. Follow his route, which doubtless took him to the scenes of his former work at Philippi and Thessalonica and thence south to Corinth, where he stayed three months. Observe that on his return he again visited his dear friends at Philippi (note his affection for this church as expressed in

Philippians 1. 1-5; and 4. 1), and spent a week at Troas, thence skirting the coast to Miletus, where he bade good-by to his Ephesian friends. Follow his entire route on the map to his landing places at Tyre and Cæsarea, whence he went to Jerusalem.

(5) Paul's Arrest in Jerusalem and Appeal to Cæsar. Read Acts 21. 17 to 28.

Note the circumstances of Paul's arrest, his address on the temple stairs, his address before the council, the plot against his life, his night ride to Cæsarea, his trial before Felix, his two years in prison, his trial before Festus, and appeal to Cæsar and his great address before Agrippa. Follow on the map the route of the ship as it sailed along the southern coast of Asia Minor as far as Fair Havens in Crete; then the general course of the tempest-tossed vessel to Melita; and finally the course of the Castor and Pollux to Puteoli and the overland journey by the famous Appian Way to Rome. Note Paul's manner of life in Rome as for two years he waited for his trial.

The details of Paul's subsequent career are uncertain. It would seem that he was released on the first charge, and later engaged once more in missionary work only to be again arrested. The most definite information is found in 2 Timothy 4. 7-22, a passage evidently written shortly before his death, which is usually dated about A. D. 68. Jerusalem was destroyed by Titus in A. D. 70.

VIII. The Books of the New Testament

The twenty-seven books are divided into five divisions, as follows:

1. Biographical (or Gospels): Matthew, Mark, Luke, John (4 books).
2. Historical: The Acts (1 book).
3. Epistles to special churches or persons: Romans, First and Second Corinthians, Galatians, Ephesians, Philippians, Colossians, First and Second Thessalonians, First and Second Timothy, Titus, Philemon, Hebrews (14 books).
4. General Epistles: James, First and Second Peter, First, Second, and Third John, Jude (7 books).
5. Prophetic, or Apocalyptic: Revelation (1 book).

IX. Memory Passages from the New Testament

NOTE. Learn any five of the following passages, as in the case of the Old Testament passages, being careful to commit them accurately:

RELIGIOUS EDUCATION AND DEMOCRACY

1. The First Christmas, Luke 2. 8-19.
2. The Beatitudes, Matthew, 5. 3-11.
3. The Lord's Prayer, Matthew 7. 9-13.
4. From Jesus's Last Talk, John 15. 1-14.
5. Paul's Address on Mars Hill, Acts 17. 2-31.
6. Rules for Life, Romans 12. 9-21.
7. Paul's Account of Love, 1 Corinthians 13.
8. Faith, Hebrew 11. 1-6, and 32-40.
9. Works, James 2. 14-26.
10. The New Jerusalem, Revelation 22. 1-14.

2. THE COLORADO PLAN

SYLLABUS OF BIBLE STUDY[1] FOR THE HIGH SCHOOLS OF THE STATE OF COLORADO

A four-year course of study is in process of preparation to meet the needs of churches in which Bible instruction is given for the purpose of credit in the public high schools. The Joint Committee of the State Teachers' Association and the State Sunday School Association has recommended for the first year a course entitled "Heroes and Leaders of Israel." The course and its syllabus of lessons has been approved by the State Council of Religious Education of the State Sunday School Association, an organization composed entirely of public school and college men. The first year's course will be followed rapidly by courses for other years of the high school, together with optional courses to meet as occasion demands the varied needs of different faiths.

First Year—Heroes and Leaders of Israel
AIM OF THIS COURSE

The aim of this course is to suggest, develop, and establish in young people high moral and religious ideals. Students of child life are agreed that biographical material is especially well suited to accomplish this aim in the early high school period. The course should deepen the sense of duty and responsibility for right individual conduct and develop habits and attitudes of practical service.

SUGGESTIONS AS TO METHOD OF TEACHING

While the central aim of the course is to present vividly ideals of life through the study of concrete examples of right living, with all that they can furnish of inspiration and to illustrate in the concrete the consequences of evil as it works out in the lives of actual men and women, nevertheless the current of history and the background of geographical fact are not to be ignored. The details of history and geography are necessary to an understanding of conditions that affect the lives of individuals and to give the tang of reality to the biographical facts. These are not

[1] Copies may be obtained from the Colorado State Sunday School Association, 312 17th Street, Denver, Colorado.

the main things to be emphasized in the course, but the good teacher will try to carry on historical and geographical lines of work continuously in intimate correlation with the more fundamental studies of human nature.

The aim of this course will not be most fully realized by homiletical treatment of the subject matter nor by the study of critical questions; but, rather, by the vivid presentation of the lives of the men and women discussed, the reconstruction of the situations which confronted them in as concrete terms as possible, and the bringing home to the pupil the truth or particular lesson to be learned through the inevitable connection which he sees and feels for himself between conditions and consequences in the life and conduct of individuals. Make the students of these lessons feel that they are dealing with real men and real women struggling with real problems and that the ideals and attitudes that dominated their lives had something very definite to do with their successes and their failures. Do not be afraid to use extrabiblical material for purposes of comparison and emphasis of the reality of the principles of conduct involved.

Lesson Materials

The topics selected for the course are adapted from the First Year Intermediate Course of the International Graded Sunday School Lessons. Consequently the publications of the various denominational publishing houses, in so far as they have prepared lesson helps for the graded lesson series, will be available for this course. It is not the intention of the committee to recommend these lesson helps, but to leave the field wide open for the selection of any kind of lesson materials that will best realize the aim of the course and cover the ground indicated in the outline. The following books will be found useful in dealing with the biographical material:

Chamberlain, Georgia—Hebrew Prophets; or Patriots and Leaders of Israel.

Gates—Heroes of the Faith.

Kent—Heroes and Crises of Early Hebrew History.

Robinson, George L.—Leaders of Israel.

Soares, T. G.—Heroes of Israel.

Rutland, J. R.—Old Testament Stories.

Wells, Amos R.—The Bible in Miniature: Character Sketches of One Hundred and Fifty Heroes and Heroines of Holy Writ.

Willman, Leon K.—Men of the Old Testament.

CURRICULA IN RECENT EXPERIMENTS

SUPPLEMENTARY REFERENCE MATERIAL

Smith, George Adam—Historical Geography of the Holy Land.
Calkins—Historical Geography of Palestine.
Stewart—Land of Israel.
Leary—The Real Palestine of To-day.
Vincent and Hurlbut—Bible Geography and Atlas.
Kent and Madsen, or Eiler—Map of the Ancient World.
Schaff-Herzog Encyclopedia.
Hastings—Bible Dictionary.

FIRST YEAR'S COURSE IN DETAIL

1. The Land Where Hebrew History Began.
  Biblical Material: Genesis 2. 10-15; 10. 10-11; 11. 1-9, 31, 32.
  (A preliminary geographical and historical study of the
  Tigris and Euphrates regions.)

2. Abraham the Pioneer.
  Biblical Material: Genesis 11. 31, 32; 12. 1-10; 13. 1-4, 18.

3. Abraham the Man With a New Vision of God.
  Biblical Material: Genesis 13. 14-17; 15. 1-6; Hebrews 11. 8-19.
  (To show how Abraham was faithful to his vision.)

4. Jacob a Winner With God.
  Biblical Material: Genesis 25. 19-34; 28. 10-22; 32. 24-32;
  35. 9-20. (Note: In connection with a study of Joseph
  attention should constantly be paid to the land of the Nile.
  Biblical Material for this historical and geographical background: Genesis 41. 54-57; 42. 1-3; 45. 10-13; 47. 29-31; Exodus 1. 1-14; Isaiah, chapter 19.)

5. Joseph the Boy Who Was True to His Trust.
  Biblical Material: Genesis 37. 2-4, 12-27; 39. 1-6, 20-23; 41.
  33-45.

6. Joseph the Man Who Overcame Evil With Good.
  Biblical Material: Genesis 42. 1-6, 13-17; 44. 18-34; 45. 1-15.

7. Moses the Prince Who Chose Exile.
  Biblical Material: Exodus 2. 11-22; Acts 7. 17-29; Hebrews
  11. 24-27.

8. Moses Emancipator and Lawgiver.
  Biblical Material: Exodus 2. 23-25; 3. 1-22; Acts 7. 30-36;
  Exodus 12. 21-23, 29-36; Psalm 105. 23-45.

9. Joshua Scout and Conqueror.
  Biblical Material: Exodus 17. 8-16; Numbers 13. 1-3, 17-33;
  14. 5-10; Joshua 1. 1-9; 3. 5-17; 6. 1-20; 24. 1, 2, 14, 15, 29-31;
  Acts 7. 45; Hebrews 11. 30.

10. *Gideon the Man Whom Responsibility Made Great.*
    Biblical Material: Judges 6. 1-8, 22.
11. *Ruth the True Hearted.*
    Biblical Material: The Book of Ruth.
12. *Samuel Trained for Service.*
    Biblical Material: 1 Samuel, chapters 1 to 12.
13. *Saul the Leader Who Lost His Chance.*
    Biblical Material: 1 Samuel, chapter 11; 14. 47 to 15. 35;
    chapter 31.
14. *David the Kingly Youth.*
    Biblical Material: 1 Samuel, chapters 16 to 20.
15. *David the Youthful King.*
    Biblical Material: 1 Samuel, chapter 21; 2 Samuel, chapters
    1 to 4.
16. *David Israel's Greatest King.*
    Biblical Material: 2 Samuel, chapter 5; Kings 2. 11.
17. *Solomon Famed for Wisdom, Wealth and Peace.*
    Biblical Material: 1 Kings, chapters 2, 3, 4, 5, 6, 9.
18. *Rehoboam a Youth Who Despised Good Counsel.*
    Biblical Material: 1 Kings, chapter 12.
19. *First Semester Review.*
20. *Jeroboam a Champion Who Forsook the Lord.*
    Biblical Material: 1 Kings 11. 26-40; 12. 1-33; 13. 33, 34.
21. *Elijah the Champion of Jehovah.*
    Biblical Material: 1 Kings, chapters 17 and 18.
22. *Elijah Learning a Better Way.*
    Biblical Material: 1 Kings, chapters 19 and 21. 17-29.
23. *Elisha the Plowman Prophet.*
    Biblical Material: 2 Kings 2. 1-13; 4. 8-37; 5. 1-15; 13. 14-20.
24. *Jehu the Vengeful King.*
    Biblical Material: 2 Kings, chapters 9 and 10.
25. *Jonadab a Man Who Dared to Stand Alone.*
    Biblical Material: 1 Chronicles 2. 55; 2 Kings 10. 15-28;
    Jeremiah 35.
26. *Amos the Herdsman Preacher.*
    Biblical Material: Amos 1. 1; 7. 10-17; 6. 1-11.
27. *Hezekiah and Josiah Religious Reformers.*
    Biblical Material: 2 Kings, chapters 18 and 20, 22 and 25 and
    35; Isaiah, chapters 36 and 39.
28. *Isaiah Prophet and Statesman.*
    Biblical Material: Isaiah 1. 1-20; chapter 6; 7. 1-9; 8. 21;
    9. 7; 39.

CURRICULA IN RECENT EXPERIMENTS

29. *Jeremiah the Man Who Suffered to Save His City.*
Biblical Material: Jeremiah 1. 1-19; 39. 1-18; 40. 1-6; 42. 1-22; 43. 1-7; 45. 1-5; 47.
30. *Daniel and Ezekiel, Heroic Hebrew Captives.*
Biblical Material: Daniel, chapters 1 and 4; Ezekiel, chapters 1 and 2; 3. 4-27; 6. 8-10; 14. 1-5, 21-23; chapter 27.
31. *Cyrus the Liberator of the Jews.*
Biblical Material: Isaiah 44. 28; 45. 1-4; 13; Ezra 1. 1-8; 3. 1-7.
32. *Haggai the Inspirer of Discouraged Builders.*
Biblical Material: Ezra 3. 6-13; 4. 1-5, 11-24; 5. 1; Haggai 1. 1-8; 2. 1-4; Zechariah 4. 1-10; Ezra 5. 2-5.
33. *Nehemiah and Ezra the Founders of Judaism.*
Biblical Material: Nehemiah, chapters 1, 2, 4, 6, 9, 13.
34. *Judas the Jewish Conqueror.*
Material: The First Book of Maccabees.
35. *John the Last Prophet of the Old Dispensation.*
Biblical Material: Matthew 3; Mark 1. 1-12; Luke 3. 1-22; John 1. 6-8; Matthew 11. 2-14.
36. *Second Semester Review and Final Examinations.*

The Founder and Disciples of the Christian Religion
SECOND YEAR'S COURSE IN DETAIL
First Semester—The Friends and Followers of Jesus.
Second Semester—The Life and Labors of Jesus.

FIRST SEMESTER OUTLINE

1. *The Roman Empire and Christianity.*
A geographical and historical lesson to furnish a background for the semester's study.
Biblical Material: Acts 2. 5-12.
Reference Material: The Roman Empire in the Time of Christ.
2. *Mary the Mother of Jesus.*
(a) Chosen to be the Mother of Christ. Luke 1. 26-38.
(b) Praising God for this High Honor. Luke 1. 46-55.
(c) Fleeing to Save Her Child's Life. Matthew 2. 1-18.
(d) Training the Boy Jesus. Matthew 2. 19-23; Luke 2. 39-52.
(e) Calling Upon Her Son to Help a Friend. John 2. 1-11.
(f) At the Foot of the Cross. John 19. 25-27.
(g) A Believer in Jesus. Acts 1. 14.
3. *Peter the Disciple and Apostle.*
(a) Education. John 1. 40-42; Luke 5. 1-11; Mark 1. 29-39;

189

3. 13-19; Mark 5. 22-24, 35-43; 6. 7-13; 8. 27-34; 9. 2-9; John 13. 6-10.

(b) Temptation and Testing. Mark 14. 26-42, 54, 66-72.

(c) Restoration and Commission. Mark 16. 7; Luke 24. 34; 1 Corinthians 15. 5; John 21. 7-22.

(d) Leader. Acts 1. 12-22; chapters 2-5.

(c) Fellow Worker. Acts 8. 14-24; 9. 32-43; chapter 10; 11. 1-18; 12. 1-19; Acts 15. 6-11; Galatians 2. 11-16; 1 Corinthians 1. 12; 3. 22; 9. 5; 1 Peter.

(f) Pastor and Martyr—Early Traditions.

4. *James One of the Favored Three.*

(a) Called by the Master. Matthew 4. 21; Mark 1. 19; Luke 5. 10.

(b) Ordained One of the Twelve. Matthew 10. 2; Mark 3. 14; Luke 6. 13.

(c) Present at the Transfiguration. Matthew 17. 1; Mark 9. 2; Luke 9. 28.

(d) Present at the Passion. Matthew 26. 36; Mark 14. 33.

(c) Slain by Herod. Acts 12. 2.

5. *John the Beloved Disciple.*

(a) A Beginner in Service. John 1. 35-39; Mark 1. 19-20.

(b) Chosen and Surnamed. Mark 3. 17.

(c) Jesus's Love for John. John 13. 23-26.

(d) The Loving Trust. John 19. 25-27.

(e) John at the Tomb. John 20. 2-10.

(f) By the Sea. John 21.

(g) Why John Wrote. John 19. 35; 21. 24; 1 John 1. 1-4; Revelation, chapter 1.

(h) John's Work in Asia. Revelation, chapters 2 and 3.

6. *Andrew the Soul Winner.*

(a) Wins Peter. John 1. 40-42.

(b) Wins a Boy. John 6. 8, 9.

(c) Wins Greeks. John 12. 20-22.

7. *Nicodemus a Seeker After Truth.*

(a) A Timid but Earnest Seeker. John 3. 1-15.

(b) Coming into the Light. John 7. 45-52.

(c) A Firm Believer, Not Ashamed of His Faith. John 19. 38-42.

8. *Thomas the Doubter, Who Became a Firm Believer.*

(a) Called to be an Apostle. Luke 6. 12-16.

(b) Refuses to Forsake Jesus in an Hour of Danger. John 11. 7-16.

(c) Seeking Light. John 14. 1-7.

(d) Overwhelmed by Doubt. John 20. 24, 25.

(e) The First to Acknowledge the Deity of Jesus. John 20. 26-28.

9. *Mary and Martha, a Contrast in Service.*

   (a) The Two Sisters. Luke 10. 38-42.

   (b) The Raising of Lazarus. John 11.

   (c) The Feast and the Anointing. John 12. 1-11.

10. *Mary Magdalene a Loyal Helper of Jesus.*

   (a) Ministering to Jesus. Luke 8. 1-3.

   (b) Standing by the Cross. John 19. 25.

   (c) A Witness of the Death and the Interment. Mark 15. 40-47; Luke 23. 55, 56.

   (d) The First to See the Risen Lord. John 20. 1-18; Mark 16. 9.

11. *Stephen, Preacher and Martyr.*

   (a) Chosen Deacon. Acts 6. 1-6.

   (b) Interpreter of Christ. Acts 6. 8-10; 7. 44-53.

   (c) The First Christian Martyr. Acts 7. 54 to 8. 1.

12. *Philip the Evangelist.*

   (a) A Colleague of Stephen. Acts 6. 1-6.

   (b) A Pioneer Evangelist. Acts, chapter 8.

   (c) The Host of Paul and Luke. Acts 21. 7, 8.

13. *Barnabas the Large-hearted.*

   (a) Consecrating His Money. Acts 4. 36, 37.

   (b) Befriending Paul. Acts 9. 26, 27.

   (c) Taking Charge of the Work in Antioch. Acts 11. 19-23.

   (d) Companion of Paul. Acts 11. 25-27; 12. 25; chapters 13 to 15.

   (e) The Secret of His Goodness. Acts 11. 24.

14. *Saul the Pharisee and Persecutor.*

   (a) Student; (b) Pharisee; (c) The Enemy of the Christians. Acts 22. 3, 28; 23. 6; 26. 4; Galatians 1. 14; Philippians, 3. 3-6; Acts 7. 54 to 8. 3; 26. 9-11.

15. *Paul the Disciple and Preacher.*

   (a) A Convert and His Zeal. Acts 9. 1-30; 26. 12-23.

   (b) A Missionary Evangelist. Acts 11. 27-30; 12. 25; chapters 13 to 26.

   (c) A Life Victorious. Romans 8; 1 Corinthians 9; 2 Corinthians 11. 16 to 12. 10; 2 Timothy 4.

16. *Luke the Early Historian.*

   (a) Paul's Call to Macedonia. Acts 16. 9-18.

(*b*) Paul's Travels and Counsels. Acts 20. 5 to 21. 19.
(*c*) Paul on His Way to Rome. Acts, chapters 27, 28.
(*d*) Luke the Beloved Physician. Colossians 4. 14.
(*e*) The Companion of Paul. 2 Timothy 4. 11.
(*f*) A Fellow-Laborer. Philemon 24.
(*g*) A Faithful Narrator. Luke 1. 1-4; Acts 1. 1, 2.
17. *Timothy, Paul's Son in the Faith.*
(*a*) A Chosen Companion of Paul. Acts 16. 1-5.
(*b*) "Faithful in the Lord." 1 Corinthians 4. 17.
(*c*) His Work Commended. 1 Corinthians 16. 10, 11.
(*d*) A Messenger with Good Tidings. 1 Thessalonians 1. 1; 3. 2-8.
(*e*) Paul's Letters to Timothy.
18. *Semester Review.*

SECOND SEMESTER OUTLINE

The Life and Labors of Jesus

PART I.

The Thirty Years of Private Life

1. *The Sources of Our Knowledge of Life of Jesus: The Origin and Purpose of the Four Gospels.*
(*a*) Prologue of John's Gospel. John 1. 1-18.
(*b*) Preface of Luke's Gospel. Luke 1. 1-4.
(*c*) The Gospels—Meaning of the Name. Matthew 4. 23: Luke 4. 18.
When, why, and by whom written?
Authorship, purpose, and differences of the four Gospels.
(*d*) Other Sources for the Life of Christ. 1. Jewish History. 2. The Christian Church. 3. The Land of Palestine.
2. *From the Birth of Jesus to the Coming of John the Baptist.*
(*a*) The Annunciations. Luke 1. 5-56.
(*b*) Birth of John the Baptist, and of Jesus. Matthew 1. 18-25; Luke 1. 57-80; 2. 1-20.
(*c*) The Infancy of Jesus. Matthew 2. 1-23; Luke 2. 21-39.
(*d*) His Life in Nazareth. Luke 2. 39-52.

PART II

The Opening Events of Christ's Ministry

3. *From the Coming of John the Baptist to the Public Appearance of Jesus in Jerusalem.*

192

CURRICULA IN RECENT EXPERIMENTS

(a) The Ministry of John the Baptist. Matthew 3. 1-12; Mark 1. 1-8; Luke 3. 1-20.

(b) The Baptism of Jesus. Matthew 3. 13-17; Mark 1. 9-11; Luke 3. 21-23.

(c) The Temptation. Matthew 4. 1-11; Mark 1. 12, 13; Luke 4. 1-13.

(d) The Beginnings of Faith in Jesus. John 1. 19-51; John 2. 1-12.

PART III

The Early Judæan Ministry

4. *From the Public Appearance in Jerusalem to His Return to Galilee.*

(a) Cleansing the Temple. John 2. 13-22.

(b) Discourse with Nicodemus. John 2. 23 to 3. 21.

(c) Baptizing and Teaching in Judæa and Samaria. John 3. 22-36; 4. 1-42.

PART IV

First Period of the Galilæan Ministry

5. *From the Return to Galilee to the Choosing of the Twelve.*

(a) The Beginning of the Ministry in Galilee. Matthew 4. 12, 17; Mark 1. 14, 15; Luke 4. 14, 15; John 4. 43-45.

(b) The Nobleman's Son. John 4. 46-54.

(c) First Rejection at Nazareth. Luke 4. 16-30.

(d) The Call of the Four. Matthew 4. 18-22; Mark 1. 16-20; Luke 5. 1-11.

(e) First Preaching Tour in Galilee. Mark 1. 35-45; Luke 4. 42-44.

6. *Growing Hostility of the Scribes and Pharisees.*

(a) The Paralytic Borne of Four. Matthew 9. 1-8; Mark 2. 1-12; Luke 5. 17-26.

(b) The Call of Matthew. Matthew 9. 9-13; Mark 2. 13-17; Luke 5. 27-32.

(c) The Question about Fasting. Matthew 9. 14-17; Mark 2. 18-22; Luke 5. 33-39.

(d) The Infirm Man at the Pool of Bethesda. John, chapter 5.

(e) The Disciples Plucking Grain. Matthew 12. 1-8; Mark 2. 23-28; Luke 6. 1-5.

(f) The Man with the Withered Hand. Matthew 12. 9-14; Mark 3. 1-6; Luke 6. 6-11.

RELIGIOUS EDUCATION AND DEMOCRACY

Part V.

Second Period of the Galilæan Ministry
From the Choosing of the Twelve to the Withdrawal into
Northern Galilee

7. *The Choosing of the Twelve, and the Sermon on the Mount.*
   (a) The Widespread Fame of Christ. Matthew 4. 23-25;
   12. 15-21; Mark 3. 7-12.
   (b) The Choosing of the Twelve. Matthew 10. 2-4; Mark
   3. 13-19; Luke 6. 12-19.
   (c) The Sermon on the Mount. Matthew, chapters 5, 6, 7,
   and 8. 1; Luke 6. 20-49.
8. *Further Conflict with the Scribes, and Lessons Concerning
   the Kingdom.*
   (a) Warnings to the Scribes and Pharisees. Matthew 12.
   22-45; Mark 3. 20-30; Luke 6. 43-45.
   (b) The True Kindred of Christ. Matthew 12. 46-50; Mark
   3. 31-35; Luke 8. 19-21.
   (c) The Parables by the Sea. Matthew 13. 1-53; Mark 4. 1-34;
   Luke 8. 4-18.
9. *Miracles and Ministry in Galilee.*
   (a) The Stilling of the Tempest. Matthew 8. 23-27; Mark
   4. 35-41; Luke 8. 22-25.
   (b) The Gadarene Demoniacs. Matthew 8. 28-34; Mark 5.
   1-20; Luke 8. 26-39.
   (c) The Raising of Jairus's Daughter. Matthew 9. 18-26;
   Mark 5. 21-43; Luke 8. 40-56.
   (d) Second Rejection at Nazareth. Matthew 13. 54-58; Mark
   6. 1-6; Luke 4. 16-30.
   (e) The Mission of the Twelve. Matthew 9. 36 to 11. 1; Mark
   6. 7-13; Luke 9. 1-6.
   (f) Death of John the Baptist. Matthew 14. 1-12; Mark 6.
   14-29; Luke 9. 7-9.

Part VI

Third Period of the Galilæan Ministry
From the Withdrawal into Northern Galilee to the Final
Departure for Jerusalem

10. *A Northern Journey, and a Brief Stay by the Sea of Galilee.*
   (a) Journey toward Tyre and Sidon. Matthew 15. 21-28;
   Mark 7. 24-30.

194

CURRICULA IN RECENT EXPERIMENTS

(b) Return through Decapolis; Miracles of Healing. Matthew 15. 29-31; Mark 7. 31-37.

(c) The Feeding of the Four Thousand. Matthew 15. 32-38; Mark 8. 1-9.

(d) The Pharisees and Sadducees Demand a Sign. Matthew 15. 39 to 16. 12; Mark 8. 10-21.

(e) The Blind Man near Bethsaida. Mark 8. 22-26.

11. *Journey to Cæsarea Philippi; Peter's Confession, and the Transfiguration.*

(a) Peter's Confession. Matthew 16. 13-20; Mark 8. 27-30; Luke 9. 18-21.

(b) Christ Foretells His Death and Resurrection. Matthew 16. 21-28; Mark 8. 31 to 9. 1; Luke 9. 22-27.

(c) The Transfiguration. Matthew 17. 1-13; Mark 9. 2-13; Luke 9. 28-36.

(d) The Demoniac Boy. Matthew 17. 14-20; Mark 9. 14-29; Luke 9. 37-43.

(e) Christ Again Foretells His Death. Matthew 17. 22, 23; Mark 9. 30-32; Luke 9. 43-45.

PART VII

The Peræan Ministry

From the Final Departure from Galilee to the Final Arrival at Jerusalem

12. *Jesus at Work for Mankind.*

(a) The Final Departure from Galilee. Matthew 19. 1, 2; Mark 10. 1; Luke 9. 51-62.

(b) The Mission of the Seventy. Luke 10. 1-24.

(c) The Good Samaritan. Luke 10. 25-37.

(d) The Visit to Martha and Mary. Luke 10. 38-42.

(e) The Good Shepherd. John 10. 1-21.

13. *An Earnest Teacher and Preacher.*

(a) Discourse on Prayer. Luke 11. 1-13.

(b) Concerning Trust in God, and Coming Judgment. Luke, chapter 12.

(c) Teaching by Ministry and Parable. Luke, chapters 15, 16.

(d) Concerning Forgiveness and Faith. Luke 17. 1-10.

(e) Further Teachings in Peræa. Luke 17. 11 to 18. 14.

14. *Closing Events in the Period of Peræan Ministry*

(a) The Raising of Lazarus, and its Effect on the Jews. John, chapter 11.

195

(b) The Parable of the Pharisee and the Publican. Luke 18. 9-14.

(c) Christ Blessing Little Children. Matthew 19. 13-15; Mark 10. 13-16; Luke 18. 15-17.

(d) The Rich Young Ruler. Matthew 19. 16-20; Mark 10. 17-31; Luke 18. 18-30.

(e) Christ Foretells His Crucifixion. Matthew 20. 17-19; Mark 10. 32-34; Luke 18. 31-34.

PART VIII

The Passion Week

From the Final Arrival in Jerusalem to the Resurrection

15. *The Triumphal Entry, and Conflicts with the Jews.*

(a) The Triumphal Entry. Matthew 21. 1-11; Mark 11. 1-11; Luke 19. 29-44; John 12. 12-19.

(b) Christ's Authority Challenged. Matthew 21. 23-27; Mark 11. 27-33; Luke 20. 1-8.

(c) The Questions by the Jewish Rulers. Matthew 22. 15-40; Mark 12. 13-34; Luke 20. 20-40.

(d) Christ's Unanswerable Question. Matthew 22. 41-46; Mark 12. 35-37; Luke 20. 41-44.

(e) Gentiles seek Jesus, while Jews Reject Him. John 12. 20-50.

(f) Judas Conspires with the Chief Priests. Matthew 26. 1-5, 14-16; Mark 14. 1, 2, 10, 11; Luke 22. 1-6.

16. *Jesus's Last Day with the Disciples.*

(a) The Last Supper. Matthew 26. 17-30; Mark 14. 12-26; Luke 22. 7-30; John 13. 1-30.

(b) The Farewell Discourses. Matthew 26. 31-35; Mark 14. 27-31; Luke 22. 31-38; John 13. 31 to 16. 33.

(c) The Intercessory Prayer. John, chapter 17.

17. *The Arrest and Trial; the Crucifixion and Burial.*

(a) The Agony in Gethsemane. Matthew 26. 36-46; Mark 14. 32-42; Luke 22. 39-46.

(b) The Betrayal and Arrest. Matthew 26. 47-56; Mark 14. 43-52; Luke 22. 47-53; John 18. 1-11.

(c) The Trial by the Jews. Matthew 26. 57 to 27. 10; Mark 14. 53-72; Luke 22. 54-71; John 18. 12-27.

(d) The Trial before Pilate. Matthew 27. 11-31; Mark 15. 1-20; Luke 23. 1-25; John 18. 28 to 19. 16.

(e) The Crucifixion. Matthew 27. 32-56; Mark 15. 21-41; Luke 23. 26-49; John 19. 16-37.

CURRICULA IN RECENT EXPERIMENTS

(*f*) The Burial.   Matthew 27. 57-61; Mark 15. 42-47; Luke 23. 50-56; John 19. 38-42.

(*g*) The Watch at the Sepulcher.   Matthew 27. 62-66.

PART IX

The Forty Days
From the Resurrection to the Ascension

18. *Christ's Resurrection, Special Appearances, Ascension.*
   (*a*) The Resurrection Morning.   Matthew 28. 1-10; Mark 16. 1-11; Luke 23. 56 to 24. 12; John 20. 1-18.
   (*b*) The Report of the Watch.   Matthew 28. 11-15.
   (*c*) The Walk to Emmaus.   Mark 16. 12, 13; Luke 24. 13-35.
   (*d*) The Appearance to the Disciples in Jerusalem, Thomas Being Absent.   Mark 16. 14; Luke 24. 36-43; John 20. 19-25.
   (*e*) Appearance to Thomas with the Other Disciples.   John 20. 26-29.
   (*f*) The Appearance to Seven Disciples by the Sea of Galilee.   John 21. 1-24.
   (*g*) The Appearance to the Eleven on a Mountain in Galilee.   Matthew 26. 16-20; Mark 16. 15-18.
   (*h*) Christ's Final Appearance, and Ascension.   Mark 16. 19, 20; Luke 24. 44-53.
   (*i*) The Conclusion of John's Gospel.   John 20. 30, 31; John 21. 25.

REFERENCE MATERIAL

Any standard life of Jesus adapted to high school students, such as Burgess's Life of Christ.

Biblical History and Literature

THIRD YEAR'S COURSE IN DETAIL
First Semester—Great Epochs and Events in Bible History.
Second Semester—Biblical Literature.

FIRST SEMESTER OUTLINE

1. *The Great Beginnings.   The Mosaic Account.*
   (*a*) The Universe.   Genesis 1. 1-19.
   (*b*) Organic Life.   Genesis 1. 11, 12, 20-25.
   (*c*) The Human Race.   Genesis 1. 26-31.
   (*d*) The Sabbath.   Genesis 2. 1-3.

197

2. *Dispersion of Mankind.*

(*a*) The Story of Noah. Genesis, chapters 6 to 9.

(*b*) The Sons of Noah. Genesis, chapters 10 and 11.

(*c*) The Distribution of the Races of Man. From History or Encyclopedia.

3. *Seeking "The Promised Land."*

(*a*) The Migration of Terah. Genesis 11. 27-32.

(*b*) The Call to Abram. Genesis 12. 1-3.

(*c*) Through Canaan to Egypt. Genesis 12. 4-20.

(*d*) From Egypt to Hebron. Genesis 13. 1-18.

(*e*) Abraham, Isaac, and Jacob. Genesis (selected).

Their relationship, God's covenant with each, and what each contributed to Hebrew history.

4. *Israel in Egypt.*

(*a*) The Story of Joseph. Genesis, from chapters 30, 37, 39 to 41.

(*b*) Seeking a New Home. Genesis, from chapters 41 to 46.

(*c*) Dwelling in Egypt. Genesis 47. 11-31; 50. 22-26.

(*d*) The Israelites Oppressed. Exodus, chapter 1.

(*e*) A Deliverer Called. Exodus, chapters 2 and 3.

5. *From Egypt to Canaan.*

(*a*) The Exodus from Egypt. Exodus 12. 29-42; 14. 5-9, etc.

(*b*) Life in the Wilderness. Exodus 15, 16, 17, etc. (selected).

(*c*) Crossing the Jordan. Joshua, chapters 1 to 4.

(*d*) The Conquest of Canaan. Joshua 5 to 12 (selecting main events).

6. *Israel Under the Judges.*

(*a*) Fifteen Judges—a period of about 350 years. See Bible History.

(*b*) Their Appointment Directed. Judges 2. 16; Deuteronomy 16. 18.

(*c*) Qualifications and Duties. Exodus 18. 21; Leviticus 19. 15, etc.

(*d*) The Last of the Judges. 1 Samuel 8. 3.

7. *Israel Ruled by Kings.*

(*a*) A King Demanded. 1 Samuel 8. 1-18.

(*b*) Saul—Appointment and anointing. 1 Samuel 9 and 10. Disobedience and Rejection. 1 Samuel 15.

(*c*) David Anointed to be King. 1 Samuel 16. 1-13. Becomes King of Judah. 2 Samuel 2. 4.

CURRICULA IN RECENT EXPERIMENTS

King of all Israel. 2 Samuel 5. 3.
Character and Career. Bible History.
(d) Solomon—Succeeds David as King. 1 Kings 2. 10-12.
God's Covenant with Him. 1 Kings, chapter 9.
Buildings, Writing, Character. Bible History.

8. *A Divided Kingdom.*
   (a) The Cause, under Rehoboam. 1 Kings, chapters 12.
   (b) The Revolt, under Jeroboam. 1 Kings, chapters 11 and 12.
   (c) The Two Kingdoms—Israel and Judah. Location, Chief Cities, etc. From Bible History and Encyclopedia.

9. *The Overthrow of Israel.*
   (a) Governed by Nineteen Kings. 1 and 2 Kings, Bible History, Encyclopedia.
   A Good King—Your Own Selection.
   A King Who Did Evil—Your Own Selection.
   (b) The Fall of Samaria. 2 Kings, chapter 17.
   (c) The "Ten Tribes" Captive to Assyria. 2 Kings, chapter 17.

10. *The Conquest of Judah.*
    (a) Ruled by Twenty Kings. 1 and 2 Kings, History, Encyclopedia.
    A Typical Righteous King—your selection.
    A Typical Evil King—your selection.
    (b) Jerusalem Taken. 2 Kings, chapter 25.
    (c) The People Captives to Babylon. Kings, chapter 25.

11. *The Return to Palestine.*
    (a) Permitted by Cyrus. Ezra 1. 1-11.
    (b) Rebuilding the City and Temple. Ezra, chapters 3 to 6.
    (c) Liberty under Judas Maccabæus. Jewish History.
    (d) Brought under Roman Dominion. Bible Encyclopedia.

12. *The Coming of Christ.*
    (a) The Prophecies. Isaiah 7. 1; 11. 1-10; Micah 5. 2.
    (b) The Annunciation. Luke 1. 26-33.
    (c) The Birth: time and place. Luke 2. 1-16.
    (d) The Infancy and Boyhood of Jesus. Luke 2. 21-52.
    (e) The Meaning to the World; the Gospel and Its Influence.

13. *The Divine Life of Service.*
    (a) His Words of Wisdom: The Sermon on the Mount; the Parables; Messages of Forgiveness.
    (b) His Works of Grace: Miracles of healing; blessing the children; loving sympathy.

(c) His Human Fellowship: With his disciples; in the home at Bethany; with the needy.

(d) His Remonstrance Against Evil: Cleansing the Temple; denouncing the scribes and Pharisees.

(e) His Sufferings and Death: A life of self-denial; persecution, and a heroic end.

(f) His Resurrection and Final Words of Promise.

14. *The Commission of the Twelve.*
   (a) Chosen as Apostles. Matthew 10; Mark 3.
   (b) How Selected. Read the several accounts.
   (c) Trained for Service. By the Master himself.
   (d) Sent Forth to Duty. Matthew 10.
   (e) The First Christian Missionaries. The Books of the Acts.

15. *The Day of Pentecost.*
   (a) The Promise of Power. Acts 1. 4, 5.
   (b) The Promise Fulfilled. Acts 2. 1-4.
   (c) The Gift of Tongues. Acts 2. 5-13.
   (d) The Testimony of Peter. Acts 2. 14-36.
   (e) The Power of the Spirit. Acts 2. 37-47.

16. *The Power of Persecution.*
   (a) Stephen a Martyr for Christ. Acts 6. 8-15; 7. 54-60.
   (b) A General Persecution. Acts 8. 1-3.
   (c) The Gospel Spread Abroad. Acts 8. 4-8, 14-16, 25.
   (d) The Persecutor Preaches Christ. Acts 9. 1-20.

17. *The Great Messenger.*
   (a) A Loyal Hebrew. Acts 22. 1-4; 26. 4, 5.
   (b) Converted to Christ. Acts 26. 12-20.
   (c) Consecrated to Service. Acts 22. 10-20.
   (d) Establishes Christian Churches. The Acts of the Apostles.
   (e) Writes Christian Counsel. Paul's Epistles.
   (f) Triumphant in the Faith. 2 Timothy 4. 6-8; Romans 8. 37-39.

18. *Semester Review.*

REFERENCE MATERIAL

Peritz—Old Testament History.
Rall—New Testament History.
Gilbert—Christianity in the Apostolic Age.
Kent—Historical Bible Series.
Kent—Students' Old Testament.
Y. M. C. A.—Life of Paul.

CURRICULA IN RECENT EXPERIMENTS

1. The Bible and Its Makeup.

Lesson.

Old Testament—39 books, Hebrew, Story of the Jews.

New Testament—27 books, Greek, Story of Christianity.

Kinds of Literature: History, Law, Prose Narrative, Romance Stories, Parables, Letters, Pastoral, Lyric, and Epic Poetry, Philosophy, Prophecy, Orations, Sermons, Prayers —Examples of each.

A. PROSE I. HISTORY

2. The Story of Solomon. A Study in Biography.
A. Parentage and Training.
B. Anointed to be King. 1 Kings 1. 32-40.
   (*a*) His Religious Zeal. 1 Kings 3. 2-14.
   (*b*) Extent of His Kingdom. 1 Kings 4. 20-25.
C. His Administration.
   (*a*) Organization of His Aids. 1 Kings 4. 1-7.
   (*b*) The Fame of His Wisdom. 1 Kings 4. 29-34.
   (*c*) His Alliance with Hiram of Tyre. 1 Kings 5. 1-18.
   (*d*) The Building of the Temple. 1 Kings 6. 1-14.
D. The Decline of His Power.
   (*a*) Idolatry and Its Rebuke. 1 Kings 11. 1-13.
   (*b*) His Adversaries and His Death. 1 Kings 11. 14-26, 41-43.

3. The Early Christian Church. Acts 1. 8.
A. The Promise of Power. Acts 2. 1-8.
B. The Promise Fulfilled. Jerusalem. Acts 4. 32; 5-11.
C. First Called Christians. Antioch. Acts 11. 26.
D. The Gentile Church. Samaria. Acts 8. 14-25.
   Greece. Acts 16. 12-31.
   Italy. Acts 28. 16-31.

II. LAW

4. A. The First Code.
   (*a*) Prologue. Exodus 20. 2.
   (*b*) The Duty of Reverence. Exodus 20. 3-7.
   (*c*) Respect for the Sabbath. Exodus 20. 8-11.
   (*d*) Respect for Parents. Exodus 20. 12.
   (*e*) Prohibited Sins. Exodus 20. 13-17.
B. The Second Code.
   (*a*) The Master Questioned. Matthew 22. 34-36.

(*b*) Our Love for God. Matthew 22. 37-38.

(*c*) Our Duty to Our Fellows. Matthew 22. 39-40.

III. PROSE NARRATIVE

5. *A. A Loyal Listener.*

    (*a*) The Characters in the Story. 1 Samuel, chapters 1, 2.

    (*b*) A Servant to the Priest. 1 Samuel 3. 1-3.

    (*c*) The Call in the Night. 1 Samuel 3. 4-7.

    (*d*) The Call Interpreted. 1 Samuel 3. 8-9.

    (*e*) The Loyal Response. 1 Samuel 3. 10.

  B. An Effective Worker.

    (*a*) A Miracle Wrought. Acts 14. 8-10.

    (*b*) False Worship Prevented. Acts 14. 11-13.

    (*c*) God Honored. Acts 14. 14-18.

IV. ROMANCE STORY

6. *Rebecca, a Prose Idyl.* Genesis 24. 1-67.

  (*a*) A Devout Mission. Genesis 24. 1-9.

  (*b*) The Mission Undertaken. Genesis 24. 11-14.

  (*c*) The Damsel Appears. Genesis 24. 15-20.

  (*d*) The Messenger Received. Genesis 24. 31-33.

  (*e*) His Story Told. Genesis 24. 34-49.

  (*f*) His Mission Accomplished. Genesis 24. 50-61.

  (*g*) A Godly Home Established. Genesis 24. 62-67.

V. PARABLES

7. *The Kingdom of Heaven.*

  A. The Sower and the Seed.

    (*a*) The Story Told. Matthew 13. 1-9.

    (*b*) The Explanation Given. Matthew 13. 18-23.

  B. The Wheat and the Tares. Matthew 13. 24-30.

    (*a*) The Explanation Given. Matthew 13. 36-43.

  C. The Mustard Seed. Matthew 13. 31, 32.

  D. The Leaven. Matthew 13. 33.

  E. Other Parables. Matthew 13. 44-52.

  F. Why Jesus Taught in Parables. Matthew 13. 10-17; 13. 34-35.

VI. CHRISTIAN LETTERS

8. *Admonitions for Right Living.*

  (*a*) Bible Standards for the Christian Family. Ephesians 6. 1-18.

  (*b*) Practical Suggestions of Duty. Romans 12. 1-21.

(c) The Nature and Work of Faith. Hebrews 11. 1-23.
(d) The Beauty of Christian Love. 1 Corinthians 13. 1-13.

B. POETRY. I. PASTORAL

9. *Ruth, an Idyl of Human Love.*
   (a) What is Poetry? A Pastoral Poem? An Idyl?
   (b) Time and Place Location of This Story?
   (c) Leading Characters and Their Characteristics?
   (d) Main Incidents in the Story?
      1. Naomi and Her Family. Ruth, chapter 1.
      2. Boaz and His Interests. Ruth, chapters 2 to 4.
   (e) The Interest and Beauty of the Poem?

II. LYRIC POEMS AND COMPOSERS

(Deborah, Moses, Miriam, Hannah, Mary)

10. *Songs of Faith and Trust.*
   A. An Introductory Meditation. Psalm 1.
      (a) Happiness the Result of Godliness.
   B. Confidence in God's Grace. Psalm 23.
      (a) The Shepherd Psalm.
   C. The Blessings of the Righteous. Psalm 91.
      (a) Trust in God's Providence.
   D. A hymn of Thanksgiving and a Prayer for Guidance.
      Psalm 139.
   E. The Helpfulness and Beauty of the Psalms to the Early
      Jews and to Us of Today.

III. EPIC POEMS AND COMPOSERS

(Joseph, David, Saul, Ruth, Naomi, Esther, Job)

11. *"An Epic of the Inner Life" or the Mystery of Human*
    Suffering.
   A. The Prologue.
      (a) A Godly Man Grievously Afflicted. Job 1. 1; 2. 10.
      (b) His Three Friends Come to Bring Comfort. Job
          2. 11-13.
   B. The Poem.
      (a) They Argue That Only the Guilty Suffer. Job 4.7.
      (b) Job Claims That He is Innocent. Job 23. 10-12.
      (c) Elihu insists that Chastisement is:
          1. An Expression of Divine Goodness. Job 34. 10-17.
          2. A Cure but also a Prevention. Job 36. 9-13.

    (*d*) God Shows Job the Wonder and Mystery of the World. Job 38. 1-7.

    (*e*) Job's Humility and Trust. Job 42. 1-6.

C. The Epilogue.

    (*a*) God is well pleased and Restores Job's Prosperity. Job 38. 1-7.

C. PHILOSOPHY AND THE WISDOM LITERATURE

(Proverbs, Job, Ecclesiastes, James and the Books of Ecclesiasticus and of Wisdom from the Apocrypha)

12. A. *The Hebrew Sage.*

    (*a*) Against Suretyship and Idleness. Proverbs 6. 1-11.

    (*b*) Concerning the Mischief Maker. Proverbs 6. 12-15.

    (*c*) Seven Things Hateful to God. Proverbs 6. 16-19.

    (*d*) Filial Obedience a Protection Against Impurity. Proverbs 6. 20-35.

B. The Preacher's Sayings.

    (*a*) Remember God in Youth. Ecclesiastes 12. 1-7.

    (*b*) The Value of Wisdom. Ecclesiastes 2. 8-12.

    (*c*) The Chief Concern of Man. Ecclesiastes 12. 13, 14.

C. The Christian Philosopher.

    (*a*) The Cause of Strife and War. James 4. 1-3.

    (*b*) Choose Between God and the World. James 4. 4-10.

    (*c*) All Evil Speaking is Forbidden. James 4. 11-12.

    (*d*) The Uncertainty of Human Plans. James 4. 13-17.

D. PROPHECY

13. A. *The Messiah Foretold.*

    (*a*) The Promises of Christ's Coming. Isaiah 55. 1-5.

    (*b*) Calls to Repentance. Isaiah 55. 6, 7.

    (*c*) The Providence of God. Isaiah 55. 8-13.

B. The Vision of a Christian Prophet.

    (*a*) The Holy City. Revelation 22. 1-5.

    (*b*) The Word and the Book. Revelation 22. 6-10.

    (*c*) The Permanency of Character. Revelation 22. 11, 21.

E. PUBLIC ADDRESSES. I. ORATORY

(Masters of Eloquence: Moses, Elijah, Amos, Isaiah, Peter, Paul, Jesus)

14. *Patriotism and Devotion.*

A. The Speaker and His Audience. Deuteronomy 5. 1.

B. He Recalls God's Covenant. Deuteronomy 5. 1-3.

CURRICULA IN RECENT EXPERIMENTS

C. He Urges Loyal Obedience. Deuteronomy 5. 32 to 6. 2.
D. Advises to Love God and His Word. Deuteronomy 5. 3, 6-8.
E. Warns Against Idolatry. Deuteronomy 5. 9-16.
F. Exhorts to True Righteousness. Deuteronomy 5. 17-25.

II. SERMONS

15. *Early Preachers of Christ.*
  A. Peter at Pentecost.
    (a) The Time, the Place, the Occasion. Acts 2. 1-13.
    (b) The Appeal to Prophecy. Acts 2. 14-21.
    (c) Jesus, the Risen Lord. Acts 2. 22-36.
  B. Paul on Mars' Hill.
    (a) Conditions That Called Forth the Sermon. Acts 17. 16-21.
    (b) The Athenians and Their Unknown God. Acts 17. 22, 23.
    (c) Paul Preaches the True God. Acts 17. 23-29.
    (d) He Urges Repentance and Faith in Christ. Acts 17. 30-32.
16. *Jesus on the Mount.*
    (a) Suggestion: Read Matthew, chapters 5, 6, and 7. Select special sections for intensive study.
    (b) The Beatitudes. Matthew 5. 1-12.
    (c) The Nature of Discipleship. Matthew 5. 13-20.
    (d) Duties Under the Moral Law, on Anger, Purity of Life, Good for Evil, etc. Matthew 5. 21-48 and 6. 12.
    (e) Counsel as to Prayer. Matthew 6. 5-15; 7. 7-12.
    (f) Standards of Life and Conduct on Display, Sincerity, Wealth, Service, Trust, etc., chapter 6.
    (g) Further Appeals for Righteousness, chapter 7.

F. PRAYER

17. *The Soul's Communion with God.*
  A. A Patriot's Prayer for His People.
    (a) An Exile Hears News from His Home. Nehemiah 1. 1-3.
    (b) His Sorrow for the Sins of His People. Nehemiah 1. 5-7.
    (c) He Dwells on God's Mercy. Nehemiah 1. 8, 9.
    (d) He Asks for God's Blessing. Nehemiah 1. 10, 11.
  B. The Saviour's Prayer for the World.
    (a) His Prayer for God's Glory. John 17. 1-5.

RELIGIOUS EDUCATION AND DEMOCRACY

(*b*) His Prayer for His Apostles. John 17. 6-19.

(*c*) His Prayer for All Other Believers. John 17. 20-26.

18. Semester Review and Examination.

REFERENCE MATERIAL

Gardiner—The Bible as English Literature.

Harold B. Hunting.—The Story of the Bible.

Moulton—The Bible as Literature.

Wood and Grant—The Bible as Literature.

For General Reference—Hastings' Dictionary of the Bible.

3. THE GARY PLAN

CURRICULA OF DENOMINATIONAL RELIGIOUS DAY SCHOOLS[1] IN GARY, INDIANA

Eight different denominations have conducted week-day religious schools.

For the most part the church school accepts the graded Sunday school curriculum of its own denomination as a basis. The task of making a proper correlation of the Sunday school and week-day church-school program is, however, far from solution. The Presbyterians follow an independent curriculum. The Congregationalists have an independent curriculum but hope to correlate later. The Disciples of Christ base their work on the International Graded Lessons, but on account of peculiar local conditions do not correlate their work with that done on Sunday. The Methodists, like the Disciples, base their work upon the International Graded Lessons, but are still far from a complete correlation of Sunday school and week-day church school work. The Episcopalians use the curriculum of their General Board of Religious Education, but their Sunday school follows an entirely different program, resembling in some respects a Junior Church under the leadership of the rector. The Baptists correlate closely and are doing this successfully.

When a completely satisfactory curriculum is worked out the church day school and Sunday school will be studying a common curriculum. The division of labor may be one of study on week days and auditorium period on Sundays or it may be a curriculum with three lessons of similar nature each week. The Baptists are now working at the latter and the Methodists have been inclined to favor the former, but a great deal of work must be done before any satisfactory conclusion is reached.

ATTITUDE OF THE LOCAL CHURCHES

The attitude of the local churches for the most part has been sympathetic from the beginning. Any hesitancy to take up the work or to promote it zealously has been due more to fear of

---

[1] From a Survey of the Gary situation by Arlo A. Brown, in Religious Education vol. xi.

adding burdens in times of financial stringency than to anything else. However, it is to be regretted that there has not been closer cooperation between all the church schools and between some individual churches and their schools, but the difficulties have not been inherent in the experiment. At the beginning there was a feeling on the part of some congregations that this was an experiment to be conducted by an outside agency (a general Sunday school board) for the benefit of the outside world. At the end of the first year a joint conference was held between pastors, directors, and general Sunday school officers, in which each of the groups showed a warm appreciation of the work of the others. But the experiment needs for the best results a more united and aggressive effort upon the part of the local churches than has yet been put forth. Such a united effort would secure larger enrollment and closer cooperation between the church schools, the homes and the Sunday schools.

HOME COOPERATION

The relation of the church school to the home thus far depends very largely upon the personal activity of each director. The local churches for the most part have not seriously undertaken to put this work upon the hearts of the parents, and the directors have been too overloaded with duties to do much calling. Parents' meetings are also contemplated, but the plans for such have not yet been worked out. It is true, however, that the interest of the pupils and the personal work of the directors have brought many parents to feel that they know the directors intimately. More than one parent has told how his boy got up out of a sick bed to go to church school when he said he was not able to go to public school.

TEACHERS AND METHODS OF SUPERVISION

In most cases the teacher or director is appointed by a general Sunday School Board, which pays the salary and supervises the work, giving for the most part, however, large liberty to the individual director.

TESTIMONY CONCERNING RESULTS

The best testimony concerning results so near the beginning of the experiment is that by Superintendent Wirt himself, who says that he has not tried to study the content of the various curricula used in the church schools nor to investigate closely the quality of the teaching, but that he has tried to test the work by its effect upon the community life. From this standpoint his observation leads him to feel that the church schools have naturalized religion, so that instead of being a thing remote from the everyday lives of the pupils it now takes its place naturally along with other interests. Religion and the church schools have also become natural subjects of conversation. Secondly, he has tried to compare pupils who have been in church schools with those who have not availed themselves of this privilege to see if there is any evidence of a difference in reverence or ideals or purpose, and he feels that there is an appreciable difference in favor of the church-school pupil.

It has been clearly demonstrated that pupils will attend the church school even in the face of strong counter attractions. In the first year of the experiment (1914-1915) the pupils made a choice between church school and auditorium periods at the public school, and the record of attendance was excellent. The next year (1915-1916), in order to avoid the criticism that the public school was sending children to church school and then calling them back, thereby practically guaranteeing the attendance of all who enrolled, the church school was allowed to have the pupil at the time when he was not actually compelled to be at public school; in other words, when the home controlled him. When the directors became aware of this plan they thought it would mean the death of their schools, but as a matter of fact their fears were groundless. The pupils still came with good regularity, though the competition with play hours was generally deemed unfortunate. It must be remembered, however, that each pupil has two hours of play or application work regularly in his school day in addition to possible play periods after school hours; in other words, the pupils will come, and parents are glad to have them come when the public school schedule permits this without an unreasonable loss of play time.

Again, there seems to be no legal obstacle to such a plan, and no violation of the principle of complete separation of church and state. The pupil goes from home to the church school or from the church school to his home.

The indictments against the Gary plan, charging it with fostering sectarian influences within the public school system, do not seem to be well founded. This plan meets every requirement for the separation of church and state in education, and takes away the last excuse for a division of school funds. It permits time in the pupil's daily schedule for instruction in religion, and leaves the churches untrammeled as to the form which this instruction may take.

Moreover, the Gary public school ideal is right. Education should take into account the whole life. The lengthened school day is a success, and the Gary schools do provide for the needs of individual children better than the usual schools which give little but formal discipline. There are, however, a few outstanding difficulties which thus far prevent the Gary church schools from being a complete solution of the problem of religious education. One is the difficulty of getting all the children of church families into the church schools, to say nothing about reaching the unchurched families. In Gary there are three large public schools—Emerson, Jefferson, and Froebel. The church schools are practically all near Jefferson and too far from the others to secure satisfactory attendance. The Disciples, Presbyterians, and Methodists, by confining their work very largely to Jefferson school pupils, get good results, but Jefferson contains only eight hundred and thirty-two pupils, Emerson has eight hundred and sixty-two, and Froebel eighteen hundred and eleven. In a city where a church draws from practically the same area as a single public school the problem will be less difficult, but in Gary there is no way of reaching all the available children without having a church school, one in common or many, adjacent to each public school.

A community school of religion in which the denominations would combine their work under a common faculty would most easily solve the problem of reaching all, and no doubt very greatly improve the work because then it would be possible to have a faculty where each teacher is a specialist in the work which he is teaching. As it is now, most of the church schools remind one of the old-fashioned country school in which one teacher is compelled to teach all grades and all subjects. Here one teacher handles all grades but deals with one subject.

But the denominations insist that a child to be properly religious must know how to take his place in a religious institution, namely, some church. Hence, they consider training in denominational history and organization as essential. There seems to be no reason why the material which the denominations hold in common could not be taught in a common church school on week days, and denominational points and forms of worship at the Sunday school hour. But there is no move toward this end in Gary as yet, although certain denominational boards would be willing to make such an experiment.

The second problem is that of securing enough teachers for a church school. The plan of one paid teacher for all grades is not considered by anyone a success. No matter how good the teacher, the task of being a specialist with all ages is impossible. The Baptists have a plan by which four of their own workers who have had teaching experience are engaged at fifty cents an hour. The Congregationalists also use local talent.

There is little difference of opinion on the part of those promoting the experiment concerning the ultimate source of the teaching staff. Most of it must be developed within the local congregation. However, there will doubtless be a growing number of churches which can afford to engage directors of religious education to organize the work and supervise and train their teachers.

The third problem, What to study, is far from solution. From the standpoint of the Methodists this is the most urgent of all. They believe that teachers could be secured and other difficulties solved very readily if what to study were properly determined.

The last problem is that of schedule. If some pupils are to be changed at the end of two weeks, others at four weeks, etc., it makes grading in the church school practically impossible. The promotion of pupils at the end of each term is hard enough. If church school courses were planned on the term basis and public school schedules were left unchanged after the first two or three weeks of adjustment, then graded work with examinations and promotions would be possible; as it is now the task is next to impossible. If a fixed schedule is impossible in Gary, then the statement very frequently heard to-day may be true, that the Gary plan could be worked more easily in many other places than Gary. But the fact that eight of the nine church schools in operation two years ago are continuing and that practically all of their directors and pastors are enthusiastic over the plan indicates that they expect this difficulty to be overcome some time in the future.

The directors on the field and the people who are backing them, feel that the experiment is exceedingly worth while. The discouragements which have arisen have come not from any lack of enthusiasm for the opportunity but from high ideals and an impatience with imperfection in the face of so great an opportunity. They generally feel that as soon as suitable curricula have been worked out the plan can be duplicated immediately in hundreds and thousands of communities with every assurance of success. The Gary plan of school administration is not necessary to the success of this method of religious education, but something like the Gary ideal and the longer hours for school work are necessary. What the church school asks of the community is a definite number of hours a week for each pupil while he is unfatigued. Given this, the church week-day school of religion in cooperation with the church Sunday school can and will perfect its work.

SCHEDULES AND CURRICULA

BAPTIST

Schedule	Monday Grades	Tuesday Grades	Wednesday Grades	Thursday Grades	Friday Grades
8.15	6, 7, 8	....	....	6, 7, 8	....
9.15	....	....	....	....	....
10.15	2, 4, 5	....	....	2, 4, 5	....
1.15	3	....	....	3	....
2.15	4, 5, 6, 7, 8	....	....	4, 5, 6, 7, 8	....
3.15	1	....	....	1	....

Enrollment— Grades | Number | Grades | Number
1.............. 10 | | 4, 5.......... 10
2.............. 10 | | 6, 7, 8........ 25
3.............. 11 | | —
| | Total....... 66

Curriculum—International Graded Lessons, Keystone Series, supplemented by especial helps from American Baptist Publication Society.

Equipment—Two rooms in the church building, equipped with tables, chairs, blackboard, maps, library cabinet, organ, etc.

Teachers—Mrs. G. D. Rummell, Graduate of Normal School, Terre Haute, Indiana.

Mrs. H. H. Dills, Graduate of Normal School, Danville, Illinois.

Mr. L. W. Carlender, Graduate of Ottawa University, Ottawa, Kansas.

Miss Jennie Cathcart, Graduate of High School and Teacher Training Course in Alabama.

Supervision—The entire educational work of the church is under the direction of the Committee on Religious Education of the local church. The Rev. S. L. Roberts, State Sunday school director, spent several weeks here, helping to organize the work and arrange courses of study. The Educational Department of the American Baptist Publication Society has assisted in preparing courses of study, and has provided the greater part of the financial support. Mr. Roberts has general supervision of the work, and visits the schools frequently.

CONGREGATIONALIST

Schedule	Monday Grades	Tuesday Grades	Wednesday Grades	Thursday Grades	Friday Grades
8.15	....	7, 8, 9, boys	....	....	7, 8, 9
9.15	....	7, 8, 9, girls	....	....	7, 8, 9
10.15	....	4, 5, 6	....	....	4, 5, 6
1.15	....	1, 2, 3	....	....	1, 2, 3
2.15	....	4, 5, 6	....	....	4, 5, 6
3.15	....	2	....	....	2

Enrollment—

Grades	Number	Grades	Number
1, 2, 3	9	7, 8, 9, Boys	5
2	3	7, 8, 9, Girls	4
4, 5, 6	15		—
		Total	36

Note.—Eight high school pupils who met regularly last year at 8:15 A. M. will probably be scheduled for an evening.

Curriculum—

Grades 1, 2, 3. Freedom given to teacher, who is an expert kindergartner.

Twenty-third psalm now being taught by story, pictures, and hand work. Memory work is given emphasis.

Grades 4, 5, 6. Life of Christ in Mark.

Grades 7, 8, 9. Connected study of Gospels of Luke and The Acts of the Apostles. Pupils use their Bibles for textbooks.

High School. Historical Outline of Entire Bible.

Equipment—Basement of church. Chairs, table for little ones, blackboard, pictures, etc.

Teachers—

The Rev. E. I. Lindh, Harvard, B.A., '93; B.D., '95; Graduate school, '96-'97.

Mrs. Frank Cargill (Teacher Grades 1, 2, 3), Graduate of State Normal, Kalamazoo, Mich. Formerly public school teacher in Chicago.

Mrs. James Graham (Teacher Grades 4, 5, 6). Formerly public school teacher in Philadelphia.

214

CURRICULA IN RECENT EXPERIMENTS

SUPERVISION—Under Pastor in consultation with the Moral and Religious Education Commission of the National Council of Congregational Churches.

DISCIPLES OF CHRIST

SCHEDULE	Monday Grades	Tuesday Grades	Wednesday Grades	Thursday Grades	Friday Grades
			Glen Park School		
8.15	....	6, 7, 8	....	....	6, 7, 8
9.15	3, 4	....	5, 6	3, 4	....
10.15	1, 2	3, 4	3	1, 2	3, 4
1.15	1, 2, 3	5	1, 2	1, 2, 3	5
2.15	5, 6	6, 7	7, 8	5, 6	6, 7
3.15	....	....	....	....	....

ENROLLMENT—

Grades	Number	Grades	Number
1	14	6	8
2	19	7	4
3	21	8	6
4	10		—
5	11	Total	93

Total, boys, 35; girls, 58

CURRICULUM—"The course of study in use in this school is based principally on the International Graded Series, though it might be said that no present existing course is followed invariably. I take the International themes for the most part, changing the order of groups of themes at times, in the interest of clearness and logical order, but drawing on as many sources as my library affords for the material and methods. In this way I make use of the International, Scribners, University of Chicago, and other courses."

EQUIPMENT—One room 22x28 in a frame apartment house, second floor. Blackboard on three sides. Good light. Hat rack in hall, running water and toilet adjoining. Steel desks. Hand work material, etc.

TEACHER—Myron C. Settle, three years in Butler College, two summer sessions in University of Chicago, one summer session in Columbia, one full year in Hartford School of Religious Pedagogy, eight years as field worker for his denomination in Kansas and Ohio.

RELIGIOUS EDUCATION AND DEMOCRACY

Supervision—All support from the American Christian Missionary Society. All local details in the hands of Mr. Settle.

METHODIST EPISCOPAL

Schedule	Monday Grades	Tuesday Grades	Wednesday Grades	Thursday Grades	Friday Grades
8.15	5, 6	7, 8	....	5, 6	7, 8
10.15	1, 2	3, 4	....	1, 2	3, 4
1.15	1, 2	3, 4	....	1, 2	3, 4
3.15	5, 6	7, 8 ·	....	5, 6	7, 8

Enrollment— Grades   Number   Grades   Number

     1, 2............ 35   7, 8.......... 21

     3, 4............ 33   —

     5, 6............ 22   Total.......111

Curriculum—A modification of the International Graded Lessons to suit the church school, grouping, supplemented by denominational history.

Equipment—Small room with thirty Moulthrop desks, blackboard, maps, pictures, song charts, hand work materials, etc.

Teacher—Harry Webb Farrington, A. B., Syracuse University B. D., Boston University Graduate study, Harvard.[1]

Supervision—Director appointed and salary paid by Board of Sunday Schools of the Methodist Episcopal Church, local expenses paid by local church with help of the Board. Details of work under supervision of the Board of Sunday Schools.

PRESBYTERIAN

Schedule	Monday Grades	Tuesday Grades	Wednesday Grades	Thursday Grades	Friday Grades
8.15	....	2A	....	2A	....
9.15	....	7c, 6b, 8c	....	7c, 6b, 8c	....
10.15	....	2c, 3c, 2b, 3b	3b, 4b	2b, 3b, 2c, 3c	3b, 4b
1.15	....	1c, 1a, 2c	5c, 4a, 4c, 3a	1c, 1a, 2c	5c,4a,4c,3a
2.15	....	....	5b, 6c	....	5b, 6c
			5a, 6a, 7a		5a, 6a, 7a
3.15	....	....	1c, 1b	....	1c, 1b

[1] This work is now in charge of Miss Mary Elizabeth Abernethy (1916).

CURRICULA IN RECENT EXPERIMENTS

ENROLLMENT—
Grades	Number	Grades	Number
1c, 1b	8	3b, 4b	8
1c, 1a, 2c	7	5c, 4a, 4c, 3a	23
2a	6	5b, 6c, 5a, 6a, 7a	21
2b, 3b, 2c, 3c	16	7c, 6b, 8c	15
		Total	104

CURRICULUM—

Grade 1, Mutch's Bible Stories.

Grades 2, 3. Judges, Kings, Prophets, Missionary Heroes, Scripture, prayer and songs.

Grades 4, 5. Life of Christ. Comrades in Service. Material from Bible followed by teacher's comments taken largely from the New Century Bible. Scripture, prayers, hymns.

Grades 6, 7. Same.

EQUIPMENT—Room in church used by an organized Sunday school class on Sunday, equipped during work with red primary chairs, small movable blackboard, lap boards for pupils, hand work materials, piano, cabinet, some picture chosen by the organized class.

TEACHER—Thomas Owens. Graduate of Ripon, where he majored in education and philosophy under Dr. William J. Mutch; and B.D. from McCormick Seminary.

SUPERVISION—All support and final supervision comes from the Synod of Indiana. Curriculum, textbooks, etc., left to Mr. Owens.

PROTESTANT EPISCOPAL

SCHEDULE	Monday Grades	Tuesday Grades	Wednesday Grades	Thursday Grades	Friday Grades
8.15	....	7	8	7	8
9.15	....	6	....	....	6
10.15	1, 2, 3	....	....	1, 2, 3	....
1.15	1, 2, 3	....	....	1, 2, 3	....
2.15	4	5	4	5	....
3.15	7	....	7	....	....

ENROLLMENT—
Grades	Number	Grades	Number
1, 2, 3	27	6	6
4	9	7	10
5	5	8	2
		Total	59

CURRICULUM—
Grades 1, 2, 3 (Primary). First year Junior International Graded Series Work Book. The Church of God.
Grade 4 (1 Junior). God speaking through the Christian seasons.
Grade 5 (2 Junior). God speaking by Church Attendance.
Grade 6 (3 Junior). Hearing God speak by knowing and living with Jesus Christ.
Grade 7 (4 Junior). Hearing God speak through the Church by the Holy Spirit.
Grade 8 (5 Junior). Hearing God speak to the whole world by Christ's church.
All Junior Courses are furnished by the General Board of Religious Education of the Protestant Episcopal Church.
EQUIPMENT—Basement of church, corner screened off. Chairs around tables, pictures on wall, blackboard, maps, handwork material.
TEACHER—Vera L. Noyes, Graduate of Saint Mary's Academy, Knoxville, Illinois.
Graduate (1910) Chicago School of Applied and Normal Art, Chicago.
Taught in Saint Mary's and Saint Martha's one year each. Taught in private studio, Lexington Kentucky, Superintendent of Sunday School, Saint Paul's, Chicago.
SUPERVISION—Support, textbooks, and teacher from the General Board of Religious Education. Immediate supervision by rector of Christ Church.

JEWISH (ORTHODOX)

SCHEDULE	Monday Grades	Tuesday Grades	Wednesday Grades	Thursday Grades	Friday Grades
2.30	5, 6	5, 6	5, 6	5, 6	5, 6
3.30	1, 2, 7	1, 2, 7	1, 2, 7	1, 2, 7	1, 2, 7
	3, 4	3, 4	3, 4	3, 4	3, 4
4.30	Confirmation Class	Confirmation Class	Confirmation Class	Confirmation Class	Confirmation Class

ENROLLMENT—
Grades	Number	Grades	Number
1, 2	18	7	6
3, 4	14	Confirmation Class	6
5, 6	12	Total	56

218

CURRICULA IN RECENT EXPERIMENTS

CURRICULUM—

Grades 1, 2. Hebrew Alphabet.

Grades 3, 4. Advanced Readers, Writing, Translation.

Grades 5, 6. Bible study (especially the five books of Moses). Translate Hebrew Periodicals. Speak Hebrew.

Grade 7. Advanced Prophets, Grammar, Jewish History in Hebrew Language, Periodicals, including Hebrew Dailies.

Confirmation Class, Duties and responsibilities of Hebrew boy when he becomes a man. The Levitical code.

EQUIPMENT—Two rooms in basement of Synagogue, with desks, etc.

TEACHERS—D. Almond, Graduate of London University, teaches three upper classes.

Mrs. D. Almond, a graduate in the Old Country, teaches Grades 1, 2, 3, 4.

SUPERVISION—All the work supported and supervised by Board of Education of Temple Beth El.

NOTE.—Hebrew language and literature, Monday to Friday (except Confirmation Class). Religion taught Saturday and Sunday two hours each with 70 enrolled.

JEWISH (REFORMED)

SCHEDULE—		Wednesday Grades	Enrolled
8.30	10	4, 8	18
2.30	4	4, 8	13
4.30	5..30	4, 8	5
		Total	36

CURRICULUM—Hebrew Language and Old Testament history arranged by the Rabbi.

EQUIPMENT—Back of store room, two tables and chairs.

TEACHER—Rabbi Harold F. Reinhart, Cincinnati University, B.A. '12 Hebrew Union College (Cincinnati) Rabbi, '15.

SUPERVISION—Entirely under Rabbi Reinhart.

NOTE.—Have 50 enrolled in Sunday School 10 to 12 A. M. Program: Hebrew, 45 minutes; Assembly, 30 minutes; History, 45 minutes. Hebrew the same as on Wednesday. History lesson given on Sunday, and no new material given Wednesday. Pupils write up in story and other form the Sunday school lesson.

CHAPTER III

OUTLINE OF CURRICULA USED IN THE RELIGIOUS DAY SCHOOL AND THE DAILY VACATION BIBLE SCHOOL

1. THE RELIGIOUS DAY SCHOOL[1]

THE ASSEMBLY

THE following is the general order of the assembly and period of daily worship, which may be varied to suit conditions.

1. Singing one or more hymns.
2. Prayer by some pastor.
3. Story or address by an adult not to exceed eight minutes is occasionally put here.
4. Bible or other story, by one or more of the pupils, selected from some lesson which he has had.
5. Hymn or dismissal.

The pupils should come into the assembly in perfect order, always taking the same seats. They should remain standing until all are in their places, when all sit together at a signal from the piano.

The assembly is the heart of the school. It unifies and inspires it. Nothing must drag, nothing must come in which is not thoroughly substantial and germane. Nothing but standard hymns should be used and no pains must be spared to secure the best leader for the singing; and the whole period must be made radiant with life.

ASSEMBLY MUSIC: All teachers are expected to give adequate time to assist their pupils to memorize the assembly hymns, and where classroom conditions will permit, it is advisable to give them some training in the singing. The main object of the assembly hymns is to teach the pupils some of the great hymns in such a manner that they will never forget them. The following are suggested: "God of All Being Throned Afar," "All Hail the Power of Jesus' Name," "The Church's One Foundation." Others may be substituted, if desired.

DAILY PROGRAMS should so be arranged that memory drills,

---

[1] Supplied by Rev. H. R. Vaughn, Urbana, Ill.

physical exercises, supplementary readings, etc., shall serve to vary the program and avoid danger of fatigue and monotony. Special care must be taken in the first few grades not to keep the pupil too long on one subject.

PERIODS OF STUDY are often provided for all beyond the second grade to good advantage. The work, at best, is intensive; the purpose being to put five hours' work in three, thus obviating the necessity of an afternoon session.

NOTE BOOK AND HAND WORK: In the first two grades the note-book work consists largely in drawing pictures such as will "illustrate" or call to memory the points in the lesson and also help to impress the lesson on the mind. Paper cutting and clay modeling are also sometimes employed to advantage. The rest of the grades write the principal points in the lessons in brief suggestive sentences. The notebook is used in connection with missions and church history as freely as with the Bible lesson.

TEXTBOOKS AND TEACHING:[1] Pupils under high school grades need no books except the Bible and notebook. The teaching is oral. The teacher must make such thorough preparation that the teaching will be vital. No one should attempt to teach who has not first received some suggestions from those who have had experience in the work. The textbooks are in the hands of the teacher, though the latter is not supposed to use it in class. Other courses than those recommended can, of course, be substituted if desired. It is better not to attempt many changes the first year. The courses recommended provide in most instances for four weeks' instruction. It is usually better to have but two weeks the first year, but several schools wishing for a longer course will be no longer embarrassed for lack of material.

GRADING, NUMBER OF TEACHERS, LOCATION OF SCHOOLS: The grading follows exactly that of the public schools. The number of teachers will average about one to every twenty-five pupils. In the larger schools, of course, each grade can have a separate teacher, while in most cases each teacher has to care for two or more grades. The schools are preferably held in school buildings where that is feasible, otherwise in churches. Each class must have a separate room unless the churches are too far apart. The teachers are usually paid a salary of $5 a week and upward. Local and traveling expenses must, of course, be provided for out-of-town teachers in addition.

---

[1] The Kindergarten course can be obtained by applying to Miss Lorena Church, Rockford, Illinois. All Books in the courses can probably be ordered from any denominational publishing house.

RELIGIOUS EDUCATION AND DEMOCRACY

SYNTHETIC LESSONS. The object of these lessons is to give the pupil a knowledge of the subject-matter as a connected whole. It is our purpose to so arrange the Bible instruction as to cover the whole Bible in eight summer terms. This can be easily done when we have three-week terms. This will give the pupil a knowledge of the whole Bible as a connected whole, which is quite essential. Teachers must take great care to go carefully over the subject-matter for the pupils in detail in as interesting manner as possible and have them reproduce it, as fully as possible.

SMALL SCHOOLS. Schools of less than thirty pupils are sometimes conducted by one teacher. The classes are divided so that two and sometimes three grades are put in one class. Such schools usually have both a morning and afternoon session. Sometimes a part of the school comes in the morning and the remainder in the afternoon. Some of our best schools have been very small.

A LOCAL EXECUTIVE COMMITTEE should be appointed as long as possible before the school is held. The founding of a school so that it is well established is the work of years rather than months. The committee should always be permanent in character and be composed of representatives of all the churches cooperating where the school is a union movement as is usually the case. It is wise to appoint members of the committee for terms of three years, allowing one-third of the terms to expire each year. The best committees are made up of members whose service has been continuous.

THE MORNING CALL BELL should ring at 8:55 so that all the pupils can be in their places at 9 o'clock sharp. While perfect order must be preserved in going in and out of the assembly, great care must be observed in arranging the movements of the individual groups so that no time be wasted.

2. DAILY VACATION BIBLE SCHOOL

The daily program adopted by the National Association and used almost universally by the local city organizations is as follows:[1]

FIRST HOUR

8:30 Preparation and visitation by staff.
9:15 Doors open and registration.

SECOND HOUR

9:30 Opening exercises, all present.
Hymn.
Psalm or other portion repeated in concert.
Lord's Prayer—said or sung.
Bible Verse and Hymn.
Kindergarten goes out.
Health and Habit Talk.
Thank Offering for Extension.
9:40 Music period.
Vocal and breathing exercises.
Singing lesson.
Calisthenics and music.
10:05 Bible Period.
Lesson represented by children; or
Taught by sand-table; or
Given with stereopticon; or
Told as story by teacher.

THIRD HOUR

10:30 Manual Work and Play in Sections.
Hammock-making.
Elementary Sloyd work.
Raffia work.
Basketry.
Sewing.
Weaving.
Work for Children's Hospital.

---

[1] College Ministry, Manual with Music and Songs, p. 3. For fuller account see Chapell, The Church Vacation School.

Bible Blank Book Work.
First Aid for Hygiene.
Play, all.

11:25 Closing Exercises—School Reassembles.
Daily salute to flag.
America or Hymn.
Children's Benediction.
March out to Music.

2:30 Open Air Games Organized and Directed.
Excursions.
Visitation of Homes.
Teacher Conference, Monday.

CHAPTER IV

OUTLINE OF CURRICULA FOR WEEK-DAY RELIGIOUS INSTRUCTION BY INDIVIDUAL CHURCHES OR DENOMINATIONS

1. LUTHERAN PAROCHIAL SCHOOLS

"An evangelical Lutheran Congregational school is formed by voluntary agreement and resolution of a Lutheran parish, or local church organization, to gather its children of prescribed age in a locality, properly fitted up for the purpose, to the end of having them thoroughly instructed, within certain prescribed hours, by a common teacher, chiefly and primarily, in the wholesome doctrine of the Divine Word according to the Lutheran Confessions, and to advance them in true godliness; next, to give them instruction and training as far as practicable in such knowledge and accomplishments as are necessary for all men in their civil status."[1]

The parochial school is organized on the same basis as the public school, having for its aim to equal its eighth grade instruction, but with this difference, that it devotes the first hour of each day to religious instruction, or about one sixth of the school period. Outside of the material used during this first hour of the school session, the parochial school is conducted in the same way and uses the same materials[2] of instruction as the public school. The materials of religious instruction are church prayers, the most important Lutheran hymn, Bible stories, Bible reading, and the text of Luther's Small Catechism with proof-texts and explanations.

In the first three grades, from about six to nine years, the children are taught simple Bible stories, the text of the chief parts of the Catechism with Luther's explanation, and morning and evening prayers.

The fourth and fifth grade instruction presupposes a ready use of German and English, since religious instruction is given in

---

[1] Lindemann, Schulpraxis, p. 3, No. 2.
[2] The textbooks on general subjects are published partly by educators of the church, the purpose being to make all subjects taught harmonize with the general doctrinal position of the church.

both languages. The children are now taught more Bible stories, which are applied to the experiences of the child. The Small Catechism is supplemented by explanations and proof-texts in question-and-answer form, which the children memorize, together with Lutheran hymns.

In the sixth, seventh, and eighth grades the text of the Catechism is gone over again, to which is added the Table of Duties and Explanations, all-in-all about thirty-five questions and answers, together with about eight hundred proof-texts. The Bible stories already learned from both the Old and the New Testament are reread, together with additional stories, about sixty from the Old and seventy from the New Testament. Important psalms and additional hymns are also memorized. Church history covering the first three centuries is touched upon, while the Reformation period is studied in detail.[1]

LUTHERAN SCHEME OF INSTRUCTION FOR CLASSES IN RELIGION[2]

The following scheme is suggested, no plan having been framed for all churches. The classes are divided into the following groups:

Infants .... 5 to 7 years.
Primarians .... 8 years.
Juniors.............. 9 to 10 years.
Intermediates........11 years.
Preparatorians.......12 years.
Catechumen ....13 years and over.

All children are invited to attend the regular church service. When nine years of age they are required to do so. An important part of the work is the report of last Sunday's sermon, given orally by the younger children and in written form by the older ones.

SCHEME OF INSTRUCTION FOR CLASSES IN RELIGION

	Catechumens	Preparatorians	Intermediates	Juniors	Primarians	Infants
Bible Study	Review New Lesson Bible Readings Texts	Review New Lesson Bible Readings Texts	Review New Lesson Bible Readings Texts	Review New Lesson Bible Readings Texts	Review New Lesson Texts	Review New Lesson Texts

[1] Religious Education, February, 1916, p. 8.
[2] Religious Education in the Public School, George U. Wenner, p. 80.

SCHEME OF INSTRUCTION FOR CLASSES IN RELIGION—*Continued*

	Catechumens	Preparatorians	Intermediates	Juniors	Primarians	Infants
Catechism	The Creed and Means of Grace Explained	The Commandments and the Lord's Prayer Explained	The Lord's Prayer Explained	The Commandments Part I Explained	The Ten Commandments	The Lord's Prayer
Church Service	Morning Service Evening Service	Morning Service Evening Service	Morning Service Evening Service	Morning Service Evening Service	Select Parts	Select Parts
Hymns	Ten chief hymns	Ten chief hymns	First verses of ten chief hymns	First verses of ten chief hymns	Ten children's hymns	Ten children's hymns
Prayers	Morning Evening Table On entering church On leaving church	Morning Evening Table On entering church On leaving church	Morning Evening Table On entering church On leaving church	Morning Evening Table On entering church On leaving church	Children's Prayer	Children's Prayer
Sermons	Written Report	Written Report	Oral Report	Oral Report		
Bible Study	Books Geography Antiquities	Books Geography Antiquities	Books of N. T. Geography	Geography		

2. THE DEMONSTRATION SCHOOL
(EPISCOPALIAN)[1]

Saint Mary's Church School, on Lawrence Street, New York city, is the official experiment station in matters of Religious Education for the Province of New York and New Jersey. It is called the Demonstration School of the Province.

TIME—The week-day classes meet afternoons and evenings, according to the age of the pupils. They meet after public school hours, some classes as early as 3:30, some as late as 4:45, in the afternoon. The evening classes are composed of those who are no longer in school, or those who are in their last year of grammar school.

COURSE OF STUDIES—The material issued by the General Board of Religious Education is used as the basis of the curriculum. It furnishes a program for much besides informational teaching. It is a series of plans calculated to set a school in motion along lines of progressive studies, acts of worship, acts of service, familiarity with Church usages, etc., and other phases of life which comprise loyal, enlightened Churchmanship.

[1] Leaflet supplied by the Episcopal Board of Religious Education, 289 Fourth Avenue, New York.

RELIGIOUS EDUCATION AND DEMOCRACY

DEPARTMENTS

This curriculum suggests the organization of the school under the four following Departments:

PRIMARY—
This includes the Beginners' Class (Kindergarten), ages 4, 5, and three years in the Primary grade, ages, 6, 7, 8.

JUNIOR—
Five years; ages, 9, 10, 11, 12, 13.

SENIOR—
Four years; ages, 14, 15, 16, 17.

GRADUATE—
Ages 18 and over.

PRIMARY DEPARTMENT

This includes the Beginners' Class (Kindergarten), ages 4, 5, and three years in the Primary Grade, ages, 6, 7, 8.

AIM

To teach that having been made through Holy Baptism the children of God we have a Father in heaven who knows and loves us, and who wants us to love and obey him.

TABULATED STATEMENT OF PRIMARY LESSON MATERIAL AND MEMORY WORK

GRADE	AGE	SUBJECTS FOR STUDY	MEMORY WORK
Beginners	4—5	Simple Bible Stories Nature Stories	Simple Bible Texts Simple Prayers Hymns: 534, 553
I	6	Bible Stories Nature Stories Elementary Truths	Simple Bible Texts The Lord's Prayer and other short Prayers Hymns: 540, 544, 537
II	7	Above Continued	As Above
III	8	Bible Stories in Chronological order	The Lord's Prayer Psa. 23, 121 St. Mark 10. 13—16 Catechism through Commandments Bible Texts

DENOMINATIONAL WEEK-DAY CURRICULA

The study material in the chart above comprises simple stories from the Holy Scriptures with illustrations and applications from the experience and knowledge which the children have gained from the natural world and their companions. In the Beginners' Class and in the Primary Grades I and II (ages 6, 7), these stories should be very elementary. The children of the Bible should be presented, as far as possible; also elementary truths, as the love, power and wisdom of God, in such manner as children can receive them.

CHURCH KNOWLEDGE

1. The parts of the church building and their use (simply).
2. The Christian Year in outline, emphasizing the great festivals and their chief significance.
3. Various simple missionary incidents.

DEVOTIONAL LIFE

1. Attendance at children's services, and as soon as possible with adults at the regular services.
2. Systematic weekly offerings, birthday offerings.
3. Personal prayers and thanksgivings.
4. Occasional attendance by classes at baptisms and church worship, preceded and followed by an explanation of the services.
5. Anticipation of Confirmation and Holy Communion.

CHRISTIAN SERVICE

1. Acts of loving kindness to people and animals, helpfulness to parents and teachers and pleasantness in home life.
2. Ministry to sick and needy.
3. Interest in the Font Roll.

JUNIOR DEPARTMENT

(This includes five years; ages 9 to 13)

AIM

To quicken boys and girls in love for the Lord Jesus Christ as the source of blessing and help to his people; to develop in them the habit of obedience to God's holy will and commandments as the aim of their personal life, to train them into a life of service for others and of worship of our Lord, and to lead them on to Confirmation and Holy Communion.

RELIGIOUS EDUCATION AND DEMOCRACY

GRADE	AGE	SUBJECT FOR STUDY	MEMORY WORK
IV	9	Old Testament Biography	Review Catechism through Commandments Versicles (Evening Prayer) Gloria Patri
V	10	Old Testament Biography	Catechism through "My Duty to My Neighbor" Te Deum Benedictus Magnificat Nunc Dimittis Beatitudes Books of Bible
VI	11	The Life of Our Lord	(Above continued)
VII	12	Personal and Social Duties taught from the Catechism, illustrated from the Bible	Catechism Selected Psalms Selected Collects
VIII	13	Missions of the Church	Nicene Creed Gloria in Excelsis General Confession from Communion Office

LESSON MATERIAL

Grade IV—Old Testament Biography.

Grade V—Old Testament Biography.

Grade VI—Stories on the Life of our Lord taken mainly from the Gospel according to Saint Mark, as setting him before the children in his active life among men.

Grade VII—Personal Duty and Social Duties, taught through a series of lessons from the Bible. These lessons, based upon Holy Scripture, should be largely extended expositions of our duties to God and to our neighbor, as set forth in the Catechism.

Grade VIII—Missions of the Church.

DENOMINATIONAL WEEK-DAY CURRICULA

CHURCH KNOWLEDGE

Grade IV—The Christian Year and Catechism explained.

Grade V—Ability to find the places in the New Testament, and in the Prayer Book for Morning and Evening Prayer.

Grade VI—(1) The Holy Days and Days of Abstinence.

2. Ability to find the places in the Old Testament.

3. Further and more detailed study of Missions.

Grade VII—The fabric, furniture and vestments of the Church; the clergy and their duties.

Grade VIII—(1) Ability to find the places in the service for Holy Communion, Baptism and Confirmation.

2. Detailed knowledge of certain mission fields.

DEVOTIONAL LIFE

1. Daily prayer and reading of Holy Scripture should be emphasized at this time; also definite prayer and thanksgiving for others.

2. Confirmation and faithful attendance at the Holy Communion, ownership of Bible, Prayer Book and Hymnal, and attendance at the regular services.

3. Systematic weekly offerings.

4. Birthday thank offering.

5. Loyalty to Christ whose cross is upon our foreheads.

6. Emphasis should be laid upon the duty and blessedness of Personal Purity and Temperance.

CHRISTIAN SERVICE

1. Share in the corporate life of the parish through the various parochial activities and guilds, e. g., Junior Auxiliary, Candidates' Class for the Girls' Friendly Society, Boy Scouts, Knights of King Arthur, etc.

2. Efforts to bring others to Church and Sunday school.

3. Gifts to Missions based upon concrete information.

4. Taking part in Mission Plays, and making articles to be sold for the Lenten offering.

5. Collecting magazines for homes and hospitals.

6. Giving to specific local needs.

7. Making friends and being friendly to new boys and girls in the schools, playgrounds and other social centers.

8. Visiting the sick and needy and institutions as far as suitable.

RELIGIOUS EDUCATION AND DEMOCRACY

SENIOR DEPARTMENT
(This includes four years; ages 14 to 17)

AIM

To develop in the pupils an intelligent love for Christ's Church, personal devotion to him in serving him in and through his church.

To give the pupils proper materials for, and instruction in, the way by which they may come to a right judgment in matters of faith and duty during this period of questioning.

To lay a strong basis for the development of Christian consciousness and faithful Churchmanship.

LESSON MATERIAL

Grade IX—A more advanced study of the Life of our Lord Jesus Christ.

Grade X—The History of the Church, beginning with the Days of the Apostles.

Grade XI—Christian Doctrine as Taught in the Catechism, Bible and Prayer Book.

Grade XII—The Story of the Hebrews as a nation setting forth faith in God, obedience to him and faithfulness to his worship as conditions of success, and the preparation of the world for the Messiah.

NOTE.—The order of the Lesson Material may be altered to suit local conditions.

TABULATED STATEMENT OF SENIOR LESSON MATERIAL AND MEMORY WORK

GRADE	AGE	SUBJECT FOR STUDY	MEMORY WORK
IX	14	Advanced Study of Life of Our Lord Jesus Christ	Collect for each Sunday, Selected Hymns Selected Portion of the Scripture
X	15	History of the Church	
XI	16	Christian Doctrine	
XII	17	History of the Hebrews	

CHURCH KNOWLEDGE

During these years careful instruction should be given with

232

DENOMINATIONAL WEEK-DAY CURRICULA

references to the sacraments, their meaning, value and use; the Church's rules for her people; her organization and Apostolic Ministry.

Careful knowledge of the missionary activities of the Church systematically arranged.

DEVOTIONAL LIFE

Emphasis should be laid upon the corporate life of the Church, her common worship, common fellowship, and common service, as something in which each pupil should have an active part. Care should also be taken for the deepening of the spiritual life, and establishing definite devotional practices as part of the soul life of each scholar. There should also be presented the personal call to the ministry and service of the Church.

CHRISTIAN SERVICE

Encourage the pupils to fulfill their responsibility to other scholars as leaders, helpers and examples, especially in bringing others to Church, Confirmation and Holy Communion; and to continue their share in the parochial and general activities of the Church, such as membership in missionary societies and mission study classes.

Older scholars should be interested in matters pertaining to the public welfare as expressions of their Christian faith and life.

GRADUATE DEPARTMENT

(This includes at least five years; ages 18 and over)

AIM

To enable the older scholars to give a reason for the hope that is in them, to build them up in their most holy faith, to strengthen their love for the Church and to prepare them for earnest service for Jesus Christ.

LESSON MATERIAL

The Life and Teachings of our Lord Jesus Christ; The Church, her history and work; The Epistles of the New Testament; The History and Use of the Prayer Book; Christian Evidences; The Principles of Sunday School Pedagogy and Organization; Missions at home and abroad; Old Testament Prophecy.

CHURCH KNOWLEDGE

Instruction should be given concerning ecclesiastical symbolism, and in the diocesan and national organization of the Church.

233

DEVOTIONAL LIFE

Emphasis should be laid upon the social and civic duties of the Christian, and the part the Church should take in the corporate life of the community.

CHRISTIAN SERVICE

All members should be engaged in some definite active service in the Church and for the community, and should prepare themselves to become teachers in the Sunday school. This is the period at which definite Social Service in theory and practice should be undertaken along the lines indicated under Christian Service.

HOME DEPARTMENT

FONT ROLL

The Board suggests the formation of a Home Department in every Sunday school. The aim of such a Department will be three-fold:

1. To complete the work of the Sunday school by enabling the home to cooperate with the Sunday school in the training of those who either will be or now are members of the school.

2. To extend the educational advantages of the Sunday school to persons connected with the home who are unable to attend the school.

3. To help cultivate in the home an atmosphere and customs favorable to Christian nurture.

Suggestions for organizing a Home Department are given in the course on this subject prepared by the Board for its Correspondence School.

The Home Department, as conceived above, not only provides lessons for adults unable to attend the Sunday school, but includes the formation of a Font Roll, which secures to the Sunday school the income of individual lives as soon as they enter the home, and helps the Church to fulfill its sponsorship.

SUMMER COURSES

The Committee is considering the preparation of summer courses, as this Curriculum provides schedules for the winter season of forty weeks.

TEACHERS

The teachers of the week-day classes are for the most part those who have had some training and experience in teaching in day schools, Sunday schools, or both. While at present the teaching staff is large, the plan is to arrange ultimately for a few teachers to do the work on week days for the entire school, each teacher meeting five or six classes separately at different times throughout the week. This scheme requires that the small staff of week-day teachers be supplemented on Sundays by a much larger staff of auxiliary teachers, for the reason that on Sundays, like the other days, all the classes meet at the same time. The course of studies for each class is continuous on week days and Sundays, there being no break in the sequence of the work. Thus the Sunday teaching continues, enlarges, reviews or "fixes" the lesson taught in the previous week. To take a concrete example: here is a teacher who holds four different classes of boys at four different times through the week, teaching each class once. On Sunday this same teacher takes one of those classes, while the other three are taught by three auxiliary teachers who carry out the directions given them by the week-day teacher. If necessary, the week-day teacher, who is in every case the controlling factor, can, while his own Sunday class is engaged in writing, visit his other three classes for a short time in order to see that their work is progressing as he would have it, or in order to give incidental help to the auxiliary teacher.

Among other things, this plan provides opportunity for a teacher in training to work in cooperation with, and under the guidance of, a more experienced teacher who has an intimate knowledge of what the former is trying to do. It may be that in this way a very practical and effective means will be found of adding concreteness and vitality to the process of teacher-training. The nature of the teaching on Sundays is somewhat different from that conducted during the week. The week-day session is the longer of the two, lasting fifty minutes. Here the "advance work" is done, the main part of the teaching. On Sunday half an hour is spent in the church, where the school as a whole has its exercises, worship, etc. Then follows the shorter teaching period, of half an hour, which is devoted largely to drill-work, review, discussion. Such, in brief, is the plan that is in progress, by way of experiment, at Saint Mary's. It will be noticed that the matter of the relation of the church school to the public school has hardly been touched upon. The description would have been just as complete if the public school had not been mentioned. Nothing that goes on in Saint Mary's Church school could not have been put into practice as well ten years ago as now. The present Saint Mary's program depends on no peculiar, or new, system of public education, be it the much-discussed Gary Plan, or a part-time plan, or any other form of schedular flexibility. The opportunities for week-day religious instruction in Saint Mary's parish are about what they have always been, just as the opportunities for it in almost every other parish in the country are about what they have always been—no more, no less. The interesting point is that recent discussions in the press and elsewhere are opening the eyes of church people to those opportunities. There are some Americans who have seen the opportunity for years, and who, seeing it, have thought it worth seizing for the sake of their religion. "About ten years ago," wrote a prominent Lutheran in 1907, "after several years of experiment on a smaller scale, I established week-day classes for all the children of the congregation, from five or six years upward. Attendance was made obligatory."

But while the week-day work at Saint Mary's is not dependent upon any peculiarity of public school routine, the question of week-day religious classes cannot be discussed to-day without some reference to the larger subject of the general relation between church schools and public schools. Indeed the very fact that Saint Mary's Church school is maintained during the week without reference to the public school is itself a comment on the subject. It suggests that the question of whether Episcopal (or any other) parishes shall conduct religious instruction on week days is one for those parishes to decide for themselves, regardless of whether the public schools of their respective neighborhoods are of the Gary type, the regular five-hour type, or any other. Any parish that wants to hold week-day classes can do so. Some parishes will find it expedient, others will not. In a community where most of the children and youth of a parish live near together, and have comparatively limited advantages, the church will be hard put to it to find any convincing argument against extending its educational offices into the week, if by so doing she will be giving a better, fuller, and more effective training to her children. At any rate the church can decide the question on its own merits.

The church can have all the time she wants for religious instruction, subject only to the demands of parents. It is to the homes, not to the public schools, that we must go for " a chance to influence the child." It is they, not the schools, who are to give to the church "more of the child's time."

3. HEBREW RELIGIOUS SCHOOLS

There is no uniform course of study for all Hebrew schools, but the following is taken from a curriculum for Jewish religious schools by Eugene H. Lehman[1] as representing the tendency among more liberal educators:

Course of Study—*First Grade* (Ages about six to eight). General title of the year's course: "How God Shows His Love for His Children." (1) About twenty simple biblical and rabbinical stories that abound in the imaginative and wonderful, and that reveal God's care and love. (2) Several nature stories, showing how in a most marvelous manner, God provides food, clothing, shelter, etc., for all of his creatures, and how his love is revealed also in the vegetable and mineral kingdoms. The children use Bloch's cards for coloring.

Second Grade (ages about seven to nine). General title of the year's course: "Things God Wants His Children to Learn and to Do." (1) A series of ethical lessons upon such topics as obedience, helpfulness, habit of prayer, etc., copiously illustrated by stories from the Bible, the Talmud, from nature, biography, history. (2) Simple stories of the Jewish and American holidays. Owing to the want of satisfactory textbooks, teachers are urged to follow the course offered by the correspondence school of the Jewish Chautauqua Society.

Third Grade (ages about eight to ten). General title of the year's course: "The Heroes Who Founded Israel." (1) From Abraham to David. Textbook, The Junior Bible for Jewish School and Home. Series I, by Kent and Lehman. (2) Nature stories, historical incidents, fables showing how God cares also for non-Jewish people.

Fourth Grade (ages about nine to eleven). General title of the year's course: "The Heroes Who Guided Israel through Dangers." (1) From David to Amos (B. C. 1100 to B. C. 927). (2) Several stirring incidents from history and real life that tend to rouse a feeling of bravery and self-sacrifice. Textbook, The Junior

---

[1] In the Encyclopedia of Sunday Schools and Religious Education.

237

Bible for Jewish School and Home, Series II, by Kent and Lehman.

Fifth Grade (ages about ten to twelve). General title of year's course: "Israel's Later Kings and Earlier Prophets." (1) From Amos to the Babylonian Captivity (B. C. 927 to B. C. 586). (2) Several biographical studies of such men as Moses Mendelssohn, Isaac M. Wise, Theodore Herzl. Textbook, The Junior Bible for Jewish School and Home, Series III, by Kent and Lehman.

Sixth Grade (ages about eleven to thirteen). General title of the year's course: "Israel's Later Leaders and Teachers." (1) From the Babylonian Captivity to Judas Maccabæus (B. C. 528 to B. C. 165). (2) Explanation of the Jewish calendar and of the orthodox ceremonial life and customs. (3) Discussions on the sanctity of the body and personal hygiene. (4) Biographical stories of such men and women as Moses Montefiore, Abraham Geiger, Emma Lazarus, George Eliot. Textbook, The Junior Bible for Jewish School and Home, Series III, by Kent and Lehman.

Seventh Grade (ages about twelve to fourteen). General title of the year's course: "The Defenders and Early Rabbis of Judaism." (1) From Judas Maccabæus to the Completion of the Talmud (B. C. 165 to A. D. 500). (2) Discussions on life problems and personal purity under the leadership of a well-balanced physician, or of a specially trained and sympathetic teacher. (3) Discussions of contemporary Jewish problems, such as the ghetto problem, orthodoxy and reform, the relationship between Jew and Christian. Textbook, M. H. Harris, Thousand Years of Jewish History.

Eighth Grade (ages about thirteen to fifteen). General title of the year's course: "Great Men and Movements in Mediæval and Modern Judaism." (1) From the completion of the Talmud to the present time (500-1913). (2) Talks on social hygiene by a physician or trained teacher. (3) Discussion of contemporary Jewish problems, such as intermarriage, the Jew at college, anti-Semitism. Textbook, C. Deutch, History of the Jews.

Ninth Grade (confirmation classes—ages fourteen to sixteen). General title of the year's course: "The Jewish Religion—Its Meaning, Its Demands, and Its Ideals." (1) The fundamental teachings of Judaism. (2) Discussions of current religious problems, such as Zionism, the position of the Jewish woman, the Jewish Home. (3) The discussion of moral, social, and personal problems, such as child labor, personal purity, moral standards in business, etc. The textbook used is Morris Joseph's Judaism as Creed and Life.

The curriculum also provides for optional courses in Hebrew, for a considerable amount of memory work, and contains numerous suggestions for social service activities to be carried on by the pupils. Postconfirmation classes are found in a more or less flourishing condition in the various schools.

CHAPTER V

PROPOSED CURRICULUM OF RELIGIOUS EDUCATION COR-RELATED WITH PUBLIC SCHOOL CURRICU-LUM—PRIZE ESSAY

THE scheme presented herewith is contained in the essay of Prof. Rugh which received the first prize of $1,000 from the National Education Association in 1915.

GENERAL SCHEME FOR ANY GRADE[1]

I. SCHOOL PLAN.
　1. *Subjects.*
　　A. Religious material in present curriculum.
　　B. Additional material of religious nature.
　　C. Specific religious instruction and training.
　2. *Discipline.*
　　D. School government—democratic—developing institutional loyalty.
　　E. Punishment religious—restoring broken spiritual unity by inducing
　　　(1) Repentance.
　　　(2) Confession.
　　　(3) Consecration to the right. (Example: Prodigal Son.)
　　F. Philanthropic enterprises.
II. CORRELATION AND COORDINATION WITH THE HOME.
　　A. Bringing home experiences into the school.
　　B. Sending vital school work into home, both subject-matter and discipline.
　　C. Fellowship through parents' days, exhibits, and other social gatherings.
III. CORRELATIONS AND COORDINATIONS WITH CHURCH.
　　For the present mostly a church problem. The Sunday

---

[1] For presentation of the scheme in full, together with other suggested schemes, see The Essential Place of Religion in Education, a Monograph published by the National Education Association, Ann Arbor, Michigan. Copies may be obtained from D. W. Springer, secretary.

school and young people's societies can use some of the
material of school for their work. Some essays, debates,
music. Church schools may come to conform in plan
and organization to the best public school. Pastors must
come to know more about the schools.

HIGH SCHOOL AGES IN DETAIL

I. SUBJECTS.
  A. Present curriculum.
    1. Science and mathematics. Study and measure-
      ment of great forces of nature and physical life.
      Great lessons in sense of proportion and values.
      With the devout teacher the science pupils
      "think God's thoughts after him," as Agassiz
      said. "God geometrizes from all eternity."
      Mathematics deal with eternal, universal prin-
      ciples.
        "Physical science leads to a knowledge of God
        and an admiration of his power."—*Karl E.
        Guthe, Professor of Physics, University of
        Michigan.*
        "Biology and religion have a common mission
        in the regeneration of man; . . . both are
        needed to achieve highest possible expres-
        sion of human power."—*John M. Coulter,
        Professor of Botany, University of Chicago.*
        "In spirit and aspiration, in motive and aim,
        science and theology, philosophy, religion,
        and art are one with mathematics; all of
        them consciously or unconsciously aim at
        congenial goods that shall be everlasting;
        . . . All of them seek to vindicate the world
        as a world of abiding worth."—*Cassius J.
        Keyser, Professor of Mathematics, Colum-
        bia University.*
    2. History and literature. Every good teacher uses
      these as means of culture and character.
    3. Music and drawing. These are also means of
      culture in the hands of the religious teacher.
    4. Vocational subjects. These subjects are some-
      times dubbed "materialistic," but not so by
      those who have seen them as taught in good

        schools. The social service aspect of a life
work dominates much of the vocational education. Making an honest living is part of living
a religious life.

B. Vitalizing Present High School Curriculum.

The greatest possibility for religious education is
involved in this problem. First the high school
must offer work into which the youth may throw
his whole soul. This is necessary for integrity
of life. The science work must couple up with
life. The supreme problems of life must be faced
and studied—struggle for existence; survival of
the fittest; selection and reproduction; the eternal
principles of right and character; one's total science must develop the fixed disposition to try to
adapt the self to one's total environment. This
will always include the religious and divine aspect.
Mathematics must be practical and help solve
vital and social problems.

Both science and mathematics will be vitalized by
being made to include biographies of the great
souls who gave their lives to these problems. They
were devout men. History must include the life
and contributions of the Hebrews as well as the
Greeks and Romans. History will be made vital
and religious for the high school age when made
to explain the development of the five historical
institutions: (1) The home, (2) The industries,
(3) The church, (4) The state, (5) The school.
The high school literature may be made to include
the best religious literature of the world. Already
schools offer the Psalms, Job, etc., without objection.

Music offers a distinct opportunity because the best
music is religious.

So with architecture and painting.

Study of civics and community problems.

C. Elective courses in the Bible. Gary plan. North
Dakota plan.

II. DISCIPLINE AND GOVERNMENT.

D. The development of school spirit and institutional
loyalty through individual and group responsibility

for the good name of the school and community. Democratic school government.

E. Reformation of wrongdoers. Study of Prodigal Son. The development of the method of restoring oneself to unity with the right after wrongdoing: (1) Repentance. (2) Confession. (3) Consecration to the right and the good of the school. This is distinctively a religious process. If the youth does not learn this process when it involves human beings, how can he do it with his heavenly Father?

F. Philanthropic enterprises. The modern high school is coming to develop many forms of social service. The poor and needy are always with a school. Thanksgiving and Christmas may offer occasions. Sickness, suffering, sorrow, and death offer occasions for delicate and religious training. Community problems may be discussed. The high school may become the social and civic center of the community, and when the principal and teachers are religious they spread not only religious contagion but have opportunity to give individual religious help to adolescent boys and girls.

CHAPTER VI

TYPICAL PLANS OF CHURCH AND COMMUNITY PRO-
CEDURE TOWARD MORE ADEQUATE RELIGIOUS
INSTRUCTION

1. PLAN OF ORGANIZATION OF INTERDENOMINA-
TIONAL FORCES AS EMBODIED IN THE INTER-
DENOMINATIONAL COMMITTEE ON WEEK-
DAY RELIGIOUS INSTRUCTION,
NEW YORK CITY

THE Interdenominational Committee on Week-day Religious
Instruction, composed as far as possible of official representatives of all religious bodies, submits the following report.

I

STATEMENT OF AIM

This Committee, representing as far as possible all religious
bodies in New York city, has been organized for the purpose of
stimulating, unifying, and promoting week-day religious instruction in the city of New York, along lines that shall conserve religious liberty, and maintain every possible safeguard against
proselyting.

Acting through its Borough Committees, and in cooperation
with denominational committees and with local churches and
synagogues, it seeks to have week-day schools for religious instruction established in different parts of the city to demonstrate:

1. Ways by which all school programs can be taken advantage
   of without infringing upon the sectarian neutrality of the
   public schools;
2. Ways by which individual churches can organize their educational work so as to include therein week-day religious
   instruction;
3. Ways by which churches of several denominations can cooperate in the management of a community school; and
4. Ways by which religious instruction can ultimately be provided on week-days for all children of any community.

CHURCH AND COMMUNITY COOPERATION

II

PRINCIPLES INVOLVED

1. The development of the child's life should be a unitary process in the light of modern psychology and education. That development should include in proper correlation the physical, mental, and religious training of child-life.
2. The American principle of the separation of church and state is reaffirmed.

III

THE SITUATION

The general situation in this country and city emphasizes the inestimable duty and privilege of the church in its own ministrations and through the home to give each child an adequate religious education. Its resources and influence make this its imperative service to the city and nation. Though the church has enormous responsibilities to meet in its charitable enterprises and missions at home and abroad, it is incumbent upon it for this very reason to raise in this city and nation God-fearing citizens, and thus to strike at the root of much of the poverty, injustice, and crime in our civilization by adequate preventive work through the religious instruction of children. In New York city, especially, the following elements of the situation should be kept in mind:

1. Upon the public school has devolved to a large extent the moral training of the child. In this city, only about 383,000 out of 831,000 children of the public schools are known to have their public school training supplemented at their places of worship by training in religious knowledge and experience.[1]
2. Of these 383,000 children, many are probably in the habit of reporting on week days out of school hours for various forms of club work, young people's societies, and children's organizations. About 60,000 are receiving more than one period weekly of formal religious instruction.
3. The time is come when, in the interests of our city and nation, all religious bodies should unite in recognizing their obligations not only to the children now enrolled, but to the hundreds of thousands at present apparently neglected.

---

[1] Exact statistics not compiled. The Roman Catholics report about 108,000; the Jews about 50,000; the Protestants, about 225,000.

245

4. The need is urgent for all religious bodies to increase the number of weekly periods, to broaden the curriculum, to improve the equipment and method, and to raise up a body of teachers as well equipped for their work as are teachers of secular subjects.

IV

SCHEDULES IN NEW YORK CITY

In order to facilitate an understanding about the possibility of extending week-day religious instruction in this city, the Inter-denominational Committee on Week-day Religious Instruction submits for consideration the findings of a subcommittee, composed of Jewish, Protestant, and Roman Catholic representatives, appointed to study the following problem: Under the existing policy of separation of church and state, what plans for week-day religious instruction are legal and feasible under the various school conditions now obtaining or likely to obtain in New York.

1. *Five-hour Schedule Including Lunch-hour.*
   No legal problems involved.
   Time for religious instruction: after 2 P. M.
   Place for religious instruction: private property.
   Teachers: provided by religious bodies.
2. *Six-hour Schedule Including Lunch-hour.*
   No legal problems involved.
   A. School hours from 9 to 3 o'clock.
   B. Double School Plan: School X, 8:30-2:30; School Y, 10:30-4:30.
   Time for religious instruction: A—after 3 o'clock.
   B—School X, after 2:30.
   School Y, before 10:15
   and after 4:30.
   Place: private property.
   Teachers: provided by religious bodies.

Practice already established and feasibility of afternoon hours demonstrated by Episcopalians, Jews, Lutherans, and Roman Catholics. Other bodies are already giving considerable time to week-day work in the form of clubs, young people's societies, and children's organizations. This only needs to be organized and scheduled, and improved in method and scope, to become effective week-day religious instruction.

3. *Seven-hour Schedule Including Lunch-hour.*
   The Committee is now awaiting the outcome of the experi-

CHURCH AND COMMUNITY COOPERATION

mentation with the seven-hour and eight-hour schedule, and
will bring in a supplemental report.

V

Recommendation

The consultations of the Committee during the past year have
centered chiefly on the legality and feasibility of extending week-
day religious instruction. In order that the Committee may proceed to further study of the methods, it respectfully recommends
its findings to the respective religious judicatories of the City
that, as far as possible, plans for an active campaign of religious
education in the City may be adopted by all bodies.

VI

Outline of Problems Connected with Week-day Religious
Instruction in New York

1. *General Preliminary Problems.*
   1. What different types of school are possible from the point
      of view of the churches?
      a. The week-day session of the church school.
      b. Denominational schools. (Preferably demonstra-
         tion schools.)
      c. Community schools for cooperating denominations.
      d. Schools for the unchurched.
   2. What are the different situations to be met owing to—
      a. Differences in population, race, church, etc.?
      b. Differences in school schedules?
      c. Differences in the distribution of churches?
   3. What type of day-school schedule best suits the community?
   4. What type of religious week-day school is appropriate to
      each of the different situations?
   5. How can the unchurched children best be reached in any
      community?
      Shall there be separate schools, or shall they go to a com-
      munity school?
      By what methods shall these children be brought into the
         various week-day schools? How can suggestions of
         proselytism be avoided?
   6. When it is decided under what auspices the week-day reli-
      gious school is to be run, it will probably be found that
      the types of schools will be reduced to two:

247

RELIGIOUS EDUCATION AND DEMOCRACY

    A. The school of the local church in week-day session.
    B. The community school attended by either—
        1. Children from different churches of the same denomination, or
        2. Children from churches of several denominations.
Children of unchurched parents are likely to be present in each type of school.

II. *The Problems of the Local Church Organization.* (See I, 6, A.)
    1. How can pastors and people be informed and interested?
    2. How can teachers be trained and secured?
    3. How can adequate support be obtained?
    4. How shall the church be organized for comprehensive work in Religious Education?
    5. How can materials for week-day instruction be secured?
    6. How can the unchurched of the community be reached?
    7. How can proper relations be maintained with day-schools, without exceeding legal restrictions?
    8. How can adequate time be secured without depriving children of the time needed for outdoor play and exercise?
    9. What shall be the relation of the Sunday sessions to the week-day sessions?

Steps toward the solution of these problems are suggested in the Report of the Subcommittee on Week-day Religious Instruction of the Interdenominational Committee (Protestant) on Religious Education.

III. *The Problems of the Community School.* (See I, 6, B.)
    A. For the solution of what problems related to Community Schools can all churches cooperate?
        1. Community surveys. How shall they be conducted? What shall be the objective? See method employed by the Federation. How can the information be made available for all?
        2. Districting of the City and locating suitable centers. See report of the Subcommittee of the Manhattan Committee.
        3. Decision of types of public school and religious school appropriate to each district.
        4. Preparing and securing teachers.
        5. Relations with school authorities: The problems of "cooperation," and of legal interpretation.
        6. Publicity.

CHURCH AND COMMUNITY COOPERATION

7. Provision of a "clearing house" for the exchange of experience among denominations.
B. For the solution of what problems will Jews, Catholics, and Protestants tend to work independently?
Thus: When a district is located for a community school,
1. How shall such a school be started?
2. How shall it be supported?
3. How shall it be supervised and controlled?
4. Where can it get teachers? Pay or volunteer?
5. What is the purpose of each of these schools, as determined by the social and religious needs of the community?
6. What shall be the curriculum?
7. What programs are suitable?
8. What social activities can be used?
9. What standards shall be set up?
10. How can these schools cooperate with the churches from which the children come?
11. What shall be done with the unchurched? See above, I, 5.
12. How many hours should each child come?
13. How can the school cooperate with the schedules of the public schools (Gary, Ettinger, etc.), and which schedules are adapted to church conditions in each community?

Suggestions on some of these problems have been made in the Report of the Subcommittee on Week-day Religious Instruction of the Interdenominational Committee on Religious Education.

COMMENT ON THE NEW YORK EXPERIMENT[1]

The following problems are defined by the Committee:
1. Different types of religious day schools:
   (a) Week-day session of the Church School.
   (b) Denominational Schools (preferably demonstration schools).
   (c) Community Schools for cooperating denominations.
   (d) Schools for the unchurched.
They feel that the types in practice will probably reduce to
   A. The school of the local church in week-day session.
   B. The Community school, attended by

---

[1] By Rev. Lester Bradner, Ph.D., at the Annual Convention of the Sunday School Council, Boston, January, 1917.

RELIGIOUS EDUCATION AND DEMOCRACY

1. Children of different churches of same denomination.
2. Children from churches of several denominations.

So much for the hypothesis of the interdenominational committee in New York. What is actually happening? Besides the Jews, who have 600 centers of instruction with a director, and some 50,000 pupils, and the Roman Catholics, who have 44 centers with an attendance of 8,000, the Protestant denominations are maintaining about 25 centers, distributed as follows:

The Dutch Reformed Church, 8, with a Demonstration School and a Director of Religious Education.

The Episcopal Church, 7, with a Demonstration School and a plan for a Director.

The Methodists, 4, with a Demonstration School, a Director and a Supervisor of the movement.

The Presbyterians, 3, with a Demonstration School in connection with Teachers College, and the Reformed Presbyterians, 1.

In the light of the experiments already made in connection with these centers in New York city, I desire to discuss briefly—

1. The question of a Community School. Theoretically it has seemed a possible and feasible project to establish one school in a locality or community to serve in competent fashion a number of Protestant denominations. This was proposed in Gary some time ago. It generally takes a prominent place in discussions concerning proposed systems of week-day instruction. Experience seems to show that it is less feasible than was anticipated. No Community School has ever been established in Gary. In fact there is less likelihood of it there now than there ever has been. Neither is a Community School a part of the practical operations in New York. The very fact that, in theory, the week-day work and the Sunday work of any child should be knit together so that one would be the explanation of the other, demands that the week-day instruction partake of the type used on Sunday. But Sunday instruction is always denominational. So in part is the week-day school.

On the other hand, combinations of local churches in the same denomination in a single school are surely possible from this point of view. I am not aware that this plan has actually been in operation, but it does not offer the objections raised against the Community School of combined denominations.

2. The Problem of a Teaching Force. Nearly all beginnings in this new plan of week-day religious instruction have made use of salaried teachers. This in itself tends to fix a limitation upon the work. Not every local church can afford a paid teacher. We may reach such a situation by degrees, but at present it is for practical reasons unattainable. Are we, indeed, shut up to this dilemma? Or is there some hope of a solution which will allow the use of voluntary service for the week-day work? I believe that we are really in sight of such a solution. There is a very considerable group of trained teachers and educators belonging to every denomination who have thus far held aloof from religious instruction, partly because it was given on Sundays and therefore cut into a very necessary day of rest, partly because the educational quality of the work proposed on Sunday was so low in its standard as not to interest them. The week-day religious instruction presents a different situation along both of these lines. It does not interfere with a day of rest and it is quite possible to construct it upon approved lines in educational processes. I have already referred to the fact that both Roman Catholics and Jews have marshaled a very considerable group of week-day teachers, many of them on the volunteer basis. In New York a similar movement has now begun in the Episcopal Church. There has been formed what is called "The Fellowship of Religious Education." This includes public school teachers and people of all types professionally interested in education. One of the conditions of membership is the voluntary gift of one hour a week when called for, to be devoted to religious instruction on week days. With the organization of such a volunteer force comes the possibility of a very considerable amount of week-day instruction, both teaching and supervision of teachers, practically without cost to the church undertaking it. Along such lines as this there is new hope of solving the problem of standard in administration of week-day instruction in religion.

3. The Question of Subject Material. I cannot discover at the present time that there is any unanimity of practice in the use of teaching material in the different efforts at week-day instruction in religion. Theoretically we maintain that the week-day instruction should be thoroughly correlated with that of Sunday. In point of practice the approach to such correlation has not been frequently worked out. Nevertheless, this appears to be more a difficulty of the actual furnishing of such material in printed form than an impossibility. There is every reason to believe

that if the new development of unified group life for children and young people is accomplished, such as is contemplated in the more recent reports of the Sunday School Council, it would be no difficult matter to develop the Sunday lessons in the direction of definite expression during the week-day time. It may be that the character of the Sunday instruction will be modified by this process. But our hope lies in the fact that every well-conceived curriculum of the religious development of childhood and youth, ought of necessity to include more material than can usually be handled in a school period on Sunday. I am of the opinion that an increase of week-day instruction will soon provide the stimulus necessary to accomplish this possible extension of the Sunday educational program.

2. SUGGESTIONS OF THE COMMITTEE ON RELIGIOUS EDUCATION OF THE NORTHERN BAPTIST CONVENTION

THE CHURCH AND THE PUBLIC SCHOOL IN RELIGIOUS EDUCATION[1]

This Bulletin is here reprinted in full as an admirable illustration of an effective denominational method of acquainting its constituency with the more recent experiments in week-day religious education and of defining the denominational attitude thereto.

A growing interest in the week-day religious instruction of the young has brought forward again the questions relating to instruction in the Bible and religion in public schools. Several special forms of activity in this field are to be noted:

The Daily Vacation Bible Schools. This is a plan of week-day instruction in religion during the summer vacation.[2]

The propaganda for Bible reading and study as a part of the regular work of public schools. Various plans are urged.[3]

The distinctive experiments of the North Dakota high schools, Colorado schools, Lakewood (Ohio), Gary (Indiana), and many other places. These all provide for work in religion by school pupils to be taken in churches or similar places outside the school building. The plans are given with greater detail below.

At a joint meeting of the secretaries of the church educational societies held in Chicago, January 13-15, the following resolutions were passed regarding the relation of the church to the public school:

That in view of the great importance of Bible instruction as related to public education, this council recommends to the church boards composing this body that they bring before their supreme judicatories a full statement of the situation looking toward action in the following particulars:

---

[1] From a report of the Commission on Moral and Religious Education to the Northern Baptist Convention, *Bulletin No. 4.* Copies may be obtained from the American Baptist Publication Society, Philadelphia.

[2] See Religious Education, for August, 1914. Also p. 223, *supra.*

[3] See the description of many methods in the introductory portion of Bible Stories and Psalms, prepared and published by Wilbur F. Crafts, Washington, D. C. Also pp. 158-172, *supra.*

RELIGIOUS EDUCATION AND DEMOCRACY

1. The favoring of legislation calculated to safeguard the right to have the Bible read in the public schools.

2. The favoring of academic recognition by public school authorities for academic work done in Bible study outside of school hours.

3. Requests to standardizing bodies in public instruction that they define the conditions under which academic recognition may be given for academic work done in Bible study.

4. Encouraging of churches and Sunday schools to provide for such Bible instruction and allied work as will prepare them to bear their part in the movements looking toward the proper functioning of the church and the public school in religious education.

This subject involves such important religious and political issues and is so vital to the future usefulness of the churches that it seems wise to review some of its fundamental principles.

I. STATEMENT OF PRINCIPLES

The Baptist position of the separation of church and state leads to the conclusion that it is inconsistent to use tax-supported institutions for private religious purposes.

The teaching of religion is a private responsibility. Religious instruction means instruction in some faith. Matters of faith are of private judgment and not of public choice.

The primary responsibility for religious instruction lies in the family. The secondary responsibility lies with the church.

Every church will lose one of its greatest privileges if it relinquishes the teaching of religion to the state.

It is important that the development of the child's life be a unitary process. The conception of education must include religious training, since education is the process of developing a religious person.

II. THE SITUATION

The child is already too much divorced from the life of the church. The present activities of the churches in the teaching of religion are inadequate:

As to time (usually thirty-five minutes per week).

As to subjects (fragmentary studies in Bible only, neglecting creed, church, duty).

As to equipment (very few have any special facilities).[1]

---

[1] See The Sunday School Building and Equipment, H. F. Evans, University of Chicago Press.

254

As to numbers taught (as a rule not over sixty per cent of young in church schools).

As to method (still few schools really using modern *school* methods).

Our highly developed public school system lacks the assistance of definite religious instruction in the development of character.

Leaders both of the school and of the church are awakening to the problem of religious education as a common responsibility.

III. Some Proposals and Experiments

1. *Legislation has been proposed regarding Bible reading in the public schools.* The public schools, however, are not religious institutions; they are not designed for teaching religion nor for worship. Their teachers are not selected and are not trained for religious instruction nor upon any religious qualifications. The use of the Bible for teaching religion or for purposes of worship in a public school would be an exceedingly dangerous experiment as giving the state power over religious doctrines and customs, interfering with freedom of conscience, and taking from the church its peculiar privilege of teaching religion to the young. If a majority may demand the teaching of the Bible, a majority may also demand the reading of the Koran or any other religious literature.

We would urge that efforts be concentrated on securing for the Bible the recognition of its place in literature in the regular course in the school, and that we emphasize the Baptist position of separation of church and state by insistence that the church preserve its prerogative of teaching religion and does not abandon it to the state.

2. *Academic recognition has been suggested for work done in Bible study and religion.* Certain important experiments have been made in this field which deserve attention. They illustrate methods of correlating instruction in religion with the work of general education.

(a) *The North Dakota Plan.* This plan was suggested by Professor Vernon P. Squires, of the University of North Dakota. The State High School Board authorizes a syllabus of Bible study. Study may be carried on privately or in special classes *outside the high school* and in connection with Sunday schools or other institutions. The work may be taught by any pastor, priest, or other person. An examination is given at the time of the regular State examination, papers are marked by readers appointed by the State School Board, and, to those who pass, credit is assigned to the extent of one half unit out of the sixteen required for high school graduation.

The following distinctive points are to be noted: The syllabus contains no religious instruction as such. Professor Squires says: "Important as religious instruction is, we must not violate our fundamental American idea of the separation of church and state. The justification of Bible study, so far as the schools are concerned, is found in the great value of a knowledge of scriptural history and literature as broadly cultural subjects. This idea must be constantly and consistently borne in mind and strenuously insisted on." To avoid any suspicion of sectarianism, no text-book except the Bible is prescribed. Any recognized version of the Bible will be accepted. There is no insistence on any theory of authorship or criticism. Memory passages must be committed from both Old and New Testaments. The work must be sufficient to amount to ninety hours of recitation, besides the time of preparation.

It must be noted that this system applies to high school students only, that it does not require or permit special absences from the regular high school work, and that it is not done by the school authorities or school members.

(b) *The Colorado Plan.* The Colorado plan is the outgrowth of the system conceived by the Rev. D. D. Forward, at Greeley, Colorado, and first used in connection with the State Teachers' College. The work is under a "State Council of Religious Education." In November, 1913, the committee for the State Teachers' Association recommended that high schools should give credit for Bible study of corresponding grade, in Sunday schools which reached in their classes the standards of the North Central Association, to an extent not to exceed one fourth unit for each year's work. Under these conditions a four years' elective course of Bible study is being prepared for use in Sunday schools and for high school students. This system will require that the teachers of such classes shall have at least an equivalent to the B. A. degree, and shall have special training in the subjects which they teach, that pupils shall be eligible to membership in an accredited high school, that churches shall provide such classes with separate rooms, freedom from interruption for at least forty-five minutes, desks for each pupil, blackboard, maps, and reference work. Credit is based upon forty recitations of forty-five minutes each for each year with a minimum of one hour of study to each lesson.

CHURCH AND COMMUNITY COOPERATION

Dr. L. D. Osborne, of Boulder, Colorado, writes: "The crux of the matter lies in the requirement that the work shall be conducted in the Sunday schools according to the standards of the North Central Association of Colleges and Secondary Schools. This means a forty-five-minute period, teachers who have had a college education or its equivalent, individual rooms for the classes, and a genuine study of the lesson on the part of the students."[1]

(c) *The Gary Plan.* The Gary plan provides for children of elementary and high school grades being excused from their classes for from one to six hours per week, as may be arranged, in order to attend classes in their churches. The parents elect the church, and the churches provide special teachers as a rule. On January 31, 1915, the following churches had special teachers, professionally employed, conducting classes, in some instances as many as six hours a day: Baptist, Episcopalian, United Presbyterian, Congregational, Methodist, Disciples, Presbyterian in United States of America, English Lutheran, and Reformed Jewish. It is to be noted that no school fund is used for this purpose and no instruction is given in the public school, nor are school teachers employed. The system, however, does involve certain definite provisions on the part of the church, and demands trained teachers in every church.

(d) *The Wenner Plan.* The Wenner plan is described by Dr. George U. Wenner in his book, Religious Education and the Public Schools. It provides for excusing all students one half day per week, and allowing them to go to their respective churches for instruction. This plan proposes an adaptation of the European system to American conditions.

(e) *Various plans* are described in Bible in Schools Plans, by Wilbur F. Crafts, including those mentioned above. He especially advocates the reading of the Bible and Bible lessons at the opening of school, and calls attention to the New Zealand plans. Several other valuable experiments are being tried. Austin, Texas, is working in affiliation with the State University on what is approximately the Colorado Plan. Des Moines, Iowa, is experimenting with the Gary plan. Several cities in Indiana are making similar experiments.

3. *Credit for week-day work has been proposed.*

The North Dakota plan and the Colorado plan give credit for work accomplished by high school students. Here care must be exercised that the State does not secure the right to determine

---

[1] See p. 185, *supra.*

the *content* of the curriculum. It may establish standards as to its academic character, but it ought to be ready to accept any work in any faith or doctrine provided it be of equal grade in requirements of study. The doctrines, interpretations, and precise content of the curriculum must be the responsibility of the churches.

In the elementary grade credit must be based entirely on the theory, established in fact, that the child is doing in the church school work equivalent in time and study to that which he would be doing in the school. Mr. Wirt, of Gary, goes even further, and says that "if the community is willing that the child should spend so much time in the church schools, it is no business of the school what it shall study there." There should be no thought of tests or examinations in the church school, for they are out of place in elementary work. The utmost care should be exercised to grade the work of instruction, the conditions of study, the class-rooms, apparatus, and discipline at least fully up to the standards in the public schools. Then the scheme of credit would simply be that no child should be retarded or conditioned on account of time necessarily taken in attending the church day school for the periods agreed upon with the school board.

4. *It has been proposed to enlarge the church's course of instruction in religion.*

Week-day instruction affords opportunity to complement, not to duplicate, the work of the church school on Sunday. If the child can have three periods of work in religion each week instead of one, it will be possible to arrange a fairly complete curriculum of religious instruction, something at present not yet provided in the United States.

In addition to the best work now offered in the Bible, the curriculum ought to include Christian teaching or doctrine, conduct or right living, the church—its history and present work, forms of religious activity in social relations, organization and service, modern religious literature in hymns, poems, and prose.

For convenience at present, it might be wise to consider the school on Sunday as devoted, for the lower grades at least, to the Bible, using the graded lessons already provided, and leaving graded instruction in doctrines, duties, and church history to the day school. But steps should be taken at once to arrange a fairly complete curriculum of religion for all churches able in any way to provide week-day instruction. This must be based strictly on the child's developing life and its needs.

CHURCH AND COMMUNITY COOPERATION

IV. CONDITIONS OF SUCCESSFUL WORK

1. *Plant.* A room designed and arranged as a classroom with tables, suitable seats, blackboards, and apparatus is necessary. This room must be hygienically, not ecclesiastically, lighted and ventilated.

2. *Instruction.* The teacher should be trained. Not many pastors can do this work, because it demands an exclusive devotion to a precise schedule, which they cannot give. In churches having two hundred children in the elementary school it is only common-sense provision for their future religious usefulness and for their present religious development to provide a leader, an educator, devoting himself exclusively to them.

There need be no serious difficulty in cooperating with other churches, so that one teacher serves more than one church. The points of difference may, if necessary, be taught in the separate Sunday schools.

3. *Plan.* It will not be worth while to withdraw children from the public schools unless certain definite results are to be achieved which could not be reached in any other way. We must be sure that there are specific and worth-while things to be taught, disciplines to be covered, in order to secure definite educational results. We must be as clear at least as other educators as to the purpose of this school.

4. *Schedule.* Before asking for time from the public school program, it would be wise to make certain whether the present actual needs may be met by some other arrangement. Is it not possible to find more time for instruction either on Sunday or on other days of the week? Saturday may be available for organized and directed play and social service.

V. RECOMMENDATIONS

(1) A more serious study to provide an adequate program of religious education for the young in the time now available, especially on Sunday morning. No demand should be made for the use of public school time until we make adequate use of the time now available.

(2) The raising of educational work of the church to the point of efficiency where we can claim the right of credits and academic recognition.

(3) Plan to secure community unity of action on:
    (*a*) A thorough survey of the needs.
    (*b*) A program of work in religious education.

(4) Better physical equipment for educational work in the church.

(5) Secure the employment of professionally trained directors: (a) Either for a local church or (b) for a group of churches.

(6) Prepare for week-day instruction special courses of study and plans of coordinated activity of service. This gives the opportunity for the much-needed work in history, doctrine, conduct, church relations, and general religious ideas.

(7) Develop the vacation Bible school plan. This affords opportunity to experiment in the field of week-day religious instruction.

(8) Become acquainted with the work of the public school.

SUGGESTIONS ON COURSES OF STUDY

The following suggestions are put forth tentatively at this time when no regular curriculum is organized for the week-day instruction, in the hope that they will furnish the basis for further study and work. The curriculum is predicated on the general theory that adequate instruction in biblical literature and biblical history will be given in the school meeting Sundays.

Grade 1. Memorizing hymns, brief passages of Scripture, and prayers.

Teaching by stories, principally, right attitude toward family, friends, school, etc.

Grade 2. Memorizing selected passages and hymns with training in worship.

Stories of heroes of religion since the close of the biblical canon.

Further training in forms of service in community and church.

Grade 3. Continued memorizing.

Modern religious history.

Ideas of God and religious conceptions.

Grade 4. Further training in worship and teaching of Christian conduct.

The story of the church.

Grade 5. The church and our relation to it.

Training in worship.

The life of Jesus and its meaning to-day.

Directed Christian service.

CHURCH AND COMMUNITY COOPERATION

Grade 6. What it means to belong to the church.
>The social duties in the light of Christianity.
>Introduction to modern religious literature.

Grade 7. The story of the Bible in history.
>Further studies in modern religious literature, especially poetry, worship, social duties.

Grade 8. Modern religious literature.
>The church at work to-day.
>Young people's organizations in general.

High School. Grade 1. The Bible as literature.
>Early church history.
>Conduct and life.

Grade 2. The mediæval church.
>Methods of Christian service.
>Christian citizenship at work.

Grade 3. Modern church history.
>Social problems.

Grade 4. The present-day church at work in the world.
>Ethical problems.

SUGGESTIONS AS TO ORGANIZATION

It is possible to provide for the twelve grades of elementary and high school during the five days of the week so as to have only one grade at a time, as follows:

In churches or communities where the number of pupils in any one grade would not exceed twenty-five the school week can be divided into twelve or twenty-four class periods, each grade appearing in one of the same once or twice a week.

Where the number of children in any one grade would exceed twenty-five it is better to organize, so as to have smaller classes. The school week can then be divided into twenty-four periods, five hours of each day except Friday, four hours on Friday, and, for example, one half the pupils in Grade 1 would take the first hour and the other half of the pupils in this Grade 1 would take the second hour.

This plan would require only one teacher at a time on any one day. It may be difficult to find one teacher who could take all the children of a church between the ages of six to nine on Monday and those fifteen to seventeen on Friday, but a trained teacher could do this much better than could a group of amateurs.

The simple fact ought to be recognized that almost all the teaching in the so-called "evangelical" group in any community could be done by a teacher in one church as well as by a teacher in another. The distinctive teachings which separate the churches could be left to the Sunday school, the one week-day period would be sufficiently occupied if devoted to the knowledge upon which all in the group are agreed.

VI. FURTHER INTERESTS OF THE CHURCH IN PUBLIC EDUCATION

While we agree that the public school cannot teach religion, we ought to insist that it shall count for moral character.

Any discussion of the school problem ought to be based on real knowledge of the facts. Pastors know altogether too little of the inside of these schools. They should visit the schools. As social leaders they are responsible for conditions in the schools. They will find teachers willing cooperators in any reasonable enterprise.

The churches ought to encourage the formation of parent-teacher associations or clubs.

It is possible to organize in any community what might be called "A Council of Moral and Religious Education." This holds, in a voluntary capacity, the same relation to the moral welfare of the young as a village or city council holds to civic affairs. It should consist of all pastors, public-school officers and teachers, Sunday school superintendents and teachers, librarians, Young Men's Christian Association and Young Women's Christian Association employed officers, social workers, leaders in women's clubs, etc. It would lead in the study and organization of community plans for week-day instruction in religion.

3. THE MALDEN PLAN[1]

THE MALDEN PLAN

The Malden School of Religious Education has developed from a conviction on the part of many of the active church leaders of Malden that an adequate program of religious education for the children of a community involves many problems which can only be solved by community cooperation. Chief among these problems is the training of religious teachers and leaders for the Sunday schools, week-day religious schools, midweek recreational activities, and other religious agencies. The establishing of the Malden School of Religious Education is the initial step in a program which will gradually develop into a thoroughly coordinated system of religious education for the city of Malden.

The program of the Malden Council of Religious Education will develop as rapidly as leadership and public sentiment will permit. The plan must grow out of the community's needs, it must be in every sense interdenominational, and each forward step must come as the normal development of a carefully planned and thoroughly representative community program. The following outline will suggest the work proposed by the Malden 'Council of Religious Education:

1. *The Development of a City System of Religious Education, Including:*
   a. A City Board of Religious Education, analogous to the Board of Education of the public schools.
   b. A City Superintendent of Religious Education.
   c. A City Training School for Leaders, including observation and practice teaching.
   d. Common Educational Standards for the guidance of the Church Schools in the city.
   e. A System of Week-day Religious Schools. This step involves
      (1) An adequate supply of trained lay teachers.

---

[1] From the announcement of the Malden School of Religious Education, conducted by the Malden City Board of Religious Education. Sessions held each Tuesday evening from 7:30 to 9:15 o'clock, at the Parish House of the First Baptist Church, Malden Square. The school year opens in October, and closes in April. Walter S. Athearn, Director.

(2) A curriculum suited to the needs of the various grades and related to the program of Sunday instructions.

(3) An enlightened public sentiment which will insure the necessary moral and financial support, and prevent misunderstandings and partisan controversies.

It is clear that religious week-day schools must come, but they must come slowly as the result of careful experimentation and statesmanlike direction.

2. *The unification of all child welfare agencies of the city in the interests of the largest efficiency.*

3. *The supervision of a complete religious census of the city with special reference to the religious needs of children and young people.*

4. *The direction of educational, industrial and social surveys for the purpose of securing the facts upon which a constructive community program can be based.*

5. *The study of the recreational and social conditions of the city, the training of local leaders, and the building of a scientific, well balanced program of work, study and play for the children of the city.*

6. *The creation of a community consciousness on matters of moral and religious education.*

CHARACTER AND PURPOSE OF THE MALDEN SCHOOL OF RELIGIOUS EDUCATION

The Malden School of Religious Education is a high-grade night college of religious education. It will attempt to do for the training of religious educators what a city or State normal college does for the training of secular teachers. The curriculum of the school will cover all phases of the educational work of the local church and the community. The two distinguishing features of this school are: (1) A unified educational program in which all courses will harmonize with an educational policy which the entire faculty is expected to promote; this means supervision and direction of all work by the City Board of Religious Education and by the director. (2) All courses offered by the school will contribute to a city-wide program of religious education. All lectures delivered, all literature distributed, and all bulletins issued must contribute to the building of a community ideal which will give common conceptions and unity of purpose so that an adequate system of religious education may be established.

The pupils in this school are expected to work. Regular lessons are assigned and students must study, recite, and pass examinations just as they do in all standard schools. The courses require hard work and much time, *but they will make trained teachers*. It has not been the purpose to plan courses that can be taken without effort by teachers who feel the honor of diplomas, stars, badges, or seals. The aim has been to outline courses of training that are within the range of the average teacher, but which require time, energy and some money, and whose chief incentive is a desire to become efficient in the teaching service of the church.

A church which contemplates week-day religious instruction must come to see that *a church which cannot adequately care for children on Sunday has no right to ask for their time on week days*. Church schools that are not doing creditable work must not ask the public schools for academic credit until their equipment and their teaching force equals that of the public schools. The request for high school credit for work done in local churches must carry with it assurance that the work is in every way worthy of academic credit. All these considerations demand thoroughgoing community programs of teacher training. Teacher training is serious business. Upon its success depends the future of the church. Pastors and church boards must demand trained intelligence on the part of religious teachers. They must be willing to lead their teachers to heroic efforts and financial sacrifices to the end that the children may be nurtured in the knowledge and admonition of the Lord.

COOPERATION WITH BOSTON UNIVERSITY

The recent enlargement of the Department of Religious Education of Boston University made possible the plan of cooperation announced in this bulletin. The city of Malden has been selected as a demonstration center for the university. The instructors are drawn from the regular and extension faculties, and come to Malden for regular courses in their respective fields. These specialists cooperate with the local religious leaders of Malden in the etablishing of a model city system of religious education.

ORGANIZATION OF SCHOOL OF RELIGIOUS EDUCATION

The Malden School of Religious Education has been established by the Malden Ministerial Association. This Association has vested the management of the school in a City Council of Religious Education, a City Board of Religious Education, a director, a secretary and a faculty of specialists in the field of religious education.

1. *The City Board of Religious Education.* This Board consists of seven members. This Board sustains substantially the same relation to the School of Religious Education as a Board of Education holds to the administration of a system of public schools. It will be the duty of this committee to elect a director of the school, approve the faculty and curriculum recommended by the director, formulate rules and regulations for the school, secure suitable quarters for the school, and to have general supervision of its work. This Board will select its own chairman, secretary, and treasurer. It will be the duty of this Board to make an annual report to the Malden Ministerial Association and to the City Council of Religious Education.

2. *The City Council of Religious Education.* This council consists of representative citizens of Malden including the members of the Ministerial Association, the superintendent of each Sunday school in Malden, and additional members representing the educational, civic, and religious interests of the city. All members not serving *ex officio* are appointed by the Malden Ministerial Association. The Council holds at least three meetings each year. The meetings of the council are for free and frank discussion of the problems of moral and religious education of the city, for the dissemination of information and for the projecting of new and improved methods and policies. The Council elects its own president and secretary. The meetings of the Council are presided over by the chairman of the City Board of Religious Education.

3. *Director.* The director of the School of Religious Education is the executive officer of the City Board of Religious Education in so far as its relation to the school is concerned. With the approval of the Board he selects a faculty, determines courses of study, recitation schedules, rules and regulations for the students, etc. The administration of the school rests with the director and faculty.

4. *Secretary.* The City Board of Religious Education appoints a secretary, who has charge of the records of the school, acts as secretary for the director and faculty, and is in charge of the details of the educational program of the Board.

CHURCH AND COMMUNITY COOPERATION

CALENDAR

The regular sessions of the school are held on Tuesday evenings. The year's work is divided into two semesters, as follows: first semester, October to December; the second semester, January to April.

EXPENSES

To defray the expenses of printing, postage, stenographic help, special lecture talent, etc., a tuition fee of $1.00 for each semester is charged. The tuition fees cover but a small part of the actual expense of the school. Students are required to purchase text-books and other material for class use.

REFERENCE LIBRARY

The directors of the Malden Public Library have established a Sunday school room in which are found the reference books recommended by the faculty of the Malden School of Religious Education.

SPECIAL LECTURES

A series of special lectures is given throughout the year. It is expected that at least once each month a great inspirational message may be brought to the school by specialists in different fields of religious work. These lectures precede the regular sessions, being scheduled for 6:45 to 7:30 o'clock.

FACULTY

Most of the men and women of the faculty have nation-wide reputations in their respective fields.

LOCATION OF SCHOOL

The sessions of this school are held in the Parish House of the First Baptist Church, Malden Square.

SUPERVISED TEACHING

An adequate program of teacher training will include (1) knowledge, (2) observation, and (3) practice. During the second half of the year courses in supervised teaching are conducted. These practice courses supplement and complete the classroom instruction in the theory of teaching.

INTERNATIONAL APPROVAL

This school meets all the standards of the International Sunday School Association, for Community Training Schools. Its grad-

RELIGIOUS EDUCATION AND DEMOCRACY

uates are entitled to International Community Training School Diplomas, as well as the diplomas awarded by the Malden City Board of Religious Education.

MALDEN PLAN INDORSED

Resolutions adopted by the Committee on Religious Education of the Massachusetts Federation of Churches, September 18, 1916:

Voted, that this Committee indorses "the enlargement of the Department of Religious Education in Boston University School of Theology," and commends its services to all seeking training in this line; and that it also commends the plans of the Malden Federation of Churches to cooperate with that Department in the establisment of a "Training School" and "Demonstration Center."

Voted, that we recommend that, before week-day religious instruction be undertaken by the churches of any community, especially when an understanding with the public schools is involved, there be thorough preparation and training of teachers similar to that now being undertaken by the Malden churches.

CHILDREN'S FESTIVAL OF SACRED MUSIC

Besides training the teachers in musical leadership Professor Smith conducts demonstrations with groups of children, culminating in a musical festival.

REQUIREMENTS FOR GRADUATION

A diploma of graduation is issued to students completing three years' work, provided that the following conditions are fulfilled:

First. The student must have completed satisfactorily six full courses of instruction.

Second. Not to exceed two thirds of the work may be elected from any one group of courses.

Third. Lessons missed may be made up by examination or by such other tests as the instructors may require, but no student shall be graduated who has not attended four fifths of all the sessions for a period of three years.

TEACHER-TRAINING CLASSES IN LOCAL SUNDAY SCHOOL

Each Sunday school should have as many teachers in training as it has in service. New teachers must come from the Sunday school enrollment. In order that new teachers may have oppor-

268

tunity for training, each school must maintain a teacher training class. To encourage the establishing of such classes this school will accredit toward the completion of its three-year course one year's work done in the local Sunday school, providing the following conditions are met:

First. Textbooks and teachers must be approved by the faculty of the School of Religious Education.

Second. The minimum equipment shall be: One set of Kent & Madsen maps, or equivalent; adequate blackboard space; one volume dictionary of the Bible (Hastings' preferred); ten volumes of reference books suitable to text studied, approved by this faculty.

Third. A separate classroom must be provided for the class.

Fourth. The recitation period shall be forty minutes.

Fifth. The class shall hold at least forty weekly sessions.

Sixth. The class shall not be confused with the workers' conference, which deals with the problems of the *present* school. It shall have in mind the interests of the *future* school.

Seventh. The entire year's work shall be devoted to one line of work. It is recommended that local schools attempt only the biblical instruction, leaving the professional training to this school.

WEEKLY PROGRAM

The sessions of the school will be held each Tuesday evening, beginning at 7:30 and closing at 9:15 o'clock. Two class periods and a brief devotional period will be provided as follows:

(a) First Class Period, 7:30—8:10.

(b) Assembly Period, 8:10—8:30.

General announcements and a brief devotional service. All students are urged to be present each session.

(c) Second Class Period, 8:30—9:15.

The schedule for the year, subject to change if deemed advisable, is as follows:

First Semester	*Second Semester*
7:30 to 8:15—	7:30 to 8:15—
Organization and Administration.	Organization and Administration.
Principles of Recreational Leadership.	Children's Music.
History of Moral and Religious Education.	Life of Christ.
	Apostolic Age.
	Beginners' Methods.

RELIGIOUS EDUCATION AND DEMOCRACY

First Semester
Life of Christ.
Apostolic Age.
Beginners' Methods.
Junior Methods.
Intermediate Methods.

8:30 to 9:15—
Primary Methods.
Adult Class Methods.
Practice Work in Recreation.
Senior Methods.
Elementary Psychology.
Old Testament History.

Second Semester
Junior Methods.
Intermediate Methods.

8:30 to 9:15—
Primary Methods.
Adult Class Methods.
Music and Worship.
Senior Methods.
Elementary Psychology.
Old Testament History.

COURSES OF INSTRUCTION

I. BIBLICAL

1. *Old Testament History.* It is the purpose of this course to present the literature and history of the Old Testament in as thoroughgoing manner as the time will permit.

Instructor, James T. Carlyon.

Textbook: Sanders. *The History of the Hebrews.*

Reference Books: Kent, *The Historical Bible;* Breasted, *History of the Ancient Egyptians;* Fowler, *A History of the Literature of Ancient Israel;* Cornill, *The Prophets of Israel;* Rogers, *The Religion of Babylonia and Assyria;* G. A. Smith, *The Twelve Prophets;* H. P. Smith, *The Religion of Israel;* Marti, *The Religion of the Old Testament;* Peritz, *Old Testament History;* Knudson, *Beacon Lights of Prophecy.*

2. *The Life of Christ.* This course opens with a study of the history of the Jews in the time of Christ. It covers the period from the return from the exile to the fall of Jerusalem. After this historical setting has been established the class will make an outline study of the life of Christ.

Instructor, John F. Dobbs.

Textbook: Burgess, *The Life of Christ.*

Reference Books: Mathews, *History of the New Testament Times in Palestine;* Burton and Mathews, *Constructive Studies in the Life of Christ.* Stevens and Burton, *Harmony of the Gospels;* Rall, *New Testament History;* Masterman, *Studies in Galilee;* Delitzsch, *Jewish Artisan Life in the Time of Jesus;* Sanday, *Out-*

CHURCH AND COMMUNITY COOPERATION

lines of the Life of Christ; Kent, *The Life and Teachings of Jesus;* Martin, *The Life of Jesus;* Gilbert, *Jesus;* Goodspeed, *Story of the New Testament.*

3. *The Apostolic Age.* This course covers the history of the early church giving special emphasis to the life and work of the apostle Paul.

Instructor, Heber R. Harper.

Textbook: Gilbert, *A Short History of Christianity in the Apostolic Age.*

Reference Books: Weinel, *St. Paul, the Man and His Works;* Ramsey, *St. Paul, the Traveler and the Roman Citizen;* Purves, *Christianity in the Apostolic Age;* Ramsey, *The Church in the Roman Empire;* Case, *The Evolution of Early Christianity;* Ropes, *Apostolic Age;* McGiffert, *Apostolic Age;* Weizsäcker, *The Apostolic Age of the Christian Church;* Gilbert, *Student's Life of Paul;* Peake, *Introduction to the New Testament.*

General Biblical References.

In addition to the reference books listed above there will be available for the use of students in the biblical courses Hastings, *A Dictionary of the Bible in One Volume; The Bible for Home and School Commentaries;* Hunting, *Story of Our Bible;* G. A. Smith and Bartholemew, *A Historical Atlas of the Geography of the Holy Land;* Handcock, *The Latest Light on Bible Lands;* G. A. Smith, *The Historical Geography of the Holy Land;* Lees, *Village Life in Palestine;* Soares, *Social Institutions and Ideals of the Bible.*

II. DEPARTMENTAL

For the purpose of securing unity throughout the departments of the graded church school the instructors in departmental specialization courses will follow the general outline found in Chapters IV to X of *The Church School,* supplementing the same with collateral reading and a liberal use of the curriculum material found in the various series of graded lesson courses.

I. *Beginners.*

For teachers of children four and five years of age.

This class will consider the problems of the Sunday kindergarten.

The course will include special work in the graded lessons prepared for the Beginners' Department, and a careful discussion of the room and its equipment, the teacher and her preparation,

271

RELIGIOUS EDUCATION AND DEMOCRACY

order of exercises, music and games, table work, lesson story, pictures, models and modeling, etc.

Instructor, Mrs. Willena Brown Reed.

Text Books: Athearn, *The Beginners' Department of the Church School;* Danielson, *Lessons for Teachers for Beginners.*

Reference Books: Weigle, *The Pupil and the Teacher;* Farris, *The Sunday Kindergarten;* St. John, *Stories and Story Telling;* Palen and Henderson, *What and How;* Clifford, *Ring Songs and Games;* Hill, *Song Stories for the Kindergarten;* Cragin, *Kindergarten Stories for the Sunday School and Home.*

II. *Primary.*

For teachers of children six, seven, and eight years of age. The work of this class will include a thorough study of the lesson material suitable for the three grades in this department, together with the discussion of such topics as the program, music for the primary grades, methods of presenting the lessons, special day exercises, illustrative material, pictures, models, classroom equipment, etc.

Instructor, Grace Jones.

Textbooks: Athearn, *The Primary Department of the Church School;* Thomas, *Primary Lesson Detail.*

Reference Books: Weigle, *The Pupil and the Teacher;* DuBois, *The Natural Way;* Sly, *World Stories Retold;* Wardle, *Hand Work in Religious Education;* Scantlebury, *Homes of the World Babies in Silhouette;* Beard, *Primary and Junior Songs for the Sunday Schools; Type Missionary Lessons, Teacher's Text,* 2d year, Part 3.

III. *Junior.*

For teachers of children nine, ten, eleven, and twelve years of age. This class will study the lesson material for the four years' work outlined for the junior grades, and the vital problems peculiar to the preadolescent child. Among the topics considered will be classroom equipment, class discipline, lesson plans, pupils' hand books and how to use them, illustrative material, home work for pupils, etc.

Instructor, Grace Jones.

Textbooks: Athearn, *The Junior Department of the Church School;* Baldwin, *The Junior Manual.*

Reference Books: Betts, *The Mind and its Education;* Worcester, *On Holy Ground,* Leary, *The Real Palestine of Today;* Soares, *Heroes of Israel;* Littlefield, *Hand Work in the Sunday School;*

272

CHURCH AND COMMUNITY COOPERATION

Hunting, *The Story of Our Bible;* Winchester, *Worship and Song;* Stuart, *The Story of the Masterpieces.*

IV. *Intermediate.*

For teachers of pupils thirteen, fourteen, fifteen, and sixteen years of age.

This class will undertake to study the graded lesson material for the Intermediate Department, equipment, illustrative material, pupils' handwork, classroom management, the pedagogy of adolescence, source material for teachers, material for home occupation and reading of pupils, and the social life of the class.

Instructor, James T. Carlyon.

Textbooks: Athearn, *The Intermediate Department of the Church School;* Slattery, *The Girl in Her Teens;* King, *The High School Age.*

Reference Books: Coe, *The Spiritual Life;* Betts, *The Mind and Its Education;* Jenks, *Life Questions for High School Boys;* McCunn, *The Making of Character;* Alexander, *The Secondary Department Organized;* Bradford, *The Messages of the Masters;* Kent, *The Life and Teachings of Jesus;* Hunting, *The Story of Our Bible.*

V. *Senior.*

For teachers of pupils seventeen, eighteen, nineteen and twenty years of age.

This class will study organization and management, the social life of the class and the opportunities for religious service open to students of this age.

Instructor. (To be selected.)

Textbooks: Athearn, *The Senior Department of the Church School;* Lewis, *The Senior Worker and His Work.*

Reference Books: Cressey, *The Church and Young Men;* King, *The Moral and Religious Challenge of Our Times;* Kent, *The Work and Teachings of the Apostles;* Peritz, *Old Testament History;* Sutherland, *Famous Hymns of the World;* Boone, *The Conquering Christ;* Hutchins, *Graded Social Service for the Sunday School.*

VI. *Adult.*

For teachers of pupils over twenty years of age.

Among the topics discussed in this class will be class organization and management, duties of class officers and committees,

273

class activities, available Bible study courses, adult class literature, class management, relation of class to church organizations. Instructor, Frederick L. Cleveland.

Textbooks: Woods, *Adult Class Study;* Cope, *The Efficient Layman;* Wells, *The Ideal Adult Class;* Pearce, *The Adult Class;* Coe, *The Religion of a Mature Mind;* Cope, *Religious Education in the Family.*

III. PROFESSIONAL

I. *Music and Worship in the Church School.*

The place of music in the worship of children. The study of the child voice. The organization and management of children's choir, music suitable to different departments of the church school.

Members of this class will have opportunity to observe and participate in the training of children for musical pageants and other group demonstrations.

Instructor, H. Augustine Smith.

Textbooks: Pratt, *Musical Ministries in the Church;* Benson, *Studies in Familiar Hymns;* Winchester, *Worship and Song.*

Reference Books: Lutkin, *Music in the Church;* Lorenz, *Practical Church Music;* Vosseller, *The Use of a Children's Choir in the Church;* Dickinson, *Music in the History of the Western Church;* Curwin, *The Boy's Voice.*

II. *Principles of Recreational Leadership.*

Modern conditions that make play necessary. The dangers from commercialized, professionalized and immoral forms of amusements. Reasons for supervised recreation. Play instincts and interests. Games that are suitable for each period of development. Competition and cooperation. The natural playground —nature and the simple arts of living. Camping. The Boy Scouts of America; aim, methods and programs; community aspects of scouting.

Instructor, Norman E. Richardson.

Textbooks: Richardson and Loomis, *The Boy Scout Movement Applied to the Church.*

Reference Books: Young, *Character Through Recreation;* Curtis, *Education Through Play;* Johnson, *Education by Plays and Games;* Forbush, *Manual of Play;* Lee, *Play in Education;* Fiske, *Boy Life and Self Government.*

CHURCH AND COMMUNITY COOPERATION

III. *Methods and Practice Work in Recreational Leadership.*
The care of the body in times of play. Games and contests described. Scout games. Tracking, trailing, nature study, swimming, camp-cooking. Common sense in leadership. Hiking and treking. Discovering and training leaders. Using the resources of a community. Sports that kill and sports that build character. Scouting and citizenship. Indoor and outdoor practice work and demonstrations.

Instructor, James A. Wilder.

Textbooks: *Boy Scouts of America, Handbook for Boys* (14th edition) ; and *Boy Scouts of America, Handbook for Scoutmasters.*

Reference Books: Same as for Course Two.

IV. *Organization and Management of the Modern Church School.*

A class for superintendents, officers, pastors, church officers, and others who are charged with the management or oversight of a church school. It includes a discussion of the practical problems of organization, gradation, curriculum, discipline, program, finances, records, teachers' meetings, etc.

Instructor, Walter S. Athearn.

Textbooks: Athearn, *The Church School;* and Cope, *The Modern Sunday School and its Present Task.*

Reference Books: Evans, *The Sunday School Building and its Equipment;* Hutchins, *Graded Social Service for the Sunday School;* Athearn, *The City Institute for Religious Teachers;* Meyer, *The Graded Sunday School in Principle and Practice;* Hurlbut, *Organizing and Building up the Sunday School;* Cope, *Efficiency in the Sunday School;* Lawrence, *How to Conduct a Sunday School*, (revised edition) ; Coe, *Education in Religion and Morals.*

V. *The History of Moral and Religious Education.*

The history of Moral and Religious Education from the earliest times to the present day. The significance of religious education for the Reformation. The parochial school system. The origin and development of the Sunday school and other present agencies and institutions.

Instructor, Edwin R. Bartlett.

Textbooks: Cope, *The Evolution of the Sunday School;* and Seeley, *History of Education.*

Reference Books: Laurie, *Historical Survey of Prechristian Education;* Monroe, *Textbook in the History of Education;*

Graves, *History of Education*, Vol. II; Trumbull, *Yale Lectures on the Sunday School;* Brown, *The Sunday School Movement in America;* Simons, *The Revival of Religion in England in the 18th Century;* Sampey, *The International Lesson System;* Schwickerath, *Jesuit Education;* West, *Alcuin;* Hughes, *Loyola;* Burns, *Growth and Development of the Catholic School System of the United States;* Feeney, *The Catholic Sunday School;* Brown, *The Secularization of American Education;* Crooker, *Religious Freedom in American Education;* Riley, et al., *The Religious Question in Public Education, Organized Sunday School Work in America,* Vols. XII, XIII, XIV; Hodgson, *Primitive Christian Education.*

VI. *Elementary Psychology and Pedagogy.*

This course will be helpful to public school teachers, church school teachers, and parents. It will deal with the unfolding mind and the approved methods of teaching. A nontechnical but scientific study.

Instructor, Walter S. Athearn.

Textbooks: First Semester, Betts, *The Mind and Its Education.* Second Semester, Weigle, *The Pupil and the Teacher.*

Reference Books: James, *Talks to Teachers on Psychology and Life's Ideals;* Betts, *The Recitation;* Bagley, *Classroom Management;* Calkins, *A First Book in Psychology;* Strayer, *A Brief Course in the Teaching Process;* McMurry, *How to Study;* Earhart, *Types of Teaching;* Colvin, *The Learning Process;* Adams, *Exposition and Illustration in Teaching.*

BIBLIOGRAPHY

The following titles have been selected as bearing particularly upon the subjects of the several chapters in Part One.

CHAPTER I. COMPULSORY EDUCATION AND RELIGIOUS FREEDOM

BUTLER, N. M. The Meaning of Education. Macmillan, N. Y., 1898.

CROOKER, J. H. Religious Freedom in American Education. American Unitarian Association, Boston. 1903.

HADLEY, A. T. The Education of the American Citizen. Scribners, N. Y. 1901.

RILEY-SADLER-JACKSON. The Religious Question in Public Education. Longmans, N. Y. 1911.

CHAPTER II. THE ESSENTIALS OF DEMOCRACY

ADDAMS, JANE. Democracy and Social Ethics. Macmillan, N. Y. 1902.

BUTLER, N. M. True and False Democracy. Macmillan, N. Y. 1907.

CROLY, H. D. Progressive Democracy. Macmillan, N. Y. 1914.

DEWEY, JOHN. Democracy and Education. Macmillan, N. Y. 1916.

DOLE, N. H. The Spirit of Democracy. Crowell, Phila. 1906.

ELIOT, C. W. The Conflict between Individualism and Collectivism in a Democracy. Scribners, N. Y. 1910.

HADLEY, A. T. The Relations between Freedom and Responsibility in the Evolution of Democratic Government. Scribners, N. Y. 1903.

SCUDDER, VIDA D. Socialism and Character. Houghton Mifflin Co. Boston. 1912.

CHAPTER III. THE CHALLENGE OF DEMOCRACY TO THE PROTESTANT CHURCHES OF AMERICA

ADDAMS, JANE. The Spirit of Youth and the City Streets. Macmillan, N. Y.

KING, H. C. Personal and Ideal Elements in Education. Macmillan, N. Y. 1904.

KING, H. C. The Moral and Religious Challenge of our Times. Macmillan, N. Y.

RELIGIOUS EDUCATION AND DEMOCRACY

SMITH, G. B. Social Idealism and the Changing Theology. Macmillan, N. Y. 1913.
RELIGIOUS EDUCATION ASSOCIATION. Report for 1908, Education and National Character.

CHAPTER IV. THE TEACHING INHERITANCE OF THE PROTESTANT CHURCHES

SCOTT, E. F. The Apologetic of the New Testament. Putnams, N. Y. 1907.
HARNACK, A. What is Christianity? Scribners, N. Y.
HASLETT, S. B. The Pedagogical Bible School. Revell, N. Y. 1903.

CHAPTER V. SOME PROPHETS OF MODERN DEMOCRACY AND THE NEW EDUCATION

COMENIUS. The Great Didactic.
LOCKE. The Conduct of the Understanding.
ROUSSEAU. Emile. Appletons, N. Y., or D. C. Heath, Boston.
PESTALOZZI. Leonard and Gertrude. D. C. Heath, Boston.
FROEBEL. The Education of Man. Appletons, N. Y.
HERBERT. Outlines of Educational Doctrine. Macmillan, N. Y. 1901.
CUBBERLY, E. P. Changing Conceptions of Education. Houghton Mifflin Co., Boston. 1909.
DEGARMO, C. Herbart and the Herbartians. Scribners, N. Y. 1895.
EMERSON, MABEL I. The Evolution of the Educational Ideal. Houghton Mifflin Co., Boston. 1914.
MONROE, PAUL. A Text-book on the History of Education. Macmillan, N. Y. 1905.
PARKER, S. C. A Text-book on the History of Modern Elementary Education. Ginn & Co., Boston. 1912.

CHAPTER VI. TYPICAL SYSTEMS OF STATE EDUCATION

PAULSEN, FR. German Education, Past and Present. Tr. by Lorenz. Scribners, N. Y. 1908.
SHAW. The Movement for Reform in the Teaching of Religion in Saxony.
FARRINGTON, F. E. The Public Primary School System of France. Columbia Univ. Press., N. Y. 1906.
French Secondary Schools. Longmans, N. Y. 1910.

BIBLIOGRAPHY

DE MONTMORENCY, J. E. G. Progress of Education in England. Macmillan, N. Y. 1904.
The Evolution of the Religious Controversy in National Education and National Life. 1906.
GARLAND. Religious Instruction in State Schools.

CHAPTER VII. THE AMERICAN PUBLIC SCHOOL SYSTEM IN ITS RELATION TO THE CHURCHES AND DEMOCRACY

RICE. The Public School System of the United States.
DEXTER, E. G. History of Education in the United States. Macmillan, N. Y. 1904.
BROWN, S. W. The Secularization of American Education, Teachers College, N. Y. 1912.
HALL, A. J. Religious Education in the Public Schools of the State and City of New York. Univ. of Chicago Press. 1914.
U. S. BUREAU OF EDUCATION, BULLETIN, No. 47. Digest of State Laws Relating to Public Education.
CRAFTS, W. F. Bible in Schools Plans of Many Lands. Washington, D. C. 1914.
McCAULEY. The Bible in the Public Schools.
SALTER. The Bible in Schools. Philadelphia. 1904.
BENDERLY, S. Aims and Activities of the Bureau of Education of the Jewish Community. N. Y. 1912.
The Problem of Jewish Education in N. Y. City. 1914.
BURNS, J. A. The Growth and Development of the Catholic System in the United States.
CONWAY. Catholic Education in the United States.
SHEEDY. Catholic Citizens and Public Education. N. Y. 1902.
WENNER, G. U. Religious Education and the Public School. Am. Tract Soc. 1912.
See also articles in Monroe, Cyclopedia of Education. Macmillan, N. Y.

CHAPTER VIII. THE DEVELOPMENT OF EDUCATIONAL AGENCIES WITHIN THE PROTESTANT CHURCH

BROWN, MARIANNA C. The Sunday School Movement in America. Revell, N. Y. 1901.
COPE, H. F. The Evolution of the Sunday School. Pilgrim Press, Boston. 1911.
HASLETT, S. B. The Pedagogical Bible School. Revell, N. Y. 1903.
SAMPEY, J. R. The International Lesson System.

RELIGIOUS EDUCATION AND DEMOCRACY

See also articles in Macfarland-Winchester, The Encyclopedia of Sunday Schools and Religious Education. Nelsons, N. Y. 1915.

CHAPTER IX. SOME RECENT EXPERIMENTS IN RELIGIOUS EDUCATION
Articles in Religious Education. Especially Volumes X and XI, 1915 and 1916. In these will be found a discussion of various aspects of this subject. Vol. X, No. 6, contains a valuable bibliography.

BOURNE, R. S. The Gary Schools. Houghton Mifflin Co. Boston. 1916.

WOOD, C. A. School and College Credit for Outside Bible Study. World Book Co., N. Y. 1917.

ALDERMAN, L. R. School Credit for Home Work. Houghton Mifflin Co., Boston. 1915.

CHAPELL, HARRIET. The Church Vacation School. Revell, N. Y. 1915.

CHAPTER X. THE MUTUAL RELATIONS OF CHURCH AND STATE IN PROVIDING EDUCATION FOR DEMOCRACY
RUGH-WILD-FRISBIE-REED-WEST. The Essential Place of Religion in Education. Monograph published by the National Education Association, Ann Arbor. 1916.

CHAPTER XI. STEPS OF PROCEDURE TOWARD PROVIDING A SYSTEM OF RELIGIOUS EDUCATION BY THE CHURCHES
ATHEARN. The Malden Leaflets. Malden. 1917.

CHAPTER XII. THE COMMUNITY TASK OF THE CHURCHES
STRAYER, P. M. The Reconstruction of the Church. Macmillan, N. Y. 1915.

INDEX

INDEX

INDEX

INDEX

Protestants—continued
Task confronting, 15, 29
Teaching function of, 29
Weakness of, 13, 93
Prussia, Education in, 54, 55
Psychology, John Locke and science of, 44
Public School System, American, 80, 83, 90
Democracy and, 90
English, 70
French, 65
German, 54, 55
Massachusetts and, 83–85
New York and, 86
"Not godless," 95
Pennsylvania and, 90
Perfecting of, 14
Puritan Commonwealth, 94, 146
Puritans, in England and America, 81, 82

Raikes, Robert, 96, 104
Realschule, Oberrealschule, 60
Reformation, Democracy and the, 42, 91, 145
Influence of on America, 80, 94
New forces released by, 42
Our inheritance from, 41, 145
Progress of, 40
Purpose of, 39
Religious Day School, 118ff., 139, 220ff.
Religion, Place of in education, 139, 220ff.
Religious education, Aims of, 103, 134, 138
Attitude of Jews, Roman Catholics and Protestants compared, 10–12
Attitude toward, England, 78, 79

Religious Education—continued
Community system of, 141
Cooperation in, 30, 125
Coordinate agencies of, 132
Correlation of, 138
Curriculum of, 136
Director of, 138
Divergent theories of, 13
Equipment, 135
Experiments in, 105ff.
Colorado Plan, 108
Gary Plan, 114
Lakewood Plan, 111
North Dakota Plan, 105
Religious Day School, 139,220
France and, 99
Froebel and, 51
Germany and, 54, 59–60, 62, 153f.
How safeguarded, England, 79
Germany, 61
Ineffectiveness of, 146
Interest of educators in, 15
Leadership of, 142
Need of, 16
New problem in United States, 147
No place in program, 92–93, 147
Normal schools for, 139
Not included in American public school system, 89
Obstacle to, 13
Organization needed, 135
Plans of, Australia, 167
England, 159
France, 64, 69
Germany, 153
Ontario, 169
Saskatchewan, 170
Responsibility for, 10, 93, 148, 149
Standards of, 126

290

INDEX

INDEX

INDEX